D1551406

# Roy Harris

Twayne's Music Series

# Roy Harris:
## An American Musical Pioneer

Dan Stehman

Twayne Publishers

Roy Harris:
An American Musical Pioneer

Dan Stehman

Published in 1984
by Twayne Publishers
A Division of G. K. Hall & Company
70 Lincoln Street, Boston, Massachusetts 02111

Printed on permanent/durable
acid-free paper and bound in
the United States of America

This book was designed
by Barbara Anderson and typeset
in Century Oldstyle by Compset Inc.

0-8057-9461-1

10 9 8 7 6 5 4 3 2 1
First Printing

# Contents

About the Author

Preface

Acknowledgments

Chronology

# About the Author

Dan Stehman was born in 1938 in Hermosa Beach, California, and still lives there. He began musical training at the age of eight with piano lessons and started composing at nine. His undergraduate studies were undertaken at Pomona College and at the University of California, Los Angeles. He went on to graduate work at the University of Southern California under a Woodrow Wilson Fellowship and received the Ph.D. in music in 1973.

Stehman began teaching in 1968 and is presently associate professor of music at Los Angeles Valley College in Van Nuys, California.

Stehman's interest in American music in general and Roy Harris in particular dates to his teens, and he has been engaged in intensive research on Harris's music for over a quarter century. He met the composer in 1961 and worked closely (though did not study) with him during the last eighteen years of his life. Among other tasks, Stehman has edited and prepared a number of Harris's works for publication and served as coproducer and annotator for several recent recordings devoted to the composer. Along with Robert Strassburg, he also helped establish the Roy Harris Archive in 1973 at California State University, Los Angeles, and currently serves on the executive board of the Roy Harris Society, the support group for the Archive.

The Ph.D. dissertation which Stehman wrote on Harris's symphonies is one of the most extensive scholarly studies yet undertaken on the work of a single American composer.

In addition to his teaching and continued activities on behalf of Roy Harris (which include the current preparation of a comprehensive catalog of the composer's works), Stehman has also maintained his composing activities. He has written in a number of genres and media, including orchestra, piano ensemble, studio jazz band, and chorus.

# Preface

"I think that nobody has captured in music the essence of American life—its vitality, its greatness, its strength—so well as Roy Harris" (Serge Koussevitzky); "Like the American continent rising up and saying hello" (*Time* magazine)—these are characteristic of the more enthusiastic tributes Roy Harris received during his long career. Even those less taken with his work frequently made some reference to an Americanist quality which seemed to them to permeate it: "I feel its American quality strongly, quite aside from any pioneer trappings. What Harris writes, as a rule, is music of real sweep and breadth, with power and emotional depth such as only a generously built country could produce. . . ."[1]

In an earlier passage in the same chapter of Aaron Copland's book from which the above was taken, there is another, crucial, phrase: "But I have never seen a single newspaper column that sums up and critically estimates the work of a man, who, at the moment at least, is more frequently played, more praised, and more condemned than any other living American composer."[2] The "more praised, and more condemned" part is, in a sense, a key to the Roy Harris story, with respect to both the music and the man. For the music, one need read only a selection from the articles cited in the bibliography of the present book to sample the wide divergence of opinion. As for the man, he was capable of polarizing opinion in like fashion, though this was not written about so much. He was born and grew up in rural surroundings. Much has been made of this, but such circumstances do not differ essentially from those from which other creative artists have sprung. Much more important is the fact that, possibly due in part to the isolation he experienced in his early years, Harris became an almost completely egocentric personality, always assured of his destiny, never denying himself anything, and assuming, as he once put it to me, that "time belongs to me, rather than the other way around."

Though assiduous in discovering the rich musical heritage of the past, Harris selected only those elements that he found useful and shaped them to his own ends, without, it seems, always understanding fully how they functioned in their original contexts. Just as his musical style is a rich mixture of the old (Gregorian chant, Renaissance choral polyphony, Anglo-Celtic folk music) and the new (jazz, asymmetrical rhythms, polytonality), so his perception of the America which some claim he represents quintessentially in music, was formed from an uneasy mixture of a nostalgic longing for a rural America of simple virtues and black and white issues and an increasing awareness of a rapidly changing land of ferment and torment.

Though Roy Harris's self-absorption was a simple mechanism, it produced a complex array of traits. It enabled him, for example, to lavish weeks over a large commission and bring it to performance, then allow the resulting score to languish unpublished and unperformed thenceforth, usually for want of revisions which he seldom got around to making because of occupation with new projects. It enabled him to find a way to justify anything for the sake of some accomplishment, whether it be the realization of a new work or the acquisition of a fancy car that had caught his eye, while at the same time insisting that his own music not be given disproportionate exposure at festivals which he helped organize. It caused him to show great callousness toward some of the emotional needs of his family while helping to provide them with well above average physical surroundings, including some facilities which he himself would never use. His self-absorption allowed him to plan detailed, well thought-through budgets for various major professional undertakings while his own finances remained in the realm of surrealism. It produced both a jovial, relaxed, earthy personality fond of telling stories and a haughtily dismissive one which relegated family and friends to distant corners from which they would be summoned when needed.

But this egocentricity also seems to have enabled Harris to produce a body of work which is among the richest, most distinctive, expressive, and colorful in the literature of American music. Of course, it is an uneven body of work and one which, for all its surface spontaneity, is based upon a set of principles which were carefully worked out relatively early in the composer's career and which possess a potentially limiting effect in terms of musical vocabulary and syntax. Yet the generosity of Harris's musical impulse managed to override the effects of these limitations in his best work while still allowing the lesser achievements to sing with an individual voice.

In a sense, a biography of Roy Harris is rendered superfluous by the music, for the man is there, warts and all—visionary aspiration, savage anger, lyrical effulgence, tender intimacy, ivory tower cerebration, bombast, unsuspected subtlety. Though the present book contains a good deal of biographical connecting tissue as a means of providing both a background for the origin and development of Harris's style and technique and a context within which specific works are discussed, the principal thrust is a concern with the music—how it came to sound the way it does, how it was created, how it is put together, and what it represents as a contribution to American musical culture. This last point will have to be in the form of a "progress report," for, while the music has been with us for over a half century, the man has only recently departed, and there is often a reevaluation of an important figure shortly after he has been "rowed across the river," as Harris liked to put it. This book is part of that reevaluation. It is built on both the earnest, often impressive, work of colleagues such as Arthur Farwell, Nicolas Slonimsky, and Robert Evett, who made pioneering attempts to come to grips with what Roy Harris is all about, and on my own quarter-century study of the music and close work with the composer for several years.

For this, the first complete examination of Roy Harris's life and works, I open with a pair of chapters concerning the early years (up through the late 1920s) and an examination of Harris's style and technique. These are followed by a series of chapters on the symphonies and the instrumental chamber works, which, since these categories comprise overall the composer's most substantial achievements and provide such a nearly comprehensive picture of his musical personality, are accorded the most detailed examination here. In addition, the symphonies, spanning virtually the entirety of Harris's career, provide, in the chapters devoted to them, a means of continuing the biographical thread. Next I examine Harris's achievements in other genres and media. Though these are nominally treated less intensively than the symphonies and chamber compositions, the fact that they share with these works many of the same features allows me to focus on the distinctive characteristics of each type, the background for an understanding of their style and technique having already been laid. A concluding chapter, serving as a kind of epilogue, rounds off the biographical material with a discussion of the composer's last years.

Though the publisher has generously allowed this volume to extend in length well beyond the norm established for the Twayne Musical Arts series, there are still areas I have not been able to explore as thoroughly as they warrant. Among these are the compositions for piano solo, for chorus, and for solo voice. In each of the chapters devoted to these genres, I have provided the usual overview but have restricted coverage of individual works to brief comments on a few of the more important ones. In order to accommodate even this much, I have had to leave out one category (albeit a minor one) entirely, that of Harris's ballets and film music. In the more heavily analytical portion of this book, that devoted to the symphonies and instrumental chamber compositions, I have foregone detailed analysis of a few pieces (e.g., the *American Portrait* and *Bicentennial* symphonies and one or two of the large chamber works) in order to treat with sufficient thoroughness the major efforts in these areas.

Roy Harris himself has occasionally been referred to as a kind of pioneer, a member of that generation of composers who helped forge what is sometimes thought to be an indigenous idiom of American concert music. However, this assumption is difficult to deal with—just what defines an "American" music? To what extent can it be free of European gestures when, in fact, it is still based upon principles, vocabulary, and musical syntax developed in Europe and when many of its major practitioners received their crucial musical education abroad? In the program note for his early orchestral work titled *Farewell to Pioneers,* Harris writes:

*Farewell to Pioneers* . . . is a tribute to a passing generation of Americans to which my own father and mother belong. Theirs was the last generation to affirm and live by the pioneer standards of frontiersmen. They were born of and taught by a race of men and women who seemed to crave the tang of conquering wildernesses and wresting abundance from virgin soil. . . . Consequently, this last generation inherited social and economic standards which were direct and simple. They abhored [*sic*] subtlety and nuance as evidence of an urbanity which could not survive the rigors of Nature's laws. Time has called them, and Industrialism has relegated their ideals to the shelves of *the impractical.* . . .[3]

Some of the pioneer ideals Harris describes above do indeed belong to the man and the music, as will be seen. Others, particularly the rejection of subtlety and nuance, will be found incompatible with the artistic personality he embodies.

Roy Harris adhered steadfastly to his aesthetics and the principles of his technique to the end and thus faced the inevitable charge from some quarters that he had failed to keep up with new trends, to be carried along by new currents. From avant garde to derriere garde—this is a condition that others besides Harris have faced (Richard Strauss is an example). Yet, it must always seem thus to the next generation, to the new "pioneers." However, as the process we call history sorts out and weaves the threads, allowing future generations to obtain an ever broader view of the emerging fabric, perspectives change and the old pioneers may no longer remain dust in the wind.

*Dan Stehman*

*Los Angeles Valley College*

# Note on the Music Examples

In accordance with the guidelines established by the publisher for the Twayne series, music examples extracted from ensemble compositions (e.g., works for orchestra, band, chamber media, chorus) are reduced to the minimum number of staves sufficient to make clear the point each citation is intended to illustrate. Also, because of the length of so many of Harris's melodies, I have usually been able to quote only the opening phrase or two from, or short extracts drawn from significant stages in the unfolding of, most of the thematic materials cited. A similar situation obtains with examples showing rhythmic designs, textures, scoring, etc.

Though all examples contain indications of dynamics, articulation, and phrasing, details of instrumentation are included only where they are necessary to the argument (i.e., where an example is intended to convey something concerning orchestration or the like).

In order to render the metric aspect unambiguous, I generally include a time signature, even if the example in question is not drawn from the beginning of a composition or section of a piece. Exceptions are the very brief citation (e.g., of a motive or other short figure) and the citation extracted from within the same context as a previous example for which a meter signature has already been supplied.

# Acknowledgments

I would like to thank the following publishers for allowing me to quote extracts from the compositions by Roy Harris on which they hold copyrights:

*Associated Music Publishers, Inc.* for:
*Abraham Lincoln Walks at Midnight*; *Bicentennial Symphony 1976* (Symphony No. 13); *Canticle of the Sun*; Concerto for Amplified Piano, Brass, String Basses, and Percussion; Concerto for Piano, Clarinet, and String Quartet; *Epilogue to Profiles in Courage–JFK*; Fantasy for Piano and Orchestra; *Give Me the Splendid Silent Sun*; *Horn of Plenty*; *Ode to Consonance*; Sonata for Piano; Symphony No. 7; Symphony No. 8 (*San Francisco Symphony*); Symphony No. 9; Symphony No. 10 (*Abraham Lincoln Symphony*); Symphony No. 11; Trio for Piano, Violin, and Violoncello

*Belwin Mills Publishing Corp.* for:
*The Birds' Courting Song*; *Cimarron*; *Evening Song*; *Freedom's Land* (solo voice/unison chorus version); Piano Suite in Three Movements; Sonata for Violin and Piano; Symphony No. 5; Symphony No. 6 (*Gettysburg*)

*Carl Fischer, Inc.* for:
Concerto for Violin and Orchestra (1949); *Fog*; *Fruit of Gold*; *Symphony 1933* (Symphony No. 1); Theme and Variations for Solo Accordion and Orchestra; Toccata for Piano

*G. Schirmer, Inc.* for:
*Farewell to Pioneers*; *Folksong Symphony* (Symphony No. 4); Little Suite for Piano; *Mi Chomocho*; Quartet No. 3; Quintet for Piano and Strings; *Soliloquy and Dance*; Symphony for Voices; Symphony No. 3; *When Johnny Comes Marching Home* (A Free Adaptation for Band); Three Variations on a Theme (Quartet No. 2)

*Acknowledgments*

*Shawnee Press* for:
Chorale (from Concerto for String Sextet)

I would also like to thank William D. Curtis for allowing me to incorporate some of the findings of his recent Roy Harris discography into the discography I have prepared for this book.

# Chronology

**1898**  LeRoy Ellsworth Harris born February 12 near Chandler, Oklahoma, to Elmer Harris and Laura Broddle.

**1903**  Family moves to southern California and settles on land of Lucky Baldwin estate in Covina.

**c. 1916**  Harris enlists in Army Training Corps (student division) at Berkeley, California (to c. 1918).

**1921**  Enrolls at University of California, Berkeley.

**1924**  Begins studies with Arthur Farwell (through 1925).

**c. 1925**  First trip to East Coast (New York City. Finishes Andante (first completed orchestral composition).

**1926**  Andante premiered by Howard Hanson and the Eastman School orchestra. Stays at MacDowell Colony, where he meets Aaron Copland. Goes to France for study with Nadia Boulanger.

**1927**  Premiere of Concerto for Piano, Clarinet, and String Quartet in Paris. Receives first Guggenheim Fellowship.

**1928**  Receives second Guggenheim.

**1929**  Injures spine in fall and returns to United States for surgery. Completes *Symphony–American Portrait 1929*.

**1930**  Begins composing away from piano.

**1931**  Receives Creative Fellowship of the Pasadena Music and Art Association (until c. 1932).

**1932**  Begins teaching summer sessions at Juilliard in New York (until 1938).

**1933**  Meets Serge Koussevitzky. Composes *Symphony 1933*. First commercial recording of a Harris composition: Concerto for Piano, Clarinet, and String Quartet.

**1934** *Symphony 1933* premiered by Koussevitzky and the Boston Symphony (first performance of a Harris symphony). Composes Symphony No. 2. Begins teaching at Westminster Choir School (until 1938). Contracts with G. Schirmer for publication of works (until 1940).

**1935** Helps organize Composers' Forum Laboratory.

**1936** Marries Beula Duffey (changes her given name to Johana). Writes Quintet for Piano and Strings as wedding present.

**1937** Father dies.

**1938** Completes Third Symphony. Teaches Princeton University summer session. "Let's Make Music" (first radio program).

**1939** Third Symphony premiered by Koussevitzky and the Boston Symphony. Harris firmly established in the forefront of American symphonic composers.

**1940** Contracts with Mills Music for publication of works (until (1945). Completes *Folksong Symphony* (original version).

**1941** Begins teaching (composer-in-residence) at Cornell University in Ithaca, New York (until 1943). Elected Honorary Fellow for 1941 for Stanford University. Receives honorary doctorate from Rutgers University. Begins teaching summer sessions at The Colorado College in Colorado Springs, Colorado.

**1942** Completes Fifth Symphony. Receives Elizabeth Sprague Coolidge medal for "Eminent Services to Chamber Music."

**1943** Begins teaching full time at The Colorado College (composer-in-residence; until 1948).

**1944** Elected to National Institute of Arts and Letters. Completes Sixth Symphony. Patricia, first child by Johana, born.

**1945** Becomes president of Fellowship of American Composers. Appointed Director of Music for the U. S. Office of War Information. Contracts with Carl Fischer for publication of works (until 1950).

**1948** Begins teaching at University of Utah at Logan (until 1949).

**1950** Begins teaching at Peabody College for Teachers in Nashville, Tennessee (until 1951).

**1951** Organizes first Cumberland Festival at University of the South in Sewanee, Tennessee. Contracts with G. Ricordi for publication of works (until c. 1956). Begins teaching at Pennsylvania College for Women under a Mellon grant (until 1956).

**1952** Organizes Pittsburgh International Festival of Contemporary Music. Completes Symphony No. 7 (original version). First long-playing record of a Harris work released: Symphony No. 3.

**1955** Sustains injuries in severe automobile accident, which necessitates hospitalization for some weeks.

**1956** Begins teaching at Southern Illinois University in Carbondale (until 1957). Joins Broadcast Music, Inc., and its subsidiary, Associated Music Publishers, for publication of works (until death). Symphony No. 7 wins Walter W. Naumburg Foundation Award.

**1957** Begins teaching at Indiana University as Patton Lecturer (until 1959).

**1958** Trip to USSR as part of delegation of American composers sponsored by United States Department of State. Mother dies.

**1959** Organizes the International Congress of Strings, with first session at Greenleaf Lake, Oklahoma. Begins teaching at Inter-American University in newly formed International Institute of Music in San Germán, Puerto Rico (until 1961).

**1960** Elected member of the *Academia de Bellas Artes y Sciencias de Puerto Rico.*

**1961** Begins teaching at University of California, Los Angeles, becoming professor-in-residence in 1963 (until 1971). First stereo recording of a Harris work released: *Folksong Symphony.*

**1962** Completes Eighth and Ninth Symphonies.

**1964** Receives honorary Doctor of Fine Arts degree from Westminster Choir College (formerly Westminster Choir School).

**1965** Completes Symphony No. 10 (*Abraham Lincoln Symphony*). Moves to final home in Pacific Palisades, California.

**1967** Completes Eleventh Symphony.

**1969** Completes *Pere Marquette Symphony.*

**1971** Begins teaching at California State University, Los Angeles (professor-in-residence; until c. 1976).

**1973** Roy Harris Archive founded at Cal State, L.A.

**1975** Completes *Bicentennial Symphony*. Receives third Guggenheim Fellowship.

**1976** Writes last composition: *Rejoice and Sing*. Appointed Composer Laureate of the State of California.

**1978** Elected to American Academy of Arts and Letters.

**1979** Dies October 1 in Santa Monica, California.

# 1

## The Early Years

### The Legend

Born in a log cabin in Lincoln County, Oklahoma, on Abraham Lincoln's birthday—this is the sort of ripe stuff on which an American legend of the first order might be built. And so it was, for under these circumstances one of the giants of the American musical scene apparently entered the world. I say "apparently" because for documentation of one of the best known stories in the historical background of contemporary American music we have had to rely to a large extent on the sometimes faulty memory of its central figure.

It must be remembered that, at the time of Roy Harris's birth (supposedly February 12, 1898), Oklahoma was still a territory and records in many areas concerning its citizenry are either incomplete or nonexistent.[1] When the elderly composer was honored during the spring of 1979 by the Oklahoma State Historical Society, that organization was able to locate and present him with a copy of the deed to the land his father had claimed as a result of his participation in one of the last of the Cimarron land rushes.[2] The land deed, however, is dated 1901, thus conflicting with Harris's recollection of his birth year and place. However, the problems of record keeping and of communication in those days may have delayed for some time the filing and recording of a claim of this sort.

### The Character

#### Early Influences

The uncertainty about details notwithstanding, there is little reason to doubt the essentials of Roy Harris's background and upbringing. Whatever the exact circumstances of his birth, there is no question that he was brought up in a region of the United States that was sparsely settled and in which survival was a trying affair. It is thus apparent that a closeness to the soil and a sense of profound loneliness and sadness bound up with his early perception of nature were with him almost from the beginning. As he recalled many decades later:

> As a boy, I lived quite alone for the first five years of my life, in that log cabin, when my father was working and my mother was bedridden. That tended to make me go toward nature for companionship. I also became introspective. When we moved to California, it was even easier to do that. . . . The trees were wonderful there; the mountain sunsets, the snow on old Baldy, all the bird songs. . . .[3]

Harris once told me that there seemed to be areas of human care to which even music, with all its potent qualities, could not penetrate, and indeed, underneath his outgoing exterior there lay a deep core of striving, of a yearning to achieve the unattainable, to express the unexpressible—the marks of a true visionary. However, Harris was not a wholly private man, for he often loved to be surrounded by people and much of what he was lay near the surface for all to see. He was too childlike, too naively unaware of the components of his personality to pose or dissemble. In fact, he was often highly critical of those who tried to manufacture an image, or a musical style, feeling that this should grow from within, unbidden.

## Traits

In many ways Harris was a very simple man. Though his personality was often commanding and charismatic, he could be charming, even, at times, deferential to the point of seeming shy. But he was also capable of being fearlessly outspoken on issues of importance to him. Partly, one suspects, through heredity, partly through the self-reliance learned in his lonely youth, he became, as I have indicated earlier, one of the most egocentric of men. One could only truly relate to him through an interest in his work and ideas. His supreme self-confidence enabled him to hold forth Wagner-style with the appearance of authority on subjects about which he in reality knew very little. He fancied himself a mover and primal force in areas outside of music, profferring advice to statesmen, captains of industry and finance, and sports club owners with complete lack of inhibition.

Harris evidently annoyed many of his colleagues during the 1930s and 40s with his observations about what he perceived to be the nature of

American music. As Virgil Thomson exploded on one occasion: "One would think, to read his prefaces, that he had been awarded by God, or at least by popular vote, a monopolistic privilege of expressing our nation's deepest ideals and highest aspirations."[4] But for Harris to make a conscientious effort to restrain himself in this respect would be tantamount to restricting the natural flow of spontaneous enthusiasm and the magnificent soar of the free spirit to which we owe in part such a rich artistic achievement.

Harris was an enormously physical man. According to his recollections, his paternal forebears, both male and female, were large, lusty animals and, but for a bout with typhoid fever as a child, he probably would have matured in similar fashion. However, though his growth was apparently stunted as a result of the illness, he nonetheless stood nearly six feet tall, and his rawboned features (which softened considerably as he grew much heavier with age) and earthy, out-of-doors qualities revealed that he had indeed retained many of the qualities which characterized his people.

In his youth, Harris helped his father on the farm the family had established in the San Gabriel Valley near Los Angeles, and he was eventually given his own acreage to work. He participated actively in sports during high school, distinguishing himself in tennis, baseball, and football. He recalled that he was a sufficiently accomplished tennis player to gain a local championship and excelled in baseball to the extent that he became a prospect for the American League. However, Harris was also aware of his limitations in these areas. His eyes were on bigger things even then, but what they were he did not know. He always retained this early love of sports, however, and in later years followed football, baseball, and basketball avidly as a spectator. The blistering profanity that occasionally accompanied the difficult labor pangs attending the birth of a new work was gentility incarnate compared with that directed at umpires, coaches, and players in sports events. His wife Johana sometimes had to explain to unnerved guests that the bellows and roars emanating from a room or studio at the far end of the property were not those of a charging, sexually inflamed bull, but were merely the exertions of a harmless composer having a little fun second-guessing the participants in a sports broadcast on the radio or television.

Harris had a passion for speed; for him it was as much an essential part of the American psyche at large as it was of his own.[5] He coupled this passion with an equally consuming one for fine automobiles. Being behind the wheel of a car gave him a sense of mastery, of being in complete control, of

an exhilaration and sense of momentum that doubtless tapped the same
source from which flowed the energy and organic continuity of his music.
The saga of the Harris automobiles, sometimes three or four in a single
year, could well occupy a complete, hilarious chapter in a large-scale
biography. He was the intimate of, and gullible prospect for, new and used
car dealers from one end of the country to the other.

Harris also fancied himself something of a financial wizard, with the
disastrous result that it is doubtful if the Byzantine tapestry of the family's
money concerns will ever be unwoven. But no matter—he always survived, even flourished, seeing to it that he had comfortable surroundings in
which to work, regardless of what the debt to the future might be.

Perhaps the old system of barter by which Harris's parents had lived
during the frontier days of his youth remained with him, for he often
accepted services in lieu of money from his students (at least the private
ones). Most often these activities involved doing copying (that expensive
bête noire for most composers) and secretarial work. Occasionally a
student and/or his wife would cook and perform household chores. The
"gay guild," as the Harris household, with its students, assistants, and
various supernumeraries was called during the 1940s and 50s, was a lively
place, a far distance from the loneliness of his childhood.

The self-absorption that threatened to devour many souls of less resi-
lient will who came within his sphere in the end threatened to swallow the
composer himself. As he grew older, Harris drew his creative world of
specialized vocabulary and techniques more tightly around him. This
resulted in several commentators criticizing what they sensed as a lack of
drive, of "need," to compose during the last ten or fifteen years of his life
and an equally noticeable element of self-repetition. Though these observations are misleading to the extent that they are generally based on
extremely limited acquaintance with the creative products of these years,
they have some validity in reflecting Harris's occasional lack of self-
criticism and his tendency to rely overly on tried-and-true devices and
gestures which he naively felt would always be accepted as new and fresh.

Signs of this lack of self-criticism manifested themselves quite early
in his career. As Henry Cowell observed, in an often cited remark: "He
often convinces his friends and listeners of the extreme value of his works
by his own indefatigable enthusiasm for them, when in reality they are only
mildly interesting and would not be very highly regarded by these selfsame
people if they heard them in performance without the stimulating presence
of their creator."[6] Many years later we find Virgil Thomson making a
similar observation: "His tendency to write as if the work he is writing has

already been judged a masterpiece (at least by himself) even before it has been composed is not one of Mr. Harris's most winning traits."[7] However, against these observations must be placed Harris's proclivity toward constant revising and rewriting and his tendency to speak disparagingly, once the heat of creation was off, of a work that he felt did not come off well. Harris was simply one of those creators who became possessed by whatever he was working on at the time. Thus, the naive enthusiasm that Cowell and Thomson observed did not result so much from conceit as from a desire to accomplish the best work of which he was capable, however modest the dimensions and aims of a particular project.

This enthusiasm, coupled with a seemingly inexhaustible drive and energy, led Harris beyond his own work to the consideration of the "idea" of music as a vital communal experience. This, in turn, stimulated him to develop festivals and competitions of various sorts, and to participate actively as a conductor in performances of his own compositions and works of other men, both past and present. Though self-centered, Harris was not an intriguer or a politician. Open and generous in many respects, he did a great deal from the 1930s through the 1960s to help his students and colleagues obtain performances, publication, and various types of both musical and nonmusical employment. He was always ready, even to the extent of interrupting his composing schedule on occasion, to lecture civic and educational groups and to advise young people in need of counsel.

There was also a "grass is greener" aspect to Harris's personality. He was frequently on the move to new locales, thinking nothing in later years, after siring a large family, of uprooting them all with little notice to move to a new community, often in a different section of the country. These moves generally accompanied a migration from one educational institution to another, each time with the hope of achieving the dual goals of infusing educational programs with fresh ideas and finding a congenial climate in which to create—and in which to be celebrated. During his career as an educator, Harris seemed to work most effectively not in the classroom, where his limited harmonic vocabulary and idiosyncratic approach tended to be restrictive, but rather in the relaxed give-and-take of individual or small-group instruction. He thus fulfilled a great deal of his teaching obligation at home.[8]

Harris undeniably possessed a tremendous resilience and an unshakeable optimism, both in the real world and in his music, even when confronting the darker aspect of contemporary life and some of the seemingly insoluble problems of existence. His rich and complex personality must thus be seen as a source of both the occasional weaknesses in his music and its very potent strengths. The "grass is greener" syndrome, applied in the larger, visionary context in which he so often seemed to function, may indeed have worked out for him after all, no matter what the cost to others. Johana Harris summed it up when she wrote, during the 1940s:

> Most people think of my husband as a good-natured, easygoing Westerner. And so he is. But he is many other people as well. To me he is a child—always eager—always ready to believe in everyone, always expecting miracles to happen, always being hurt and enraged by the social and economic injustices that he sees and feels everywhere he goes. And yet he is an unquenchable optimist who loves beauty in every phase of living.
>
> As a husband, friend, teacher, he is loyal and generous—I must say a spendthrift of his time and energy and talents.
>
> He is a child who will never grow old. Each new idea, situation, person, book, event, is a new adventure. . . .[9]

## Family Background

Roy Harris's ancestry is a mixture of Irish and Scottish (on his father's side) and Welsh (on his mother's). The paternal grandfather was a first-generation American, born in Kentucky. A large, powerfully built man, he sired thirteen children (ten boys and three girls). He met his wife, who was of Scottish background, in Ohio and, following the Civil War, became a Methodist circuit rider, going from one area to another trying to "save souls." He was seemingly a man of great independence of spirit and possessed a strong belief in learning young the lessons of self-reliance. Following his wife's death, he called the family together and told them they were on their own. They dispersed widely, though some later settled in southern California after their brother Elmer, Roy Harris's father, had established a home there.

Harris's mother, Laura Broddle, was born in Wales, but left for the United States at about the age of one. Her father became a pony express rider, acquiring the name "Pony Express Broddle" as a result of his colorful exploits on the dangerous routes in the frontier days of nineteenth-century America. According to the composer, Laura and Elmer Ellsworth Harris met at Lake Arrowhead, California, where Elmer was working as a cook, though I have not been able to verify this. The two were married, and Elmer resolved to provide a stable home for his young wife. His choice of a route by which to accomplish this might seem strange today, but during this period the options, and the aims, of many Americans were rather different: he learned of the large areas of unclaimed land in Oklahoma territory that had been made available for settlement and, after making his way there, took part, with his father-in-law, in one of the last of the Oklahoma land rushes or "runs." The two men staked a claim near the town of Chandler in central Oklahoma and built a log cabin on their acreage. The mother and, possibly, a son Carl, born in 1896, were eventually sent for, and it was in this rough dwelling that LeRoy Ellsworth Harris claimed to have come into existence.

## Character Traits of the Parents

Harris, at one time or another, provided somewhat ambivalent descriptions of his parents: the burly, gruff father who nonetheless possessed sufficient culture to quote large chunks of the classics in Latin but was held back by the prevailing mores of rural America and by the rough life on the frontier from showing any real understanding or appreciation of his son's artistic ambitions and subsequent accomplishments; the mother, ailing during much of Harris's childhood, who, though apparently possessing some musical gifts, which she was willing to share with the youngster, seemed at times equally uncomprehending and unsupportive of his career.

The two parents, though sharing a number of traits, nonetheless seemed at odds in important ways. As Harris recalled to me (albeit with tongue in cheek), "My father loved his wife and tolerated his kids and my mother loved her kids and tolerated her old man." One wonders how much real affection life back then could spare for a solitary youngster (nearly all the composer's siblings died in childhood). Still, the boy, even at that age, may neither have needed nor been receptive toward this sort of thing. The self-reliance and solitary universe so much in evidence later may have begun even then to place him at a distance from others.

But, the loneliness aside, Harris generally recalled the early years with affection, retaining a genuine warmth of feeling for both parents and keeping in touch with them at the family home in California until Elmer Harris's death in mid-1937 and Laura's passing in mid-1958.

## Youth

As mentioned earlier, the Harris family lived, like most of their neighbors, through a system of barter, exchanging some of the crops they had succeeded in growing for other items necessary to make life bearable. As evidence of the difficulty in surviving in this wilderness, with its snow-bound winters, the two other children born during this period died while still infants: Carl in 1897, Stanley (born in 1901) in 1903. One other brother Glenn, born after the family had moved to southern California, lived only slightly longer, from 1907 to 1910. Of the five children known to have been born to Elmer and Laura Harris, only Roy and his much younger sister, Irene (born in 1907), survived to adulthood.[10]

## The Move to California

Laura Harris contracted malaria around the time LeRoy was born and was in ill health for about ten years after that. (The composer's own bout with typhoid fever at age five has been alluded to above.) Around 1903, Elmer, alarmed by a doctor's warning that his wife would die of the lingering illness unless she were moved to a more salubrious climate, took action. He auctioned off the homestead (which was later discovered to be part of an exceptionally rich oil field), the money from which he supplemented with the winnings of a lucky gambling streak, and used this to purchase some land in California from the estate of the notorious gambler Lucky Baldwin, (land that originally had been part of a Spanish land grant). The acreage the Harrises acquired was located in the town of Covina in the San Gabriel Valley area east of Los Angeles. Elmer packed the family onto the train which left from Guthrie, Oklahoma, and they made the hard journey to their new home.[11]

Upon arriving in California, Elmer managed, with the help of some of their new neighbors, to erect a small pine house. Once settled, the family found that life was far from easy, but at least the southern California climate was much milder than where they had come from and cultivating the land seemed to present fewer problems. Though the San Gabriel Valley was primarily a citrus growing area, it was also hospitable to a variety of other crops, and Elmer started by farming potatoes.

## Early Musical Experiences

The mother's health began to improve in the new climate, and, perhaps as an added spur to her morale, Elmer bought her a piano. It was on this instrument that Laura Harris gave the future composer his first music lessons. Harris later recalled some of his earliest musical impressions thus:

> The music I took to most was Mozart—not only because I could play Mozart, because the Mozart sonatas are so much easier to play, or rather to play at, because to play them well is difficult. I couldn't play Beethoven in the beginning. . . . My mother also taught me how to play hymns, and that led me to

harmony, more than I realized at the time. There was all of this ornamentation in music, and the sounds of nature, the bird songs, and the railroads and whistles on each side of the valley. The Santa Fe ran on the north side, and the Southern Pacific on the south side; the Sante Fe ran to Chicago, and the Southern Pacific went to New Orleans. There was a tremendous sense of romantic [*sic*] in my youth, all related to sound.[12]

When he entered high school, Harris took up the clarinet and joined the band, partly, it seems, to keep the comradeship of his male classmates, who seemed deeply suspicious of the manhood of anyone who played piano. As another gesture in this direction toward acceptance, he shortened his given name of LeRoy to Roy and competed actively in sports. Full approval by his peers appears to have come when he succeeded in breaking his nose and an arm in football.

## The Young Farmer

In the meantime, Harris continued to help out on the farm. In fact, one of his most potent early memories involved the recollection of Elmer whistling the tune "When Johnny Comes Marching Home" briskly in the morning and then slowly and sadly on returning home from the fields in the evening.

The father bought the boy his own ten acres of land during the high school years, and by the time he graduated, Harris was on his way to being a successful farmer, with his own car and some money in the bank. Elmer, too, had prospered to the extent that he was able, with his son's help, to build a larger, more comfortable house on the Covina property.[13]

However, the eighteen-year-old was still uncertain about his future. Certainly music seemed to have a place in it, for he had continued to play the piano all through high school, in addition to pursuing his newly acquired skill on clarinet. As far as creative musical thinking was concerned though, he lacked sufficient vocabulary and technique actually to write anything down, but he did do a great deal of improvising. He was beginning to develop a vague perception of the properties of chord color and resonance, a perception which later became a vital part of his aesthetics.

## Early Musical Contacts

Harris was fortunate in being exposed to some individuals of above average intellectual and cultural attributes during these early years. One he remembered fondly was a professor Groom, the German-born conductor of the San Gabriel Valley High School orchestra. Groom apparently saw to it that his charges received thorough training both in reading sessions and in rehearsals for concerts. Another was an unusual gentleman named Alec Anderson. Anderson, a diminutive Scotsman who worked as a certified public accountant for the area Orange Grower's Association, seems to have had a broad spectrum of interests outside of his profession. Evidently the most important of these was music, which he pursued actively as a local church organist. Anderson was responsible for introducing the young Harris to the thrill of hearing a live symphony orchestra, the occasion being a visit to Los Angeles by the Minneapolis Symphony.

## World War I and Greener Grass

Elmer apparently hoped his son would follow in his footsteps as a farmer. The acreage he had purchased for the young man, and for which Harris was apparently expected to repay him out of earnings off of the land, was designed to help set the boy up in this occupation. However, the "grass-is-greener" virus had already infected young Harris, and he yearned more and more to surround himself with music. The place to do this was obviously the big city, and World War I gave him an unlikely assist in realizing some of his yearnings. Around 1916 he enlisted in a student division of the Army Training Corps, which was stationed at Berkeley. Naturally Harris aimed for the top—an officer's position. However, in the sometimes unfathomable ways of the military, he was trained in heavy artillery, apparently, as he recalled, because of the fact that he had had some experience working around machinery and driving trucks on the family farm.

The war ended, though, before Harris had an opportunity to see active duty. But the time served up north enabled him to become exposed to a good deal of the lively musical activity in the San Francisco Bay area. When the San Francisco Symphony Orchestra played in Berkeley, the young man was invariably in attendance. In fact, he managed to land a job as an usher at these concerts, thus enabling him to satisfy his craving for music while helping to provide a little financial sustenance. (Harris recalled that he also did some ushering at orchestral concerts in Los Angeles after his return there.)

## At Loose Ends

After the Armistice was declared, Harris returned home and sold his farm land. Not wishing to rely on the family for income, he began hunting for a full-time job, eventually finding work delivering butter and eggs for a dairy, on a route that took him from the San Gabriel Valley out to the coast near Venice. During his years on the farm, Harris had become accustomed to arising early, and this was reinforced by his stint with the dairy. The habit eventually became so ingrained that, until the last fifteen years or so of his life, he did the bulk of his composing in the early morning hours (though if trapped by an exceedingly fierce blaze of inspiration he would sometimes work at odd hours, even around the clock).

## Higher Education

In 1919 Harris decided to pursue his education further. He went back up to the Bay area and enrolled at the Berkeley campus of the University of California. Later he took some courses at the University of California, Los Angeles, when it was still called Los Angeles Normal School.

Among the studies he undertook were philosophy, sociology, and economics. He also had courses in music history and appreciation, and these further whetted his appetite to discover more about this art that was exercising an increasingly greater hold over him. He became dissatisfied with the imprecision and the lack of an absolute frame of reference inherent in verbal communication; it was only in music that he could truly find the qualities of concreteness and stability that he deemed necessary to express himself with precision.

The information on Harris's life during the early 1920s is incomplete and ambiguous. He gave contradictory accounts at various times, sometimes confusing incidents with places and jumbling time sequences. However, at one point during these years he did use some of the money saved from farming to buy a Steinway grand piano and he improvised a great deal on this instrument, as he had done on his mother's piano in Covina. Now, however, he began to realize something of the extent of the knowledge and discipline needed to acquire a technique in order to set down and develop the musical ideas which were starting to come with increasing insistence.

Harris went first to Charles Demarest, then to Ernest Douglas, both organists, and from them received his first private instruction in the fundamentals of harmony. It was not long before the ambitious young man aspired to large accomplishments and, in the foolhardy, but perhaps necessary, way of many fledgling composers, he succeeded in putting together a large work for chorus and orchestra (which has apparently been lost). He made the acquaintance of a man named Clark, who served as program annotator for the San Francisco Symphony Orchestra. During a visit with

Harris, Clark noticed the large score on the piano and inquired about it. He was evidently sufficiently impressed to ask to take the piece to show Alfred Hertz, the conductor of the San Francisco Symphony. Hertz, in turn, was perceptive enough to see through the obvious immaturities of the score and asked to meet the young man so he could offer some encouragement. He felt, however, that Harris, though talented, still needed a good deal of further instruction and gave him a letter of introduction to Albert Elkus, a prominent composer and teacher in the Bay area at that time.

Elkus, however, was not at all impressed. He had traveled abroad a good deal and had kept abreast of the younger generation of composers in Europe and of the level of music education there. He realized how much more thoroughly they had been trained by this age than had the young farmer from southern California and felt that Harris's late start in taking up music in a serious, systematic way, his lack of anything beyond a rudimentary technical training, and his exposure to a relatively narrow spectrum of music made it seem virtually impossible that he would ever be able to make it as a composer. He refused to teach Harris, a decision which did not deter the aspiring youth for long. In fact, it seemed to make him all the more determined in his ambition, but this determination was tempered by the knowledge of how much he still had to learn.[14]

## Return to Los Angeles, With New Determination

Harris left Berkeley and returned to the Los Angeles area, apparently resuming his truck driving to earn a livelihood. He sought out new teachers, studying for awhile with Fannie Charles Dillon and Henry Schoenfeld, the latter described by Slonimsky (*Cimarron Composer,* p. 13) as "a good musician who wrote good German-type music, mostly in the key of B-flat major." However, these contacts were only stopgaps who, though providing some experience in the aesthetics and mechanics of the common-practice harmony and traditional forms which were the products of a long European heritage, failed to satisfy the need the fledgling composer was beginning to feel to develop his own vocabulary and practices. He needed someone closer in character and philosophy to his own rough-hewn, expansive, iconoclastic temperament.

## Farwell

Harris found the kindred soul he was seeking in Arthur Farwell. Farwell, roughly a generation older than his future pupil, was born in Minnesota and had originally planned a career in electrical engineering. As with Harris, however, he discovered somewhat tardily that music was his destiny and, after studying in Boston at the New England Conservatory, went to Europe, where he worked with Engelbert Humperdinck and Hans Pfitzner in Germany and the organist-composer Alexandre Guilmant in Paris. Though his own music remained strongly indebted to late nineteenth-century European practice, especially in its highly chromatic harmonic idiom, Farwell nonetheless had a venturesome mind and a broad cultural outlook.[15]

He also had strong leanings toward mysticism and the contemplation of nature. He was partial to Emerson (being, in fact, a cousin of the New England transcendentalist) and Whitman. With respect to the latter, Farwell was a seminal figure in Harris's development, for it was he who introduced the young man to the epic "prose-poetry" of Whitman, thus providing a sort of philosophical focus for some of Harris's aspirations toward large forms and great breadth of expression.

In later years Harris was vague about his studies with Farwell and what specifically he had learned from this first truly intensive work with a single individual. He readily acknowledged the aforementioned introduction to Whitman's work and also indicated that some of the foundation for his mature harmonic vocabulary was laid during this period. As Harris recalled: "First thing he let me do was to develop new ideas in harmony. He encouraged me 100 percent. As a matter of fact, some of the harmony I've been teaching . . . was developed way back there, because they're basic principles. It had to do with voicing mainly."[16]

Farwell's own recollection supports the above: "He had discovered a new harmonic ocean in the years 1924–25, into which I was privileged to peer a bit. . . . I have caught up with his conception of form, I have grasped his melodic scheme, but while I have dipped a considerable distance into his harmonic waters I have as yet found no plummet long enough to sound its ultimate depths."[17] There is an implication in this statement, supported by occasional remarks Harris made to me, that Farwell allowed his student considerable latitude in structuring his own course of study. Harris remembered examining during this period a good deal of orchestral music, finding much of value in the works in this medium by Tchaikovsky and Beethoven. The latter in particular revealed to him much of what he called "dynamic orchestration," that is, orchestration which grows out of the acoustic properties and the idiomatic techniques of the instruments themselves. When writing an orchestral piece, Harris started off by writing directly into score, rather than orchestrating piano drafts, thus developing a feeling for the medium from the inside, through the means of conceiving idiomatic materials for it.

The influence Farwell may have had on his student, aside from the introduction of the Whitman stream, is difficult to assess. While Harris's early Andante revels in a harmonic idiom redolent of Franck and early Scriabin which must have been received warmly by his teacher, the mature works eschewed this style for an idiom whose principles of melodic and formal generation, diatonic harmony, and clarity of scoring seem to lie at the antipode from Farwell's post-Romantic vein.

One suspects, however, that the most lasting effects of Farwell's influence were the breadth of culture, open-mindedness, generosity of spirit, and visionary idealism that helped set the late-blooming composer firmly on the path of his pursuit, seizing his most promising traits and encouraging their development. What a different, but equally potent, ambience Harris would encounter a few years later at the Boulangerie!

## Other Teachers

During the mid-1920s Harris also took some lessons in scoring from Modeste Altschuler, a Russian conductor and orchestrator. However, the young American didn't mesh with him aesthetically. As Harris recalled: "He was great for embellishments and all kinds of ornamentation and to make something seem that which it wasn't."[18] However, some of the frequently ornamental counterpoint of Harris's mature work may constitute a weak reverberation of this contact.

Harris also made a few trips to Santa Barbara to show his work to the British composer Arthur Bliss, who was living in the area at that time. Harris remembered almost nothing of these visits except that Bliss may have given him some advice on orchestration. This would have been illuminating, for the sharply etched scoring of Bliss's work is quite a contrast to the way Altschuler's approach struck Harris.

## Marriage

Around 1922 Harris met a young girl named Davida. Her exuberance and faith in his potential led him to sense he had found someone who could provide companionship and the comfortable surroundings necessary for his creative work. The two were married that same year and settled in Los Angeles. A daughter, Jean (with whom the composer was subsequently to lose touch), resulted from this marriage. During the next decade, Harris was to marry at least twice more before his final union, with Beula Duffey (Johana). However, this is another of those "gray" areas in his life about which reasonably complete and accurate information has not yet come to light: even the full names of the two known wives between Davida and Beula (Sylvia and Hilda) are not known for sure.

Harris continued his musical studies and his truck driving. Though the work with Farwell was rewarding and illuminating and undoubtedly gave the young man his most potent encouragement to date, Harris felt the need to broaden his perspective, to seek new ground. The few small pieces he completed during the mid-1920s, some of which he had had an opportunity to hear (partly through Farwell's endeavors), had been valuable experiences, as had some of the cultural activities to which he had been exposed in the Los Angeles area. None of these, however, really fulfilled his desire to work on a large canvas, to succeed in writing something big as a means of proving himself and of showing that an American composer could indeed compete with the best Europe had to offer.

With Farwell's encouragement Harris planned a large-scale work, a symphony titled *Our Heritage*. However, he managed to complete only the Andante movement mentioned earlier, but it was this rather immature piece, with its uncharacteristic harmonic idiom, that provided the young composer with his first real breakthrough in gaining national recognition.

## New York

At about the same time he was drafting the aborted symphony, the young composer, in typically abrupt fashion, decided to go east. He hitched rides on trucks and hid away in freight cars, doing some odd jobs along the way. Though he eventually reached New York City, his exertions in accomplishing this goal were not rewarded with tangible success. Since he belonged to no union, there was difficulty in getting work. He did eventually manage, however, to obtain a job as a counselor in one of the settlement houses on the Lower East Side. As Harris recollected: "I taught chorus. . . . I stayed the winter, studied, and went to concerts. I wasn't oriented. I didn't have a place. I was just existing in a sense. I was very poor, soaking in a lot of experience."[19]

## A Breakthrough

The discouraged Harris returned to California, Davida, and Farwell. His devoted teacher found him jobs as a music critic on the *Los Angeles*

*Illustrated Daily News* and as a harmony teacher at the old Hollywood Conservatory. Farwell also introduced Harris to some local persons of influence, among them a number of music patrons. The most important of these was perhaps Artie Mason Carter, a doctor's wife who, along with Farwell and others, was responsible for the founding of the Hollywood Bowl. (Mrs. Carter remained a friend and occasional adviser of Harris until her death in the early 1970s.)

Harris decided to send the score of the Andante to Howard Hanson, who, in 1924, had been appointed director of the Eastman School of Music, a position he was to hold for forty years. Already at this early date Hanson was seriously committed to the cause of the American composer, establishing a festival in the spring of 1925 for the performance of previously unheard and unpublished compositions. He was sufficiently impressed with Harris's Andante to program it with his Eastman orchestra, thus becoming the first conductor to play a work in the orchestral medium in which Harris was later to attain such distinction.

The reception some of the New York critics gave the Andante was encouraging. Back home the small success in the East seems to have galvanized Farwell into action, for he took the opportunity during a speech given at a Hollywood Bowl Association Annual Dinner to reprimand the local citizens for the lip service they paid to culture and for their neglect of the young American composer. Artie Mason Carter was stirred to invite Harris to play the Andante for her on the piano. After hearing the work, she introduced the young man to the celebrated pianist, Ellie Ney, who was the wife of the conductor Willem van Hoogstraten. Ney also thought highly of the piece and sent the score to her husband, who was conducting the New York Philharmonic at the time, urging him to program it. Harris recalled that van Hoogstraten practically had to be "browbeaten" into doing the Andante, but he finally played it at a Lewisohn Stadium concert in July 1926. Harris quit his job, borrowed some money, and went back to New York to hear his piece.

During this second visit in the East, the composer managed a short stay at the MacDowell Colony in Peterborough, New Hampshire. The Colony had been established by Marion MacDowell, the widow of the American composer-pianist, as a place where composers, writers, painters, and other artists would have peaceful, comfortable surroundings isolated from the bustle and increasingly frantic pace of twentieth-century America. Here they could create and, if they wished, engage in stimulating artistic and social intercourse with their colleagues.

It was at the Colony that Harris met Aaron Copland, who had started his musical training in earnest much earlier than the newcomer from the west and was already on the rise to national prominence. Copland had studied in France during the early 1920s with a woman who was gaining increasing stature as a teacher of the first rank, Nadia Boulanger. Harris's somewhat more experienced colleague recognized both the young man's talent and his shortcomings and suggested a period of study abroad with Boulanger.

## "Lady Luck"

Harris, whenever reminiscing about his career, gave pride of place to "Lady Luck," as he called her, among the factors which enabled him to realize his destiny. Indeed, a confluence of events that took place at this time does seem to lend some credence to his belief in luck. In addition to the meeting with Copland and the efforts shortly prior to that of Hanson, Farwell, and Mmes Carter and Ney, Harris also found a new supporter in the person of Alma Wertheim, a New Yorker, who was a patroness of the arts and whose husband was a banker.[20] She had heard one of the Andante performances and telegrammed Harris to come and see her. The occasion was a party at her home and among those attending were several musicians who had also heard the work. Mrs. Wertheim seconded Copland's advice about studying abroad and offered to finance the undertaking for a period of four years. As the composer later recalled this important event: "I agreed to accept with the understanding that if it didn't seem I would make the grade by the time I was forty, then I'd pay it back to her. . . . She said it had never happened to her before. She said, 'You really are a rural farmer, aren't you? . . . I can't make an agreement like that.' I said, 'I can't take the money then.'"[21]

Eventually Mrs. Wertheim acquiesced in this stipulation and the young Oklahoman transplanted to California now moved across the ocean to France for the most intensive period of musical study he was ever to undertake, one that was to set him on the road to musical maturity.

## The "Boulangerie"

Nadia Boulanger had established herself during the 1920s as a musical pedagogue in France, holding classes at the *Conservatoire,* the *École Normale de Musique,* and at the recently opened *Conservatoire Américain* in Fontainebleau. Having abandoned her own musical creative efforts relatively early, feeling she lacked the depth of talent necessary for this, she turned her enormous energies to stimulating and honing the creativity of others.[22]

## Boulanger's Ideals and Commitment

Boulanger's sense of commitment to art, discipline, precision of thought and economy of means, was the beacon that guided her teaching. As another of her many American students reminisced after her death:

> She brought mental strictness and control to the fore. . . . We [Americans] needed it as an antidote, . . . because we were brought up with the democratic dispersal of energy, with no real commitment to anything. . . . The sense of rhythmic control, phrasing, and coherent structure that she taught, the elimination of unncessary notes—all these matters of discipline had a great impact on the development of a mature style in this country. It had nothing like the same effect in France. . . . Hers was but one of several "schools" in France. . . . She tried to maintain the traditional discipline of the Conservatoire, of Fauré and Dubois, and to demonstrate how it could be made pertinent.[23]

## Harris's Routine with Boulanger

Harris stayed first at Chatou, on the Seine, with his new wife Sylvia, whom he had met in New York. However, according to Virgil Thomson, "After one winter spent on the banks of the Seine, . . . he found that neither the dampness nor his wife, a worried reader of intellectual magazines, was good for his work. So he renounced them both and went to live alone on higher ground, near Gargenville, where his teacher, Nadia Boulanger, lived much of the year."[24]

Harris found a little cottage in the small village of Juziers (the same town in which Copland stayed for awhile during his studies in France). It was provided with the barest of furnishings, the most important of which was a dilapidated upright piano. Harris's lessons with Boulanger were on Friday evenings, and he commuted to Paris by train.

Boulanger typically took the least accomplished students early in the week, saving the more promising ones for the end. Harris recalled with pride his late Friday position, but one wonders, in spite of the cordial relations and mutual respect between teacher and pupil, how much fundamental mutual empathy there really was. (In fact, Harris's accounts of his relationship with Boulanger, and even of the intensiveness of his studies with her, were as inconsistent as those concerning other aspects of his early life.)

Right from the start, the young man from California resisted her regime:

> Had I known then what I subsequently learned, my first year would not have
> been such a fiasco. I would have taken advantage of the opportunities which
> Boulanger offered of meeting other musicians, . . . absorbed a sense of style and
> perspective, learned how to live and act. But no! I would have none of it. I came to
> learn to be a composer; I was like the rookie who came to France to win the
> war. . . . I was all for immediate action. I rejected Boulanger's formal teaching of
> counterpoint, harmony, solfeggio. And she had the patience of an angel. She called
> me her autodidact and allowed me to go my own way. . . . I could not accept the
> European idea of discipline wherein one learns by exercising a system of formalized
> studies in harmony, counterpoint and form. It all seemed to leave out the exercise
> of the most important element in a composer's equipment—the imagination. That
> was my belief then and still is my belief.[25]

Harris did not want the *Conservatoire* or, as he put it, *Academie Fran-
caise,* approach, which he likened to the neatly manicured gardens at
Versailles. He reportedly brought Boulanger to tears with an independence of spirit she had not experienced thus far from someone so raw and
untried. She seemed at a loss as to how to proceed, her only answer to the
young composer being that her approach was all she knew. Harris suggested that a much more efficient and productive procedure would be one
wherein he would profit from the mistakes of others: he asked that she
bring in several works by the great masters in which she felt there were
flaws; they would then discuss these and how the mistakes could have
been avoided. But this rather simple-minded, though useful, approach was
evidently only one aspect of a program that the two worked out together.
"Autodidact" though he may have been, Harris nonetheless seemed able
to engage in a give-and-take in which both he and Boulanger were able to
contribute to a useful course of study.

Boulanger fueled Harris's interest in the music of the past, and it seems
to have been through her that he first became acquainted with the magnificent literature of monophonic chant and with some of the great masters of
the Middle Ages and the Renaissance. Boulanger was interested in the
history of music as the sum of individual accomplishments, and her concern
with the styles and techniques of particular creators was another manifestation of her desire for precision and the avoidance of vague abstractions
and generalities. She assigned Harris exercises in the styles of various
composers, and he acquiesced in this (the story of his fulfilling her first
assignment for twenty melodies of this sort by coming up with over a
hundred is relatively well known).

But Harris's chief learning method seems to have been an immersion in various aesthetic principles and the gleaning of specific techniques that he might find useful in realizing his own creative efforts. One of the most revealing statements he ever made in this respect is this:

> I subscribed to a series of all the Beethoven string quartets, bought the scores and studied them in minute detail before and after each concert. Beethoven became a wise, confiding, copiously illustrative teacher. Days and nights were saturated with Beethoven's dynamic forms. I also turned to Bach's rich contrapuntal textures and long, direct musical structures. I learned about the passion and discipline of uninterrupted eloquence. . . . In short, I became a profound believer in discipline, form, both organic and autogenetic.[26]

As far as his own composition work was concerned, Boulanger provided Harris with some leeway. She suggested that he write something for an instrument with which he was familiar and, for his first major effort under her tutelage, he wrote a Concerto for Piano, Clarinet, and String Quartet, drawing upon his youthful studies of the first two instruments in fashioning their parts. Boulanger was sufficiently enthusiastic about the Concerto to arrange for a performance at one of the concerts of the *Société Musicale Indépendant* in the spring of 1927 in Paris.[27] In spite of performance problems, particularly with the rhythmic aspects, this ambitious work was generally well received and, in fact, it is still viable today in spite of its immaturities, being the earliest of Harris's works to be performed with any frequency.

## Trips Back Home; the Guggenheim Fellowships

Harris studied with Boulanger through 1929 when, as the result of suffering a fall on the steps of the cottage in Juziers, he was compelled to return to the United States for surgery (see chapter 3).

Prior to this accident, however, he did go back to New York at least twice in the Falls of 1927 and 1928. The Paris success of the Clarinet Concerto was instrumental in his obtaining a $2500 Guggenheim Fellowship, of which he received the news during the 1927 visit to the East Coast. The Fellowship stipend was renewed for an additional year in 1928.[28]

## At the Brink of Independence

Harris's union with Sylvia ended in divorce. Boulanger was sympathetic with his domestic problems, recognizing his need for the companionship of someone compatible, someone who could be of real help to him during these crucial early years of his career. In an effort to remedy the situation, she introduced him to a young lady, Hilda, who turned out to be a relative of George Bernard Shaw. Hilda joined Harris in Juziers and assisted him as a copyist, a function she continued to serve until the mid-1930s. She accompanied the composer to America after his back injury and the two were eventually married in Pasadena in 1932. Though most of the women to whom Harris was married at various times during the 1920s and early 1930s seem to have contributed something to his well-being, it was not until he met Beula Duffey in 1934 that he found united in one individual a strength of personality and an artistic vision capable of matching his own.

At this point, the beginning of 1929, we leave Roy Harris on the eve of the creation of what was certainly the magnum opus of his work with Boulanger—his first completed symphonic effort, the *American Portrait*—in order to assess the results of his studies in France and the influences that helped shape his work and to examine his style and technique.

# 2

## Style

### Influences

Before examining Roy Harris's compositional style in detail, it would be appropriate to look at some of the influences which affected its development. Many of these stem from some of the great masters of the past; however, a few influences were contributed by some of his older contemporaries.

Though in his later years Harris's knowledge of musical history and of such areas of theory as traditional harmonic practice seemed somewhat sketchy, there is no doubt that during the early years of his career he undertook an assiduous study of the major style periods in Western music and of some of the most important representatives of these periods. After his final return to the United States and recovery from the surgery which healed his spinal injury, the composer spent many hours in the Library of Congress examining studies and collected editions of early music made by the recognized scholars of the time.[1]

The distinctive Roy Harris style was indebted for many of its important characteristics to the examples provided by the magnificent bodies of Gregorian and Ambrosian chant; by masters of the Renaissance such as Josquin, Lassus, Palestrina, and Victoria; and by later composers as diverse as J. S. Bach, Beethoven, Tchaikovsky, and Franck. Among his twentieth-century colleagues, Debussy, Ravel, and Stravinsky come to mind.

### Attitude Toward Contemporaries

Harris shared some aesthetic concerns with a number of other composers of his time, openly admiring their achievements without, however, appearing explicitly influenced by them. Among these were Prokofiev, in Russia, and Vaughan Williams, in England. Harris's kinship with the latter is especially close: the American and the Britisher possessing highly individual styles marked by a strong infusion of folk idioms, seem very much counterparts of each other in their respective countries, though they came from quite dissimilar personal backgrounds.[2]

Harris also maintained a guarded appreciation of some of his American colleagues, such as Virgil Thomson, Walter Piston, Howard Hanson, Elliott Carter, and Samuel Barber. But the figure with whom he is most often associated is Aaron Copland. Copland, of course, was responsible for helping Harris on some occasions during the early years, something which the latter acknowledged publicly. Though both composers mined an Americanist vein from time to time and possess similarities in their harmonic palettes and scoring, they seemed to grow apart in their aesthetics over the years.

However, whatever differences may have developed between the two men are unimportant in the large context. Both established themselves as important creators with distinctive voices who contributed a great deal to the establishment of an indigenous literature of American concert music. In some areas their strengths and weaknesses are complementary—for example, Copland's astuteness in managing his career and business affairs contrasted with Harris's slapdash, scattershot approach; Copland's technical security vs. Harris's occasional waywardness; Copland's economy and general coolness of approach contrasted with his colleague's generosity of impulse and visionary breadth; Copland's ability to develop his musical vocabulary in some areas vs. Harris's relative inflexibility in this regard; Copland's often thin and commonplace sounding materials vs. Harris's subtle and sophisticated melodic structures.

## Relationships with Students

As far as his students are concerned, Harris seemed proud whenever they accomplished something worthwhile. As his letters from the 1930s and 40s show, he always seemed willing to make time to examine the work of a fledgling composer. He also helped organize ambitious festivals and competitions aimed at encouraging young composers.[3] He kept in touch with many of his pupils for years after they had finished their studies, regarding them as both friends and respected colleagues.

One of Harris's best known students, William Schuman, went on to considerable eminence as a composer, educator, and arts administrator.

Schuman today retains a strong affection for his teacher, with especially high regard for some of the early works, such as *Symphony 1933*.[4] Harris, for his part, retained a similar affection for Schuman and appreciated some of the latter's earlier efforts, in which the older man's influence was still evident. However, he seems not to have followed his former student's later music and had little to say about it.

As he grew older, Harris, as I have implied earlier, became increasingly insulated from developments in contemporary music, though he was generally aware of them to some extent. The influences that went into the shaping of his style, technique, and aesthetics had long been absorbed and, aside from the occasional addition of a new ingredient, such as the jazz element which entered in the late 1930s and early 40s, his idiom seemed self-sufficient. Harris felt, with his teacher Nadia Boulanger, that one lifetime was hardly long enough to master a style, and he remained true to this belief for the duration. Though it undoubtedly served him well, this conviction did not always work to the advantage of his students, for he seemed to lack the flexibility and receptivity to a wide variety of idioms that enabled him to respond effectively to the developing stylistic persuasions which those who sought his guidance revealed.

## Approaches to Examining Harris's Style

The essentials of Roy Harris's style are present in some of his earliest works. However, though the fundamental character of his music remained much the same through the decades, there is no question that the Harris of the 1930s sounds quite different from the composer of the 60s and 70s. Some of the features of Harris's development that produced this change will be taken up in the succeeding chapters. As for the basic ingredients of the style, one finds upon extended acquaintance with the music that, for Harris, the elements of melody, harmony, rhythm, form, and scoring are intimately interrelated. An examination of them as separate entities tends to give an incomplete picture. Nonetheless, each of these elements is handled with such distinctiveness that such an examination provides a relatively easy first step for the general listener toward getting inside the style and ultimately arriving at a coherent overview. I have thus selected the aspects of melody, harmony, and rhythm for detailed discussion here. Since with Harris the evolution of form is often undertaken through the unfolding of melodic and/or harmonic shapes, this important aspect can be subsumed under the discussions of these elements. Matters of scoring can be treated in the various chapters devoted to works in different media.[5]

# Melody

"Harris restores melody to its old place at the fountainhead of symphonic music, but a new-found melody of these times, of his own, of his America." Thus one finds H. T. Parker writing in the Boston *Evening Transcript* on the occasion of the premiere of *Symphony 1933*.[6] And indeed, melody is the generating force of many of Harris's structures, from the shortest a cappella choral works to the monolithic *Canticle of the Sun*.

Through an examination of the mosaic-structure of plainchant, Harris likely gained an insight into the technique of "reconstituting the germ-theme" mentioned by Farwell.[7] From Anglo-Celtic folk music and New England psalmody spring the cadences and, in some cases, the profiles of his melodies. If a distinction were to be made in the particular areas of influence in which chant, on the one hand, and folk-and-hymn-tunes, on the other, operate in Harris, one might say that the former is reflected in his more florid, rhythmically flexible utterances (such as theme II of the first movement of *Symphony 1933*) while the latter condition his slowly unfolding, songlike ideas (such as theme II of the slow movement of Symphony No. 5). From Beethoven comes Harris's early fascination with the use of the motive as a form-building device (a use which he subsequently extended to an ornamental function as well).

## Harris's Melodic Types

Harris's melodic writing falls into three types:

1. Relatively short, "finite" melodies that are repeated with internal variation, expansion, and contraction. These are generally developed from a short motive and are often used in a theme-and-variations format and in fugues, where the necessity for relative thematic conciseness is obvious. They also appear in the additive structures of some of the early compositions, such as the first movement of *American Portrait*. Folk tunes form a special category of melodies of this type, for Harris often borrowed them either for settings or as thematic materials for otherwise original compositions.

2. Long, slowly unfolding, nonrecurring melodies of an "open-ended" character. These contain numerous phrases and, like the melodies of category 1, are usually launched by

a seed-motive. This is often a simple figure outlining a major or minor triad or comprising an up-beat figure based upon the leap of a fourth, fifth, or octave. This type of melody spins out continuously, generally forming the basis of either a large section of a work or an entire composition. Each phrase of a melody of this type generally refers back either to the rhythm, and sometimes the contours, of the seed-motive or to the pitches and/or rhythm of the immediately preceding phrase or two. It is this category of melody which most truly represents Harris's so-called "autogenetic" (self-generating) melodic technique.

3. Short motivic ideas. These are frequently drawn from complete melodies (such as fugue subjects) for purposes of development. However, they are just as often of independent origin. Harris uses them for transitions, for interjections (punctuation), and for ornamental counterpoint. These ideas are diverse in character, many of them falling into classes, each of which seems to have been conceived in terms of the character of a specific instrument or instrumental choir.

## The Autogenetic Principle

Central to Harris's concept of melody, and, by extension, of form is the idea of autogenesis referred to above. He seems to have arrived at this via a number of routes in an effort to build large forms without resorting to some of the devices, especially sequence, used by composers of the Classic and Romantic periods.[8]

Virtually all of Harris's original melodies can be regarded as autogenetic to some extent. For example, the melodies of category 1, though relatively short, are nonetheless, as mentioned, often generated by a seed-motive. Theme I of the "initiative" movement of *American Portrait* illustrates this especially well:

EXAMPLE 1

*Symphony—American Portrait 1929:* I. Theme I germ-idea

This is a self-contained idea set in motion by a simple germ figure and containing short clearly defined and variously permuted phrase-components. The later appearances of this melody with internal variation and expansion, and the addition of new ideas which accumulate along the way, produce a multisectional additive structure.

The *American Portrait* idea just cited is a melody in fast tempo. However, it is in the more leisurely paced melody of lyrical character that one finds embodied most clearly the composer's autogenetic style. The theme of the slow movement of Symphony No. 2 (and of the Trio slow movement as well) is a good early example:

EXAMPLE 2

*Symphony No. 2:* II. Theme

This is still a "closed" melody that recurs (it is employed in a variations format in the symphony) and is thus characteristic of a relatively early stage in Harris's development. However, he does manage here a true spinning-out by means of a flexible technique involving two procedures: 1) back-references to the rhythm of the opening of the first phrase; 2) the repetition, at the beginning of a new phrase, of the concluding note, or notes, of the preceding phrase. This technique provides both a sense of unity and a feeling of forward momentum.

Refining the above approach, Harris was able, in his maturity, to generate enormous melodic structures. Probably the most celebrated example is the great melody of the central portion of the Fifth Symphony slow movement alluded to earlier (see Example 43). This huge utterance falls into three beautifully proportioned sections which together describe an ascending and descending arch, a design which occurs over and over in Harris's works. He sometimes referred to it as a "Gothic arch," and I have retained this term for ease of reference.

In general outline, Harris's Gothic arch entails a gradual rise to a peak of tension followed by a gradual descent. This is usually carried out not only through the ascending or descending direction of the melodic line itself, but also by accompanying changes in harmonic texture and color (for example, from dark to bright harmonies and back to dark), rhythmic activity, dynamics, tessitura, and scoring (at least in the works for large media). Also, individual phrases of the ascending and descending portions of the melody often come to rest on successively higher and lower pitches respectively, thus creating the effect of a series of spirals.

Harris employs the arch design for both large and small structures. The Fifth Symphony example illustrates its use in a single melody which defines a complete section of a larger piece. In works such as the Third and Eleventh Symphonies, one finds the Gothic arch operating, in terms of the large musicodramatic plan, over the entire composition.

Though Harris's melodies, especially the long ones, seem to have little in common with the relatively concise and symmetrical phrase and period structure of those of much of the music of the Classic and Romantic periods, they do often reveal a sense of antecedent-consequent relationships between successive phrases. These are quite traditional in their alternation of tension and relaxation, of movement and rest. This principle is found in both short ideas and long melodies. Excellent illustrations of the latter type are the passacaglia subjects of both the Piano Quintet and the Seventh Symphony. In each of these, Harris builds his melody entirely out of two contrasting phrases in an antecedent-consequent relationship which is repeated, as a whole, several times with constant variation within each component.

In some instances, the composer, instead of presenting his melodies as a fait accompli, allows them to take shape gradually through a sort of motivic accretion and foreshadowing. An example of this is the opening movement of the Sixth Symphony. Here the first three sections of the movement consist of little else, thematically, than a series of motives and short-winded phrases in various sections of the orchestra. After the nearly immobile opening, each succeeding section builds in intensity by means of increasing rhythmic activity and textural density, with the addition of new layers of quasicontrapuntal working-out of the short ideas referred to above. It is only in the final section of the movement that a full-fledged melody, incorporating some of the earlier fragments, emerges.

## Tonal Organization

Harris's idiosyncratic treatment of the old Church modes is a fundamental aspect of the tonal organization of his melodies. There is relatively little "pure" modal writing in his oeuvre, one of the most extensive examples of this being the exposition of the second theme in the slow movement of

*Symphony 1933,* a passage which lies chiefly in the Aeolian mode on A. Usually Harris chooses to construct his melodic materials tonally from a combination, or overlaying, of two modes built on the same tonic. This, of course, produces a scale of more than seven different pitches and allows for the chromatic inflections on various scale degrees characteristic of his writing. The definitive statement of the composer's concept of modality is embodied in the Third String Quartet. As mentioned in the discussion of that work in chapter 7, the subject of each prelude is formed out of the notes of a pure mode (such as the Dorian on A) while that of each fugue is based on a combination of two modes (such as the Dorian and Aeolian modes on D). An example of such a scale of "mixed modes" is given below:

EXAMPLE 3

Dorian/Aeolian scales on D

The result of the combination just cited is an eight-tone scale in which the sixth degree fluctuates between B-flat (Aeolian) and B-natural (Dorian).

In addition to this frequent use of modal combinations, Harris generally carries his melodies through a kaleidoscopic succession of changing tonalities. This sort of "modal mutation" is usually accomplished, after the opening phrase or two, through "modulation," the gradual introduction of accidentals. The process might be regarded as the tonal analogue of Harris's melodic autogenesis. In it, the original mode (or modal combination) acts as a springboard for the emergence of new tonal centers and modal formations. It is akin to a process which is sometimes found in melodies of the chant literature.

## Harmony

Harris's harmonic idiom has received more attention than any other aspect of his style. It is certainly the most immediately distinctive aspect of his music and the area about which he himself seemed most willing to talk.

## The Overtone Series

At the root of Harris's treatment of harmony is a concern with the properties of the overtone series. He believed that the best vertical structures are those which take into account the varying degrees of consonance and dissonance arising from the reinforcement of various chord factors by the overtone series generated by these factors. His mature harmonic style, which achieved its definitive state during the late 1930s, is based upon the simple major and minor triads. Each of the three positions (root, first inversion, and second inversion) of these two triad types has its own degree of brightness or darkness depending upon the degree to which the upper notes of the triad are supported by the overtone series of the lowest note. Thus, for Harris, the brightest sound is produced by a second-inversion (6/4 position) major triad. This is because some of the most important overtones of the bass note (the fifth of the triad) reinforce overtones of both upper notes:

### EXAMPLE 4

C major triad overtones

The darkest sound is given by the second-inversion minor triad, this quality due to the relatively weak support which the overtones of the top note receives from partials of the bass note:

### EXAMPLE 5

C minor triad overtones

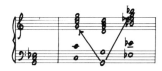

This principle extends, of course, to the case where triads built on different roots are superimposed on one another in a polychordal texture. In Example 6a the relatively bright sound results from the upper triad receiving considerable reinforcement from the overtones of the lower

triad; in 6b, the sound is darker because there is less support of this sort
for the upper triad:

EXAMPLE 6

a: A/D polychord—relationships of overtones of lower triad with notes of upper
triad

b: f/d polychord—relationships of overtones of lower triad with notes of upper triad

Harris's concept of the intervals that form the building blocks of both
harmony and melody is essentially historically-oriented. His primary intervals are the perfect fifth and fourth, which were the intervals used in the
organum compositions dating back to around the ninth century and comprising the earliest surviving examples of harmony in Western music. It
was only much later, around the late fourteenth and early fifteenth centuries, that thirds and sixths were admitted by composers and theorists as
consonances. On occasion, as in a large portion of the Third Symphony,
Harris made this historical concept explicit by starting with a texture built
on the unison and the octave and gradually expanding it to organum
harmonies, then simple triads, and finally polychords.

## Development of Harmonic Style

The development of Harris's harmonic style was marked during the 1920s
and 30s by a gradual purging of what he came to regard as "foreign"
sonorities. These included dominant seventh and ninth chords, diminished
and half-diminished seventh chords, the augmented triad, French sixth,
and other chords of this sort. This left a harmonic vocabulary restricted, as
indicated above, to major and minor triads and their associated seventh

chords. In terms of his contrapuntal writing, the development reveals a move away from a harmonic character conditioned by the interaction of individual lines (polyphonically generated harmony) to one founded upon a secure harmonic basis (harmonically generated polyphony). Two examples of the latter type follow:

EXAMPLE 7

a: *Symphony No. 5:* III. Harmonic texture

b: *Ode to Consonance.* Harmonically-generated melody

In Example 7a, the triad (oscillating between major and minor) underlies every vertical combination; in Example 7b, the fugue subject appears to emerge out of a preexisting harmonic texture created by the strings.

As far as the composer's principal harmonic structure, the triad, is concerned, one can trace three stages in the development of its use:

1. The music of the 1930s is marked by an exploration of the varying vertical spacings and relationships of both triads and seventh chords, particularly the latter. While Harris tended to regard a seventh chord as the interlocking of two

simple triads, his treatment of this type does not always bear this out. Example 22 is a good illustration of this. Here the interweaving of voices creates a linear feeling in what is really a block-chordal texture, a texture in which the seventh chords are heard as self-contained units rather than as polychordal aggregates.

2. This stage occurred during the late 1930s and early 40s. Here one finds Harris's most intensive exploration of the simple triad and of common-tone relationships among triads (I shall elaborate upon this latter aspect). There are lengthy passages, sometimes entire compositions (such as the *Ode to Friendship*) founded harmonically almost entirely upon progressions of major and minor triads, occasionally varied with polychords and chords built in fourths. In his reduction of the harmonies of a composition to simple triads, Harris often provides the variety and tension necessary to fore-stall blandness by means of the occasional use of both some of the more complex sonorities referred to above and of vertical friction stemming from relationships between chords and melody notes foreign to the chords. This por-tion of Harris's development reached its culmination during the 1950s through its metamorphosis into a fully developed polychordal idiom. (It is possible that the true germ of his later preoccupation with polychords is the "Pastoral" sec-tion of the Third Symphony, with its polytonal canonic string background which he was so fond of pointing out in his discussions of this work.)

3. In the period that began in the early 1960s, the various elements of Harris's harmonic vocabulary—triads, polychords, chords built in fourths and fifths superimposed on triads, and complete harmonies built on organum intervals—are freely intermixed in a looser and more pli-able idiom. If there is any one element which might seem new, it is the sonority based on multiple perfect fifths. Of course, the organum intervals are, as mentioned earlier, the fundamental intervals for Harris. However, he had not employed chords built entirely on multiples of these inter-vals, particularly the fifth, nearly so extensively prior to the 1960s. Example 73 shows a harmonic texture based on the fifth.

## Chord Relationships

As far as chord relationships are concerned, Harris's progressions are seldom of the same type as their counterparts in the common practice of the eighteenth and nineteenth centuries, in spite of the common denominator of the triad. Rather, his technique is based upon an extended set of common-tone relationships among chords, a set obtained between both the major and minor modes. Through an extension of this set of relationships Harris had access, from a given "tonic," to chords related in similar fashion to both the dominant and subdominant chords.

Example 8 reproduces, with slight changes, the sample table of chord relationships given by Robert Evett in his important article on Harris's harmonic style.[9]

EXAMPLE 8

Table of common-tone relationships

As one can see, the root of a given triad can serve as the fifth degree of the subdominant major and minor triads and as the third degree of the major and minor triads on the two forms of the submediant scale degree. The two forms of the third of the tonic triad can serve as root of major and minor triads on the mediant scale degree, while the fifth of the triad serves as the root of the major and minor triads on the dominant note. In addition, the subdominant and dominant major and minor triads generate their own sets of relationships which parallel those of the tonic triad. This creates the network of chord relationships and access routes referred to in Example 8.

Two things are evident from the table:

1. Harris is selective in deriving these relationships. Thus, while the root of a given triad is made to serve three functions, its major and minor third and its fifth degrees are allowed to serve only as roots of other triads. Therefore, for example, the flatted third degree, E-flat, of the C triad,

is not used by Harris as the third degree of a C-flat triad.
However, some of these "omitted" relationships are accessible through the subdominant or dominant chords. In this
case, the C-flat chord, spelled enharmonically as a B-major
harmony, is arrived at through the dominant. In practice,
Harris was apt to use a wider set of relationships from time
to time, but the table above contains his most frequently
employed, and characteristic, ones.

2. The establishment of a set of relationships based on the
concept of tonic, subdominant, and dominant function
chords implies a sense of tonality. Indeed, as I have brought
out in connection with Harris's melodic writing, each phrase
in the unfolding of a melody generally possesses a tonal
center, though one often enriched through the application
of a mixture of modes on the same tonic. A similar feeling of
tonality prevails in the harmonic aspect of the phrase, as I
illustrate subsequently, in that virtually all the chords of a
phrase can be related to what the listener perceives as the
tonic through the above set of relationships. Of course, as
indicated already, the tonality of the harmony need not be,
and often is not, that of the melody which it supports.

Roy Harris was certainly not the only composer to develop a body of
theory, whether implicity or explicitly stated, to support his musical
practices (Messiaen and his *Technique de mon langage musical* come to
mind).[10] As was so often the case with Harris and other composers,
however, an organizational structure which implied a rigidly worked-out
"system" really functioned more freely in actual practice. His ideas about
chord relationships (and about modality, for that matter) were essentially
talking points and manifestations of the cerebral aspect which is an integral
part of his music. Just as he found it necessary to arrive, during the early
1920s, at a philosophical basis for his decision to become a composer, so it
was necessary to perform a similar act in the formulation of his aesthetics
and techniques once the fundamental decisions had been made.

Two excerpts from the Little Suite for piano illustrate important aspects
of Harris's handling of chord connections, with respect especially to
tonality:

EXAMPLE 9

a: *Little Suite:* IV. Harmonic texture

cont.

b: *Little Suite:* II. Harmonic texture

cont.

In Example 9a, the melody appears to be in F major. However, the harmonization ranges far afield from F at times (e.g., the e-flat minor chord in measure 1 and the f-sharp minor chord in measure 4). Early in his career, Harris had created a concept in which "Harmony should represent what is in the melody, without being enslaved by the tonality in which the melody lies. At the same time harmony should center around a tonality sufficiently to indicate that tonality, because tonality is absolutely essential to form, and to harmonic contrast."[11] His fully developed harmonic style formed of a wide ranging set of common-tone relationships within an expanded concept of modality seems to answer this requirement, as Example 9a reveals. Here all of the chords can be related to the central tonality of F through the tonic, dominant, or subdominant chords (sometimes a combination of two of these). In addition, the recurrence of certain chords, such as the d-minor first inversion, at strategic points (phrase beginnings and/or endings), helps establish a sense of key center through emphasis.

The use of the d-minor chord referred to above to establish the key of F major rather than its own tonic may seem strange. However, Harris uses it a good deal in first inversion in this short piece, and for him the first-inversion minor triad tended to sound like a major triad (in this case F major) whose root is the bass note. The reason for this is the fact that the third and fifth of the minor triad, when placed together at the bottom of the harmony, sound like the root and third of the closely related major triad. As Robert Evett puts it in his article on Harris's harmonic practice, "It is partly because of this that it is impossible to analyze [Harris's] harmony by root progressions."[12]

Example 9b is more complex. The melody is in the Locrian mode on A. However, the harmonies seem formed from a mixture of Mixolydian, Locrian, and Aeolian (natural minor). There are one or two instances, though, such as the first two beats of measure 7, where the harmonies appear so distantly removed from any one of these scales that they may more easily be regarded as simply generated by (or originating as "resonances" of) the single melody note itself.

Example 9b also illustrates Harris's tendency to define and reinforce the emotional character of a phrase by emphasizing either the major or the minor triad in the harmony. Here the latter predominates, though the composer imparts subtle shadings to the line through the occasional use of major triads and fourth chords. This is another example of his concept of harmony quoted above. Although the complex modal inflections of the harmony are sometimes distant from the Locrian mode of the melody, the use of the dark minor triad as a defining sonority grows out of the employment of that very dark mode itself.

## Harris's Concept of the Functions of Harmony

Harris conceived that harmony should have three functions, which he defined early in his career: "first, for the architecture of tonalities; second, for melody delineation; third, for dynamic resonance."[13] For me, he was never very explicit about precisely what he meant by this, but an examination of his work in connection with other remarks made at various times seems to indicate the following:

The first of the functions relates to Harris's concept of form. Though, as indicated earlier, his structures are often generated through melody, they can also be built on, or at least reinforced by, a harmonic foundation. In numerous sketches one finds him first drafting chord progressions, which then serve as skeletons for the melodic unfolding. These structures are carefully conceived to provide the gradations in bright and dark sounds necessary for conveying the emotional tone of the work or passage in question. Illustrations of this procedure are the chiming sonorities which form the basis of the first movement of *Memories of a Child's Sunday* and the similar sounds which conclude *These Times*. Even when the melody appears to have been written first, Harris generally worked out the harmonic aspect along the line described above.

With Harris, the gradual metamorphosis of one harmonic color into another is a device which can operate over several phrases, sections, or even over entire compositions. As indicated earlier, he uses this procedure frequently to define the progress of his Gothic-arch constructions.

The cadence also forms a vital element in the definition of Harris's form, as it does in so much of the music of Western culture. Evett observes that for Harris "the greatest wealth of harmonic invention should be saved for the cadence" and points to a "merciless intensification of [Harris's] expression at the point of conclusion."[14] He cites in support of the latter point the rather dissonant cadence of Fugue III of the Third Quartet. Though this is an exceptional passage for Harris, it is true that his final cadences are sometimes points of great harmonic tension. As illustrations of this I cite the following:

EXAMPLE 10.

a: *Farewell to Pioneers.* Final cadence

b: *Fantasy for Piano and Orchestra.* Final cadence

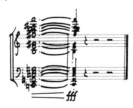

One might observe that at least in Example 10b, the brass-dominated scoring provides reinforcement of the harmonic "affect." This is an example of the manner in which the interrelationship of the various elements of music often work together for Harris to create a desired musical point.

While Harris's chord progressions, as I have stated above, seldom follow traditional patterns stressing the fundamental importance of the relationships between the primary triads (except indirectly through the common-tone connections obtained through these chords), they nevertheless help articulate the phrase structure of his melodies by providing cadences of varying sorts. Like all masters of harmony, he carefully plotted the relative strengths of his cadences during the spinning-out of a melody, determining when a strong cadence was needed to give a momentary sense of repose or the achievement of an intermediate goal and when a weaker one was required to punctuate without unduly disturbing the flow. This latter type is particularly important as the melody gathers momentum toward its apex.

Harris sometimes differentiates the bass line progression at a cadence from that which occurs during the body of a phrase, particularly if he is writing a strong cadence. He does this by employing fourths and fifths, especially descending, in the bass at such a point. A weaker cadence is often underpinned by the smaller intervals of the second and third. In this respect, he follows traditional harmonic practice. He also sometimes uses a chord-type at a cadence which contrasts with the harmonies that precede it. The dissonant polychordal cadence of Example 10b illustrates this.

One of the best and most comprehensive examples of Harris's treatment of the cadence in both its harmonic and melodic aspects is, once again, the great melody in the slow movement of the Fifth Symphony, as well as the concluding section of that movement, which is built largely on various cadential "formulae" and their expansions.

A special type of weak cadence which Harris sometimes uses is the "open cadence." This occurs at the end of a section or movement as a means of avoiding too great a sense of finality and of providing a kind of structural upbeat to the ensuing portion of the work. The Third Quartet contains some examples.

The open cadence is achieved through a number of means, of which some of the more important are: (1) a stationary bass line over which motion in the upper voices continues for another measure or two (Example 11a); (2) placement of all the voices in a relatively high register (Example 11b); (3) dropping out of all the voices but one, thus thinning out the texture (Example 11c).

However, of all the methods Harris employs to define cadences, rhythm is the most important. Every cadence, whether strong or weak, is marked

# EXAMPLE 11

a: *Quartet No. 3:* Prelude I. Final cadence

b: *Quartet No. 3:* Fugue I. Final cadence

c: *Quartet No. 3:* Fugue II. Final cadence

off by some agogic differentiation from the music which has preceded it. This nearly always takes the form of longer note values for the last chord or two. However, a complete cessation of motion in all voices is not required to create a cadence. In some instances, such as the concluding section of the Third Symphony, the cadences in the melody, marked off by both an agogic lengthening and by the successively lower resting places in the descending spiral outlined by the long string line, are defined further by bass-line motion past the cadence points coupled with motivic development in other sections of the orchestra. Thus Harris, especially in his orchestral works, uses changes of texture and musical idea as additional phrase-end punctuation. In this context, the cadence is more than simply a harmonic resting place; it also provides an "opening" for the introduction of new musical ideas or the development of old ones.

Returning to Harris's list of the functions of harmony cited above, the second item, its use "for melodic delineation," has been discussed earlier in this chapter. The third function, the use of harmony "for dynamic resonance," concerns, as set down by Evett, "problems of density, concentration, registration and voicing."[15] This, of course, arises from Harris's exploitation of the intervals of the overtone series and manifests itself in such things as the exact chord types employed in a given passage, the characteristics of interval arrangement (close or open voicing), inversion, the instrumental (or vocal) timbre for which the harmonic texture is conceived, and the positions of the chords (i.e., root position, first or second inversions). This, in turn, affects considerations as disparate as the dynamic level at which a given harmony-type is written and the speed at which it moves to other harmonies. Essentially, therefore, this function has to do with how the harmony "sounds" as an entity.

All the above reveals that, though the basic vocabulary of Roy Harris's harmonic style is limited, he employs it with great variety to carefully defined ends which interrelate with all the other elements of his music and with the forms which these elements generate. Perhaps more than any other ingredient in his style, it is harmony which creates for most listeners the distinctive Harris "sound." But it does not accomplish this alone, for the harmonic vocabulary which he employs has long become common practice, not only in the realm of concert music but also in the areas of jazz and popular music. Rather, it is Harris's tripartite concept of harmonic function, as described above, and most especially the subtle tensions set up between a melodic line and its harmonization, which render the source of a given passage almost instantly identifiable to anyone familiar in some depth with the music of the twentieth century.

# Rhythm

## Early Approach to Notation

Harris's rhythmic style is intimately bound up with his concept of melody. During the early years of his career, he employed frequent changes of time signature and many asymmetrical meters (e.g., 5/8, 7/8). This seemed to result from an attempt to match his constantly varying phrase-units with corresponding measure-units. He had to find a means of defining phrases in such a way that their articulation and relative proportions could be grasped by both performer and listener. Consequently, his early rhythmic style might be regarded as barline-oriented, in the sense that schemes of changing time signatures represent an effort to have the strong accents of the metrical groupings within a melody fall on the strong beats of measures of varying lengths.

However, the composer came to realize that this approach created difficulties in ensemble and in the spontaneity of rhythmic flow in works for large media. He therefore began exploring other possibilities. This led, at least in the orchestral medium, to the substitution within a complete work or large portions thereof of a single time signature for the changing meters he had employed previously, with the varying accentual patterns of the melodies now conveyed by means of note groupings, phrase marks, and written accents.[16] This change in approach is readily apparent in his reworking of the "Collective Force" movement of *American Portrait* into the finale of *Symphony 1933*.

The abandonment of asymmetrical meters was not complete, however. There are examples (such as the "variations in asymmetrical rhythms" in the Seventh Symphony) of such meters in Harris's mature writing. However, in later periods, he employed these meters sparingly and logically, and they either predominate through much of an entire section of a work or alternate in regular patterns with symmetrical meters.

Another development in Harris's treatment of rhythm and its notation involves a change from the quarter note to the half note, then back to the quarter note again as his standard pulse unit. This took place during the 1930s. Examples of the half-note unit (and its dotted counterpart) can be found in *Symphony 1933* (slow movement) and Symphony No. 3 (passim); of the quarter-note unit in the early Andante for orchestra and the subject of the "Passacaglia" movement of the Piano Quintet. Though Harris was later inconsistent with respect to a "standard" pulse, it is true that at least in the works of his last years the half note predominates (the *Bicentennial Symphony* is an example).

## Types of Rhythmic Character

The following examples show the two types of rhythmic character which predominate in Harris's music:

EXAMPLE 12

a: *Sonata for Violin and Piano:* III. Theme

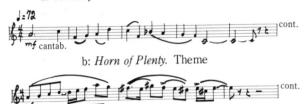

b: *Horn of Plenty.* Theme

The first type cited is typical of the composer's broadly paced lyrical unfoldings. This kind of line generally moves in a moderate to slow tempo and possesses a smooth rhythmic flow, with the central portion of each phrase built on a single note value (usually the quarter note), contrasting longer values being reserved for phrase endings and beginnings. Melodies belonging to this category begin so often with the same rhythmic design that the basic pattern of note values may seem a stereotype to some.

The type of melody represented by the *Horn of Plenty* excerpt illustrates the buoyant, aggressive sort of idea Harris often devised for his fast music. Here he frequently adopted a shorter note value (such as the eighth note) as a pulse unit and created a stronger contrast between this unit and its subdivisions, often using the latter within the phrase to break up the flow in a playful fashion.

One rhythmic characteristic virtually all the melodies of Harris's maturity possess is a deliberate lack of coordination between their strong and weak accents and the barlines. This is especially noticeable in Example 12a, where the phrase marks indicate the breaking in measure 3 of the regular four-in-a-bar rhythmic disposition of notes into a two-note group followed by a four-note group phrased across the barline, the phrase ending in the middle of the fourth measure. Harris juggles the components of the next phrase in similar fashion, this time producing a phrase ending on a weak beat. An even clearer example of this technique is found in the first theme of the Eleventh Symphony (Example 85). Harris clearly derived this style feature from the vocal polyphony of the Renaissance, as he acknowledged in one instance.[17]

## A Storehouse of Melo/Rhythmic Ideas

As he developed as a composer, Harris accumulated a store of melo/rhythmic ideas that recur again and again in his works. These are chiefly instrumental in nature and, as mentioned earlier, were often conceived in terms of the idiomatic characters of specific instruments and choirs. Such ideas are often used to help define a particular musicodramatic quality. Most are short motives and their linear characteristics and functions have been discussed earlier. The exact pitches of each figure change from one context to another, but the idea's overall shape and character generally remains constant. This is especially true of the rhythmic aspect, which, indeed, is often the most immediately recognizable feature of these ideas. Some of the most frequently occurring involve designs in 5/8 meter or one of the compound meters (chiefly 6/8). The first movement of the Fifth Symphony serves as a convenient source from which several can be extracted as illustrations:

EXAMPLE 13

*Symphony No. 5:* I. Motives

Harris seemed to find these melo/rhythmic ideas most useful in his fast music, which often involves the juxtaposition of several relatively short sections and occasional sharp contrasts. Here they provide transitions (as indicated above) as well as some of the contrasting materials. Harris's slower music generally evolves in a more continuous, organically developing fashion in which the transition from one section to the next is gradual, often not requiring specific devices for this purpose. However, there are exceptions, especially in theme-and-variations compositions in moderate tempo. Here the composer sometimes sets off individual variations or groups of variations by development of motivic ideas, which are occasionally derived from a portion of the theme.

# Summary

With Harris, each of the elements of melody, harmony, and rhythm is treated in a distinctive fashion according to clearly defined principles which he formulated early in his career. In his best music these elements work together to create a musical organism which possesses both a firm, yet pliable, forward momentum and a richly textured, kaleidoscopically colored vertical dimension.

The chapters that follow on Harris's substantial literature of symphonies and chamber music will amplify upon the matters already introduced and illuminate the process of the composer's stylistic and technical development over the major part of his career.

# 3

## Symphonies, Part I
## (*American Portrait*, Nos. 1, 2, and 3)

During the 1920s, when the generation of young composers to which Roy Harris belonged was beginning to flex its muscles in an attempt to establish an indigenous "American" style of concert music, it seemed something of a paradox that that most European of musical genres, the symphony, should have been so much on its collective mind.

Though Harris's aesthetics were still forming during these early years, it seems reasonable, on the basis of his demonstrated long term consistency of thought, to project this statement of the mid-1950s back in time to give us a clear idea of his attitude toward musical form and materials:

> In the matter of form development the modern composer has his greatest problem. Most of his audience have been conditioned to the slow, long, mosaic forms of nineteenth-century Europe, or the short 4- 8- 16-measure periods of modern dance music. These forms achieve continuity through a constant and endless repetition of small motives as well as many repetitions of periods and sections. . . . Certainly the acceptance of some old European form, as if it were an ancient vessel into which we pour contemporary materials, is no solution, no matter how often it has been done or will be done. Broadly stated, the problems of form can be successfully solved only if there is a clear musical idea in the composer's mind, and clear melodic, harmonic, contrapuntal, and orchestral vocabulary in his technique. . . ."[1]

The statement does not address the problem of what to do with European forms per se, and some of the ideas expressed, especially those of the final sentence, are obvious truisms. However, by stressing the importance of the "musical idea," Harris seems to refer to the concept of an autogenetic form which develops out of the materials, rather than one worked out within existing structures.

By the 1930s, the symphony had served, for roughly a century and a half, as the vehicle for the largest scale exposition and working out of musical ideas and as the most generous framework for the expression of diverse emotional characteristics in the realm of orchestral music. With Beethoven's addition of the chorus in the finale of his Ninth Symphony, the genre acquired a sort of mystique with special appeal to the sensibilities of many of the major Romantic period composers. Clearly, the young American lions, for all their independence of spirit, were not about to back away from the supreme challenge the European masters had flung at them.

Harris always believed firmly in the idea of an international intercentury mainstream. As mentioned earlier, during his studies with Boulanger, he examined and absorbed a wide range of musical culture and subsequently acknowledged his high regard for many masters of the past. It is likely that he responded to the symphony in terms of its importance in the tradition, its potential for large scale utterance, and the increasing freedom with which composers of the nineteenth and early twentieth centuries had treated its formal components. The symphony thus seemed to him not only to provide an opportunity to test his mettle but also to give him a means of adapting a traditional genre to his own means.

## Harris's Concept of the Symphony

Of course, as I have pointed out, the symphony had undergone a good deal of change from the type written by Haydn, Mozart, and Beethoven (though even during the Classic period the formal procedures of the individual movements were by no means as standardized as they were once thought to be). In 1920, Stravinsky, in his Symphonies of Wind Instruments, had returned to the earlier definition of the word "symphony," or "sinfonia," as a "sounding together" of various instruments and ideas, discarding the multimovement, sonata cycle format which it later came to signify. A few years later, Jean Sibelius, in his Seventh Symphony, developed a single movement structure which seems a hybrid of the four individual movements of the traditional type and a large scale sonata design. Other composers, among them Havergal Brian, Arnold Bax, Sergei Prokofiev, and Dmitri Shostakovich, developed their own approaches, experimenting with both the number of movements and with the formal designs within each movement.

By now, the symphonic genre has been treated to such a variety of approaches, some of them almost impossible to reconcile with the traditional type, that one might cynically observe that a symphony is whatever a composer wants it to be. This is certainly true in some respects of Roy Harris's symphonies. One thus finds both multimovement and single movement works and, in terms of medium, compositions for orchestra, band, chorus and orchestra, a cappella chorus, and chorus and band.

For a long time, Harris gave numbers only to those symphonies that employed the orchestra (or orchestra with chorus). Thus the a cappella Symphony for Voices and the Symphony for Band did "not count," to use his phrase (though he regarded them highly). However, by the time he came to write his *Abraham Lincoln Symphony,* which uses as its instrumental component only brass, pianos, and percussion, he abandoned this practice and numbered the work as his Tenth Symphony. Thus, in the end his numbering practices proved not to be a reliable guide to his concept of the symphony.

Neither are his formal procedures any help in this respect, for those which he employs in the symphonies are virtually the same as in his miscellaneous orchestral and band works, and his chamber compositions, for that matter.

Acquaintance with all of Harris's works in the genre reveals that his most consistent view appears to have been of the symphony as a work of greater seriousness, emotional variety, intensity of expression, and length than was the norm for him. Though, as indicated above, the elements which went into their creation were formed and treated quite similarly to those employed in other works, the materials of the symphonies are sometimes greater in number, richer in complexity, and accorded a more elaborate development, with especially prominent use of the various types of motivic working out described in chapter 2. Occasionally ideas recur in a thematic sense within a symphony (as in the Third and Seventh Symphonies), thus providing more of a sense of large scale unity than one finds, or may even deem necessary, in the miscellaneous pieces. Finally, the quality of the ideas in the symphonies, particularly the long melodies, is sometimes more distinctive than that found elsewhere in Harris's oeuvre.

## American Portrait

Harris, as mentioned, had actually begun a symphony during the mid-1920s, probably near the end of his studies with Farwell. The projected work, *Our Heritage,* was never fully realized. The Andante movement which he did complete has, however, achieved some historical distinction as his first orchestral work to be performed (see chapter 1).

In 1929, the final year of his work with Boulanger, Harris once again attempted a symphony, this time completing a four-movement work titled *Symphony–American Portrait 1929*. The movements bear the headings "Initiative," "Expectation," "Speed," and "Collective Force." It is obvious from the title of this work, and that of the earlier unfinished attempt as well, that Harris felt one way in which the symphonic genre could be approached in a fresh manner would be as a vehicle for the expression of Americanist sentiments. Harris was often to attach extramusical ideas to his symphonies, along the lines of the nineteenth-century program symphony. This aspect of his music is taken up more thoroughly in the chapters on the miscellaneous orchestral works and the band pieces. It is sufficient to remark here that the extramusical elements range from a generalized sort of program (as in the case of the *San Francisco Symphony*) to what might be regarded as a "motto" format, in which a literary source, or simply a string of movement subtitles, generates an emotional character rather than a depiction of specific events (as in the *American Portrait* and the Sixth Symphony). One should keep in mind that, though Harris often portrayed a specific activity in his music (as the building of St. Francis's church in the *San Francisco Symphony*), he did not have the born film composer's flexibility to respond to a wide variety of constantly changing activities and moods within a short span. Thus Harris generally concentrated, for a large section or a complete movement of a work, on representing what he extracted as the essence of an often complex extramusical situation.

Harris's program for the *American Portrait* is worth quoting, in part, as perhaps his earliest concrete expression of the Americanist aspect of his aesthetics:

In "American Portrait 1929," the composer chose to present the emotional aspect of Initiative, Expectation, Speed and Collective Force because they are the dominant characteristics of the American people. Whether our ancestors were early settlers or late immigrants, they came to America because they expected to realize some ideal which they had been unable to attain in Europe, and because they possessed the individual initiative to hazard their lives on those expectations. Initiative and Expectation . . . remain as permanent elements of the American temperament. On the other hand climate has stimulated our nervous energy and organization has concentrated and intensified our production until Speed and Collective Force have become the two outstanding characteristics of the American civilization. [2]

This statement, with its combination of idealism and recognition of the practical, industrial aspects of human existence in the modern world, may be viewed as an articulation of a "creed" in which strong visionary and mechanistic strains function together deep within the psyche of this most original creative figure.

Though Harris subsequently withdrew the *American Portrait,* and there is not room to discuss the work in detail here, I must nonetheless acknowledge its importance not only as his first completed symphony but also as a source of materials for some of the succeeding orchestral works, including the First and Second Symphonies.[3]

## A Liberating Injury

It was not too long after Harris had completed the *American Portrait* that he suffered the bad fall mentioned earlier, slipping on the steps of the cottage in Juziers and seriously injuring his spine. After some period of treatment in France, he eventually found it necessary to return to the United States, where he underwent the Albi operation, in which a piece of shinbone was used to replace a shattered spinal vertebrae.

Though the operation was successful, it necessitated a long convalescence, during which Harris was unable to use the piano, as had been his general practice, in completing the First String Quartet, on which he had been working. He later regarded the potentially disastrous accident as a Godsend because, in freeing him from the "tyranny of the piano," as he put it, it enabled him not only to write with greater fluency than before but also to achieve smoother continuity in his musical structures.

## The First Years Back Home

Following his return to the United States and his convalescence, Harris went for awhile to the family home in California. At about this time he received a composing fellowship from the Pasadena Music and Art Association which gave him a certain amount of financial sustenance.

However, the lure of the East Coast was strong, and the composer finally succumbed to an offer to teach composition during the summer sessions of the Juilliard School of Music in New York. He held this position from 1932 through 1938.

During this period in the early 1930s, Harris completed several orchestral and chamber works, among them the Toccata for orchestra, the *Over-*

*ture from the Gayety and Sadness of the American Scene,* and the Concerto for String Sextet (as well as the aforementioned quartet). The overture, based in part upon materials from *American Portrait,* was premiered in Hollywood Bowl, the conductor on this occasion a Russian émigré who was to become an important friend and chronicler of the composer (among his many other accomplishments) during the succeeding two decades, Nicolas Slonimsky.

## Symphony 1933

The dissatisfaction Harris felt with *American Portrait* persisted with his more recent orchestral pieces. As quoted at about this time, he was still attempting to find an orchestral style "indigenous to the line and form."[4] In the spring of 1933, the composer received what was perhaps the most decisive boost in his career since the opportunity to study with Boulanger. It was at an Elizabeth Sprague Coolidge concert of chamber music in the Library of Congress in Washington, D. C., that he was introduced by Aaron Copland to the conductor of the Boston Symphony Orchestra and celebrated champion of new music, Serge Koussevitzky. As the composer recalled it, Koussevitzky remarked: "[Aaron] Copland told me you are the American Mussorgsky. You must write for me a big symphony from the West. I will play." Harris set to work almost immediately, composing the work during the spring and summer while living in New York.

Actually, the new symphony was not so much newly composed as reworked from preexistent materials drawn from such diverse sources as the *American Portrait* (finale); the Fantasy for Woodwinds, Horn, and Piano; the Toccata for orchestra; and the First Quartet. However, Harris reshaped and polished these materials to such an extent that the symphony seems very much a new piece, even if one is armed with a foreknowledge of its "prefabricated" nature.

The *Symphony 1933,* as Harris titled his official Symphony No. 1, was something of a triumph for the composer upon its premiere by Koussevitzky and the Boston Symphony early in 1934. Until this performance by an orchestra and conductor of international stature, Harris had been recognized as one of the more gifted, though controversial and unformed, members of a rising generation of American composers, but one hardly known to the concertgoing public at large. The new work, however, put him on the map as a serious creative figure of substance and vitality, though the occasional flaws and miscalculations of timing, structure, and scoring bore out the wisdom of the note of caution sounded in the salutation with which

Arthur Farwell headed his pioneering article on the composer: "Gentlemen, a genius—but keep your hats on!"[5]

## First Movement

The symphony is in three movements. The first is an aggressive, confident statement in a large ternary form, underpinned by the almost continual oscillation between triple and duple subdivisions of the beat:

EXAMPLE 14

*Symphony 1933:* I. Introduction

The upthrusting principal theme and its continuation by means of constant back-reference to previous segments reveals Harris's attempt to achieve a semblance of variation and growth, but the movement (and the symphony as a whole) still relies on closed thematic ideas:

EXAMPLE 15

*Symphony 1933:* I. Theme I

The more flowing second theme is one of the composer's finest inspirations, revealing not only a strong unification through use of rhythmic motives but also the inflections on scale degrees so characteristic of his style:

EXAMPLE 16

*Symphony 1933:* I. Theme II

The middle section of the movement, in which Theme II is exposed and developed, is cast in a variations format, a procedure Harris was to follow in the corresponding section of some subsequent works.[6] Here the variations proceed from an initial unison statement (over a sinuous ostinatolike figure in the horns and low woodwinds), through a strange contrapuntal web bordering on atonality, to a vertical and horizontal expansion wherein the melody is harmonized and each phrase is answered by a wild melisma. This music comprises one of Harris's most original utterances.

The third part of the movement is a return, with much development and transformation, of the materials of the opening section, culminating in a tortuous three-part canon on a motive derived from Theme I.

## Second Movement

Though the first movement, in its diversity of expressive characteristics within a convincing structural tautness, is perhaps the most successful orchestral piece Harris had composed up to this time, the remaining two movements also reveal how far he had come from the stylistic and technical uncertainties of the *American Portrait*. The slow movement, like the first, can also be perceived as a ternary design, but it incorporates elements of rondo in the recurrences of some of its materials at strategic points. The first theme, like that of Example 16, is one of Harris's most distinguished and expressive ideas:

EXAMPLE 17

*Symphony 1933:* II. Theme I

It reveals a concept of line, cadence, and organic growth which demonstrates how surely, even at this relatively early stage, he was moving away from closed designs in favor of a type of melody which seems to flow outward rather than being contained within fixed boundaries.

Harris's use of rondo principles in this movement again shows him attempting to come to grips with preexisting traditional forms. Unlike the first movement, where he was content to leave the second theme as an isolated entity in the middle of the piece, he here tries to integrate his various thematic ideas. Thus, the second theme functions, after its initial statement, as counterpoint to a varied return of Theme I:

EXAMPLE 18

*Symphony 1933:* II. Theme II

Theme III, entering about midway in the movement, is interesting as an illustration of the importance Harris attaches to the changes in emotional character imparted through different harmonic colors:

EXAMPLE 19

a: *Symphony 1933:* II. Theme III (initial appearance)

b: *Symphony 1933:* Theme III (variant)

Theme IV, introduced only near the end of the movement, provides both fresh melodic interest and a sense of unity through its subtle kinship (achieved through both rhythmic and linear means) with Theme I:

EXAMPLE 20

*Symphony 1933:* II. Theme IV

As far as the overall musicodramatic design is concerned, though the initial statement of Theme III creates something of the effect of a central climactic point (with its sudden change of texture from the preceding measures and a quality of being suspended in space imparted through the relatively high tessitura of the woodwind counterpoint), it is certainly not the dramatic high climax which Harris was to achieve so effectively with his mature Gothic-arch design. Thus the slow movement, musically distinguished though it is, does seem to lack a sense of focus and goal. Perhaps the use of a number of themes is another factor contributing to this sense of diffuseness.

## Third Movement

Though all the materials of the finale are drawn from the "Collective Force" movement of *American Portrait,* so thoroughly has Harris rethought them and their working out that he has virtually written a new piece, rather than simply reworking the source. Like the earlier music, everything here grows out of the three-note motive which launches the single theme and its main variant:

EXAMPLE 21

*Symphony 1933:* III. Theme (form 1)

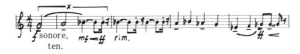

b: *Symphony 1933:* III. Theme (form 2)

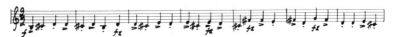

However, in its rigorous motivic development, austerity of texture, and conciseness, the movement presents a much more unified impression than "Collective Force," with a stronger orientation toward a goal.

This finale is in two large parts. Both sections involve the working out of the principal theme and motive x, usually in contrapuntal terms. However, the quasifugal procedure of the "Collective Force" source is loosened considerably here to the point where the movement might be regarded as more in the nature of a fantasia or contrapuntal study.

Harris exploits motive x a great deal in this movement. However, in spite of the ingenious dovetailings and stretti through which he puts it, it is evident, in his tendency to become stuck in repetitive patterns which smack of intellectual contrivance, that Classic period principles of motivic working out are not really native to his musical temperament. This repetitiousness tends to cause the otherwise life-asserting quality of the final pages of the symphony to veer dangerously toward the bombast which was to lie in wait for Harris at the end of many of his future symphonic journeys.

## Overview

Though *Symphony 1933* is a flawed work, it is nonetheless a fresh and, for its time, bold conception which stands up remarkably well today. It is certainly more assured and stylistically unified than *American Portrait.* Part of its originality lies in Harris's struggle to infuse new life into traditional forms while seeking simultaneously a new, more spontaneous means of structural growth. Also striking is the development in harmonic idiom which the symphony reveals. Many of the chromaticisms and other "foreign" elements of the *American Portrait,* and other works on which he drew for its composition, have been purged and one is left with an idiom based chiefly upon major and minor triads and seventh chords. A comparison of an especially felicitous passage of harmonic writing from the second movement with its ancestor in the woodwind Fantasy illustrates this:

EXAMPLE 22

a: *Symphony 1933:* II. Harmonization

b: *Fantasy for Woodwinds, Horn, and Piano.* Harmonization

## A "Premature" New Attempt: Second Symphony

Sometime after the premiere of *Symphony 1933,* Harris went to the Yaddo Estate at Saratoga Springs, New York, and, spurred on by his success, began work on another symphony. However, he had to contend with a sense of letdown which, on a number of occasions in his career, was to follow the completion of a successful work:

> Then I began to write my Second Symphony—not because it was ready for harvest, but to keep busy. It had only one good movement, the second. . . . The [symphony] was a failure, but it taught me a hard lesson: successful people should not try to keep pace with their success,' or count on it. . . .[7]

### First Movement

Like its predecessor, the Symphony No. 2 is in three movements. The first movement is one of the composer's most intriguing, not only because of its economy of materials (nearly equaling that of the finale of *Symphony 1933*), but because of the number of analytical possibilities it offers. Perhaps the description which corresponds most closely with what one hears is that of a multipartite form incorporating both additive and rondo features.

Again, a germ motive (x) generates virtually all the materials. Harris keeps the listener in suspense, however, by delaying the first complete appearance of the principal theme, building up to it by means of motivic working out:

EXAMPLE 23

a: *Symphony No. 2:* I. Theme

b: *Symphony No. 2:* I. Motivic development

This one real theme of the movement is clearly an attempt to develop a long line out of a motivic cell and is clearly modeled, both in rhythm and in structural principles, upon the first theme of Beethoven's Fifth Symphony.

The movement appears to fall into five parts, each of which is initiated by a statement or development of motive x and continues with one or more varied restatements and developments of the theme itself. In spite of a still present tendency to become bogged down in reiterated combinatorial patterns (of motive x), Harris does achieve, especially in the variations to which he subjects the theme, an advance over the finale of *Symphony 1933*. As in the earlier work, there is a new-found leanness to most of the harmonic writing and the texture. This movement seems the most "classical" of all Harris's symphonic compositions in its treatment of materials, its textures, and in its sense of key relationships, most of which revolve around the tonality of Bb.

## Second Movement

For the second movement, Harris again, as in his previous slow music, turned for his materials to a longer, more lyrical type of melody. The single theme has been cited in chapter 2 (Example 2) as an early illustration of the composer's principles of autogenesis. He employs the melody here in a structure which was to prove especially congenial to him throughout much of his career, theme and variations. Of course, the cerebral element pervades this movement as well, for, superimposed on the variations format is a scheme of canonic development. Harris referred to the movement, in fact, as a "study in canons."

The variations may be grouped, on a higher structural level, into three sections of about equal length. Section A contains two complete statements of the theme, the first with rather free, intermittent imitation, the second in strict canon (embedded in a fabric of additional contrapuntal voices freely derived from the theme). Given to the strings, this opening section builds to one of Harris's most radiant climaxes. The eloquent and skillfully devised music of this section doubtless explains Harris's particular regard for the movement.

Each of the remaining two sections comprises a further canonic development of the theme, followed by development of its head motive.

This slow movement is another early example of the Gothic arch design, though one with a clearer focus than the corresponding movement of *Symphony 1933*. Here the peak is reached relatively early rather than halfway through, as was usually to be the case.

## Third Movement

The finale is an orchestral reworking of the last movement of the First Quartet. Considering its 1930 source, it is thus a prototype of the contra-

puntal triple-fugue finale that was to become a feature of a number of
Harris's multimovement symphonies.[8] Here he imposes an additional plan
of diminishing note values on his three subjects: thus, Subject I consists
chiefly of dotted half-notes, Subject II of halves and quarters, and Subject
III of eighths. The scheme results in an increase in momentum as the
movement unfolds:

EXAMPLE 24

a: *Symphony No. 2:* III. Theme I

b: *Symphony No. 2:* III. Theme II

c: *Symphony No. 2:* III. Theme III (characteristic segments)

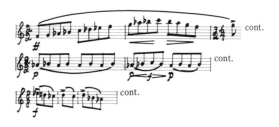

Each subject is given its own exposition in each of the first three sections
of the movement. For the fourth and final portion, Harris makes an attempt
at combining at least the salient characteristics of the three ideas.

The fugal procedure is treated freely. For example, I is developed,
following an initial unison statement, chiefly in stretti based upon a motive
extracted from it. After an initial rather free presentation, II is subsequently accorded something closer to a textbook fugal exposition (or
counterexposition). Subject III is not so much a real melodic idea as a
"figure of motion," with a constantly changing linear profile. It is harmonized
in a scheme of shifting colors.

However, the finale also points up a problem which was to plague the composer in constructing similar movements in later works, namely the fact that the various subjects are not conceived in such a way as to combine contrapuntally with one another in a natural fashion. This is often especially true of the third subject, which tends to be rather long and florid, as here.

The movement is, though, an altogether more successful piece than the finale of *American Portrait*. In addition to its importance as a structural prototype for later finales, it is also important in providing, in its treatment of Subject III, the first instance in Harris's oeuvre of the concept of creating chord successions in terms of changing color values rather than as progressions of individually perceivable harmonies. This was to reach its culmination nearly thirty years later in his chamber setting of St. Francis of Assisi's *Canticle of the Sun* and in the companion to that work, the *San Francisco Symphony*.

### Subsequent History

The Second Symphony proved to be a troublesome work for Harris in other than musical ways. He had written it, like its predecessor, for Koussevitzky. However, a rift developed between composer and conductor over matters about which the composer and subsequent chroniclers recalled differently and which are still not clear. Koussevitzky, a proud and touchy man, declined to perform the symphony. It was, however, eventually premiered, nearly two years after its completion, by the Boston Symphony under its concertmaster and assistant conductor, Richard Burgin. Following this, it received only one further performance, by a pickup orchestra in New York under Alexander Smallens, before sinking into almost total obscurity.

## The Westminster Choir School

Though disappointed with his latest symphonic effort, Harris nonetheless continued to hone his technique during the next few years by producing works in a variety of media. He also began to broaden his experience in the field of music education, an area with which he was to remain associated throughout most of the rest of his life and to which he was to contribute significantly. While continuing the summer sessions at Juilliard, he assumed a position as composition instructor at the Westminster Choir School in Princeton, New Jersey, settling in that city for a short while around 1935. This experience was especially fruitful in providing an impetus for Harris's exploration of the field of choral writing (which is discussed in chapter 14).

## First Publications and Recordings

Harris's first published compositions were issued during the early 1930s by Harold Flammer (the "Chorale" movement of the Concerto for String Sextet) and the Cos Cob Press (Piano Sonata, Concerto for Piano, Clarinet and String Quartet). Somewhat later (1936), Henry Cowell's *New Music* edition issued the Trio. It was in 1934 that Harris signed his first contract with a major publisher, G. Schirmer, and this resulted in a more systematic issuance of many of the orchestral, chamber, and choral works written between 1933 and 1940. G. Schirmer was succeeded as Harris's publisher by Mills Music (1940–1945), then by Carl Fischer (1945–1950), and finally by Associated Music Publishers (1956–present), with a brief and essentially nonproductive liaison with G. Ricordo preceding the tenure with the last-named.

The 1930s also saw the first recordings of Harris's works. His Concerto for Piano, Clarinet and String Quartet, recorded in 1933 by Columbia Records, seems to have been the first major chamber work by an American composer to be commercially recorded. A similar situation obtained in the symphonic genre with *Symphony 1933,* which was recorded by Koussevitzky and the Boston Symphony at a live performance in Carnegie Hall in 1934.

Among other works recorded at various times during this period by Columbia and RCA Victor were the Piano Sonata (Johana Harris's first commercial recording of one of her husband's works), the Quartets Nos. 2 and 3, the Trio, the orchestral overture *When Johnny Comes Marching Home* (written specifically for recording), and the Third Symphony (another Koussevitzky/Boston Symphony recording). '

## Johana

It was about this time that Harris met the young Beula Duffey, an event which was to affect profoundly the remainder of their personal and professional lives. Miss Duffey, a native of Canada, had been a piano prodigy. After studying at the Toronto Conservatory, she entered Juilliard at the age of twelve, later becoming the youngest faculty member in the institution's history when she joined the summer piano staff at fifteen. After a period of study abroad at the Hochschule in Berlin (where she received a scholarship), she returned to the position at Juilliard.

Harris recalled Beula Duffey as the "Queen of Juilliard." After his divorce from Hilda, from whom he had been separated since her disaffection with life in the United States had led her to return to her family in England, Harris married Beula, and the two talents merged into one of the most successful and formidable artistic partnerships in American musical culture. Shortly after their marriage, the composer changed Beula's first name to Johana (after Johann Sebastian Bach). The new Mrs. Harris's musical gifts called forth a number of piano works from her husband during the succeeding decades, and her warm personal qualities were an important factor not only in the eventual raising of the family which began to appear during the mid-1940s, but also in drawing many celebrities in the arts and in education to the various homes the couple established over the years.

Mrs. Harris joined her husband in Princeton following their marriage and was the recipient of the Quintet for Piano and Strings, which the composer wrote as a wedding gift. During its composition, the couple also made a trip to California, where Harris's parents had an opportunity to meet his new bride.

The Harrises left the Westminster Choir School in 1938 and moved for a while to Upper Montclair, New Jersey, then to New York City, where they subsisted for about two years on Mrs. Harris's income from teaching, supplemented by occasional money from commissions which the composer received. During this period, Harris also gave private lessons, initiating the sort of "master-disciple" relationship I have described elsewhere. Among his students during these years were George Lynn, who, many years later, succeeded John Finley Williamson as director of the Westminster Choir, and Wray Lundquist, who, after serving as one of the finest of Harris's copyists, went on to a career as a teacher and composer. One of the most notable of all Harris's students, as mentioned earlier, was William Schuman, whose compositional style is indebted in some respects to the example set by his teacher.

## Third Symphony

Around 1937 Harris was commissioned to write a violin concerto for Jascha Heifetz. He completed a one-movement work but, due to mutual dissatisfaction on the part of both composer and recipient, the piece was withdrawn. Harris then used some of its materials in a new symphony for which he had received a commission from Hans Kindler, conductor of the National Symphony Orchestra. However, after completing the work, Harris took it instead to Koussevitzky, who, after some initial coolness toward the composer, read through the piece, became enthusiastic, and offered to perform it.

This incident seemed to heal the rift between Harris and his most important early champion, and the subsequent premiere of the Third Symphony in early 1939 by Koussevitzky helped to fulfill the potent promise conveyed some years earlier by *Symphony 1933.* Though some of the critical reviews from the period indicate that the symphony was not the immediate or unequivocal success its now legendary status has made it seem, it nonetheless (with some reworking) eventually became the most often performed and one of the most widely admired of all American works in the genre.

## Form

In this work, the composer came closer to solving the problems of form with which he had wrestled in his previous symphonic efforts. The one-movement design, though not unique with Harris, provided him with the necessary framework within which he could work out a continually evolving musicodramatic continuity.

Harris provided a structural outline of the symphony, an outline which reveals how closely his purely musical conception of a work is allied with an equally potent "character" or "dramatic" scheme. He is truly a Romantic composer in this respect, though the assignment of a single character to each of the several sections of the symphony, along with a fairly consistent working out of a specific set of materials in a given section, also resembles the Baroque-period "doctrine of the affections."

Though often quoted, Harris's outline is given again here for its importance in the development of his aesthetics:

Section I. Tragic—low string sonorities.

Section II. Lyric—strings, horn, woodwinds.

Section III.. Pastoral—woodwinds, with a polytonal string background.

Section IV. Fugue—dramatic
A. Brass and percussion predominating
B. Canonic development of materials from Section II constituting background for further development of the fugue.
C. Brass climax, rhythmic motive derived from fugue subject.

Section V. Dramatic—tragic

    A. Restatement of violin theme of Section I; *tutti* strings in canon with *tutti* woodwinds against brass and percussion developing rhythmic ideas from climax of Section IV.

    B. Coda—development of materials from Sections I and II over pedal timpani.[9]

The single movement of the Third Symphony can be perceived as an arch design in terms of the progress of intensity and of emotional states. It starts with dark tragedy, moves through the increasingly brighter lyrical and pastoral states to the blazing intensity and aggressive activity of the dramatic fugue, and returns at the end to the tragic character.

The opening theme, which functions as a sort of large scale introduction to the Tragic section, is, with its long, flowing, sinuous curves, perhaps the most striking example up to this point of Harris's newfound maturity of style and technique.

Here virtually every phrase seems to be launched from the concluding notes of its predecessor, with frequent rhythmic references back to the opening measures of the melody. In addition, the building blocks of Harris's mature harmonic style are displayed in this passage: after several measures in unison, the harmonic texture is expanded to organum sonorities, then major and minor triads (first statement of Theme II), and eventually polychords (the polytonal background to the Pastoral section).[10]

Theme II (Tragic), borrowed from the First Quartet, exhibits the closed design characteristic of an earlier stage in Harris's development, though this in no way detracts from its eloquent effectiveness here:

EXAMPLE 25

*Symphony No. 3:* Theme I

*Symphony No. 3:* Theme I

EXAMPLE 26

*Symphony No. 3:* Theme II (opening phrases and later portion containing motive x)

Theme III (Lyric) is akin to Theme I, though it too exhibits something of a closed form which recurs, or, more accurately, is regenerated with variation from the opening broken-chord cell:

EXAMPLE 27

*Symphony No. 3:* Theme III

Harris also extracts motive y for independent development both here and later.

The Pastoral section is a seminal passage in Harris's oeuvre. It is the first fully realized example of the sort of sound and texture he employed subsequently to represent an open-air, nature ambience. Here, a long melodic continuity (Theme IV) is passed back and forth, in phrases of varying length, between several solo winds while the strings provide a colorful harmonic background:

EXAMPLE 28

*Symphony No. 3:* Theme IV (arpeggiated harmonic background reduced to block polychords)

The "polytonal" string background to which Harris refers in his outline quoted above—created through canonic imitation of arpeggio designs among various divisions of the strings—contains the sort of superimposed triads built on different roots which are a hallmark of Harris's style.[11]

The fugue subject (Theme V), perhaps Harris's best known tune, is an illustration of his ability to devise a concise, memorable, and very potent idea to counterbalance his longer melodies:

EXAMPLE 29

*Symphony No. 3:* Theme V

It also, however, points up the difficulty the composer experienced as a result of his tendency to formulate melodies, motives, and figuration in terms of specific instruments or instrumental choirs. Though the fugue is ingeniously worked out, the subject reiteration becomes bothersome and overinsistent because it is consistently given to the brasses rather than being passed through different instrumental colors for variety and to enable it occasionally to be subsumed in the texture in order that other ideas might be placed in relief.

The final section of the symphony (actually a new ending worked out and copied within the short space of a very few days prior to the first New York performance) very likely constitutes the pinnacle of Harris's art up to that time. This tragic denouement was a rather daring stroke for its time, for it, and the Romantic intensity of expression of the symphony as a whole, in fact, seemed to go against the aesthetic grain of a period in which an acidic satire and brittle smartness were cultivated with some success as part of a reaction against this same late 19th century expressiveness. The great melody (Theme VI), more clearly diatonic than usual for Harris, is a perfect example of the descending spiral which generally forms the final segment of his mature arch designs:

EXAMPLE 30

*Symphony No. 3:* Theme VI

Each phrase lands on a successively lower pitch, the last phrase being sealed by one of Harris's most masterfully constructed cadences:

EXAMPLE 31

*Symphony No. 3.* Final cadence

The composer manages in these final measures of the work to achieve a sense of completion while withholding the tonic triad until the very end—an excellent example of his increasing ability to use the devices of musical tradition in a fresh and individual way.

This final section also illustrates Harris's mastery in creating a sense of unity in a large and diverse structure by building a supporting texture for Theme VI out of a network of important motives from some of the earlier themes (motives x and y).

## Overview

The Third Symphony represents what is perhaps Harris's most successful early attempt to reconcile his predisposition toward continually unfolding, autogenetic form with the sectionalism which is an important feature of the Classic period aesthetic. Though he achieved equal success with the multimovement symphony (of which Nos. 1, 5, and 6 are outstanding), his idiosyncratic handling of the one-movement type is perhaps his most significant contribution to the history of the genre.

The artistic and public success of the Third Symphony doubtless formed the capstone for the increasing confidence Harris had begun to feel in his creative powers, as demonstrated in the works he had written in the two or three years prior to its composition, after recovering from his disappointment over the Second Symphony. No doubt this new assurance was due partly to the inestimable personal and artistic stimulus provided by Johana; it was also likely due to the experience provided by the increasing number of commissions for works in a variety of media which had begun to come his way and had forced him to work under pressure and with economy.

The clarity of form, directness of expression, and eloquence of the Third Symphony combined to make it the most widely performed of all Harris's orchestral works, and, in creating it, he moved securely into the front rank of American composers.

# 4

## Symphonies, Part II
## (*Folksong Symphony,* Nos. 5, 6, and 7)

### Ballet and Radio

The Harrises remained in New York throughout the rest of the 1930s and into the early 40s. The composer resumed his fulltime teaching activities in 1940, when he obtained a position at Cornell University under a Carnegie Creative Grant. The couple moved to Ithaca, New York, at this time and remained there until 1943.

It was also in 1940 that Harris began a series of ballet collaborations with Hanya Holm. These took him out west during the summers, to Colorado Springs, Colorado, where the noted choreographer had organized a summer ballet under the auspices of The Colorado College.

Somewhat earlier, in 1938, Harris had initiated another aspect of his career, one which was to last into the 1950s: an involvement with radio. For CBS he developed a weekly series titled "Let's Make Music," a program designed to acquaint the general public with both the elements and the literature of music. After moving to Colorado, the composer, along with Johana, revived the series on station KOA in Denver. For both editions of the program, Harris drew upon a wide variety of sources for materials, among them folk music.

### The Folk Element

Of course, the folk element had long been present in Harris's work. The modal characteristics, cadences, and melodic shapes of some of his melodies reveal a kinship with folksong of a certain Anglo-Celtic type (though the closest explicit association often seems to be with the hymnody contained in the psalters, some of which were of European origin or influence, used by the early settlers in North America). We know from Harris's own testimony that folksong formed part of his upbringing, and his attitude toward the idiom seemed to develop relatively early:

> I was brought up with simple folk attitudes by my pioneer parents. Folk music was as natural to our way of life as corn bread and sweet milk. My mother played the guitar and we hummed along with her after supper on the front porch or in the kitchen. . . . When I began to study music, I decided that composers were folk singers who had learned to write down the songs that took their fancy; and that therefore folk songs could be recast to suit a composer's purpose, and that they could be legitimately used to generate symphonic forms . . .
> Certain ways of musical treatment seemed to me more natural than others; the harmony should be clear in texture and intent. . . ; the rhythmic patterns should be complementary to the melodic phrases and the orchestration should be unobscured and direct. . . .
> . . . As a composer, I felt that folk songs were like the Good Earth, to be cultivated by musicians according to their tastes and skills.[1]

Harris's experience with folk music was broadened during the mid-1930s when he undertook intensive research in the collections of printed and recorded folk music in the Library of Congress in connection with his preparation, along with Jacob Evanson, of an anthology of choral music titled *Singing Through the Ages*. In fact, a glance at the table of contents of the two volumes of the collection hints at the possibility that Harris's initial introduction to some of the folk tunes he was to employ most frequently in his oeuvre may have taken place during this endeavor.

The composer also came in contact, during the early 1940s, with some of the gifted performers and scholars in the field, among them John and Alan Lomax, Burl Ives, and the Golden Gate Quartet. And, of course, there was Johana Harris. Mrs. Harris knew many folk tunes (or variants of tunes of wider dissemination) from her native Canada and was an effective folksinger. In addition, her gifts as a keyboard improviser enabled her to build imaginative harmonic textures when accompanying herself, something which strongly influenced her husband's piano settings of folk materials.

## The *Folksong Symphony*

Aside from some early uses of "When Johnny Comes Marching Home," Harris began his exploration of folk materials in earnest with a cappella choral settings made during the mid and late 1930s.[2] It was his colleague Howard Hanson, however, who was responsible for an enlargement of the scale of his folk-based efforts: Hanson commissioned from Harris a work for chorus and orchestra to be given at the Eastman School's American Spring Festival in 1940.

For this work, which he eventually titled *Folksong Symphony* and regarded as his Symphony No. 4, the composer drew most of his materials from two important anthologies: *Cowboy Songs and Other Frontier Ballads* by John and Alan Lomax and *The American Songbag* by Carl Sandburg.

## Early History; Revision

The new symphony initially had six movements. Sometime after the premiere, however, Harris added what is now the first orchestral interlude and reversed the positions of the first and last movements. Thus, in its final form the work consists of seven movements: I. The Girl I Left Behind Me, II. Western Cowboy, III. Interlude: Dance Tunes for Strings and Percussion, IV. Mountaineer Love Song, V. Interlude: Dance Tunes for Full Orchestra, VI. Negro Fantasy, VII. Welcome Party ("When Johnny Comes Marching Home").[3]

## Character and Aesthetics

Though the *Folksong Symphony* has on some occasions been dismissed as constituting mere arrangements of folk materials (in fact, Harris's original title was *Folksong Jamboree*), it is, in reality, a skillfully conceived work of large dimensions which combines elements of both arrangement and original composition. In the treatment of his borrowed tunes, Harris clearly follows the idea set forth in his statement quoted above, especially in the realization of their subtle emotional implications and in the attempts to explore some of the technical possibilities which they afford by using motives and phrases extracted from them for development of a symphonic character. These latter include the creation of orchestral introductions and interludes and the weaving of often sophisticated accompaniment textures.

## Form

The large structure of the work is beautifully planned, another indication of the symphonic thinking involved. The seven movements are arranged symmetrically around the central axis provided by the "Mountaineer Love Song." Thus, movements I and VII, fast, aggressive, and boisterous, can be perceived as two pillars of similar character supporting the main edifice.

Movements II and VI, slow and regional in character (VI decidedly ethnic, as well) match one another as large rooms of related types at opposite ends of the structure. The two interludes, relatively light, fast moving, and purely instrumental, function as corridors leading to the central fourth movement.

Most of the choral movements of the *Folksong Symphony* are cast in modified strophic form, following the structure of the original tunes with their several verses. Harris, of course, utilizes a great deal of variation from one verse setting to the next, paralleling on a symphonic scale the common practice in performances by folksingers.

## Movements I and VII

The first and last movements are excellent illustrations of the above. Movement I is, for the most part, relatively clear-cut in its treatment of the tune in the choral sections:

EXAMPLE 32

*Folksong Symphony:* I. The Girl I Left Behind Me

Harris employs similar, highly rhythmic orchestral accompaniments for most of the four verses he sets. However, he raises the key from D major to E for the last verse (which also has the first real change in accompaniment texture) as a means of increasing the tension. He also provides the movement (and, consequently, the entire symphony) with a lengthy orchestral introduction during which the tune is gradually introduced, skillfully averting anticipating the first choral entrance too much by avoiding the definitive form of the melody and by giving it a slightly different harmonic coloration than its customary straightforward major-mode setting. He also steers away from the home key of the movement here.

As evidence of his maturing technique, Harris is able to introduce an element of parody in the closing pages (a quotation of "Good Night, Ladies") with a natural, almost inevitable effect.

The finale, "Welcome Party," also employs a strophic variations format, though here the composer alternates choral and orchestral statements of the "Johnny" tune. This movement is somewhat more complex than I, for Harris subjects the theme to a greater symphonic manipulation, extracting motives from it for the accompaniment and using a wider variety of textures and harmonic colorations for the various verse settings. These include an effective major-mode treatment and a free canonic working out. The latter imparts a great sense of urgency and drive to the climax in the final pages. Harris groups the variations in such a way as to produce a large ternary structure, with the major-mode verse forming the B section.

## Movements II and VI

Movements II and VI, though differing from each other, share a common situation both in differing from the other choral movements in form and, as mentioned earlier, in their more explicitly regional associations. "Western Cowboy" is based on the following:

EXAMPLE 33

a: *Folksong Symphony:* II, The Lone Prairie

b: *Folksong Symphony:* II. Streets of Laredo

c: *Folksong Symphony:* II. The Old Chisholm Trail

The "Negro Fantasy" employs chiefly this melody:

EXAMPLE 34

*Folksong Symphony:* VI. De Trumpet Sounds It In My Soul

In "Western Cowboy" Harris employs devices of timbre and harmonic color (e.g., the sustained woodwind chords emphasizing organum intervals in measures 33ff.) to convey a spacious, "open-plains" ambience. In the "Negro Fantasy" he uses incessant motivic repetition with variation, constant fluctuation between the major and minor thirds, and *glissandi* to suggest the wild aspiration of the black revival service.

Both movements fall into a large binary form and both employ strophic variation within the sections of this form. In movement II, however, Harris bases the B section on a new tune ("Laredo"), which he eventually puts in canon. In movement VI, he uses essentially the same materials throughout but marks off the two sections of the piece by making the A section purely orchestral (a wild fantasia on "De Trumpet Sounds It") and bringing in the chorus only in section B.

These two movements and, to some extent, movement IV, are perhaps the most "symphonic" in terms of their complexity, particularly in the instrumental textures, and clearly show Harris working creatively with his given materials rather than simply arranging them. In addition, movement VI shows the extent to which the composer's by now almost completely diatonic harmonic idiom can be "stretched" to provide unexpected vertical relationships. This is demonstrated by the passage beginning in measure 89: here, both the wailing canonic ostinato in the horns and women's voices and the tortured discant in the violas and winds are borrowed from the "Tears" movement of the Symphony for Voices. However, in the present movement, they are underpinned by harmonies in strings and low woodwinds centering around g minor:

EXAMPLE 35

*Folksong Symphony:* VI. Harmonic texture

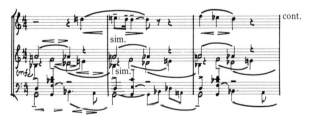

## Movement IV

The fourth movement, "Mountaineer Love Song," functions, as indicated earlier, as a sort of centerpiece for the entire symphony. Not only does it contain some of the most deeply expressive writing of the work, it also exhibits some of the richest and most complex choral and orchestral textures. Again, Harris employs the strophic variations procedure, distributed over a large ternary form, as in the case of movement VII. The folksong itself is unusual in that the various stanzas differ from one another musically, especially toward their latter portions, and this provides additional variety in Harris's treatment:

EXAMPLE 36

*Folksong Symphony:* IV. He's Gone Away

Section A opens with an orchestral introduction (containing some of the composer's most effective uses of common-tone chord relationships), which foreshadows the tune in the solo horn. The main body of section A is in two parts: (1) a choral statement of the first stanza of "He's Gone Away" followed by (2) an imaginatively conceived orchestral variation of the melody featuring changing harmonic colorblocks and phrase-end expansion.

Section B is likewise in two parts and comprises the settings of the second and third stanzas. It is somewhat more intense than section A, especially in its treatment of the second stanza, with its active, polyphonically derived orchestral accompaniment. Harris rounds the movement off in section C with a varied restatement of the first stanza of the folksong.

Throughout this piece, but especially in the B section, the composer makes much use of motives, both thematically derived and of independent origin, to develop the choral part (in various *stretti*) and to create an orchestral fabric (though free counterpoint, *stretti,* and varied repetition).

## The Two Interludes

The two orchestral interludes (movements III and V) set off movement IV, as mentioned above. They also provide contrast, not only with the movements employing chorus, but with each other as well, since the first interlude is restricted to strings and percussion while the second employs full orchestra. Further contrast with the other movements is achieved through the use of tunes of a predominantly dancelike character.

The third movement is in a clear ABA form, the second A, unusual for Harris, a nearly literal recapitulation of the first. For the A section, the composer invents original materials which spring from the essence of "hoedown" fiddling:

EXAMPLE 37

*Folksong Symphony:* III. Theme I

The B section is built on a quietly flowing modal melody:

EXAMPLE 38

*Folksong Symphony:* III. Theme II

This section, in its quotation of snatches of "The Irish Washerwoman" as phrase-end punctuation for and, later, counterpoint to Example 38, provides another touch of parody in this rich and diverse symphony.

In the second interlude, Harris ingeniously exploits the similarities between the two folk melodies employed:

EXAMPLE 39

a. *Folksong Symphony:* V. The Birds' Courting Song

b: *Folksong Symphony:* V. Jump Up, My Lady

cont.

There are six sections, in each of which both tunes appear in succession. Harris subjects them during the first four sections to increasingly complex and imaginative variations. This is especially noticeable in the case of "Jump Up," expanded in section D in a fantastic, almost grotesque manner. For the fifth (E) section, the composer draws back, restoring "Jump Up" to something closer to its original form.

In the tiny coda (section F), the "Bird" flutters briefly past the listener one last time before disappearing into the distance.

Both interludes contain some of Harris's most charming and unpretentious writing, simple on the surface but containing within rich detail and many subtleties of form. In these pieces, the relatively unfamiliar persona of Harris the miniaturist comes unashamedly to the fore. The very fact that he was able here to bring off the light touch reveals how far his mastery of technique and his stylistic assurance had grown during the previous decade.

## Overview; Harris Reaches Out to the Community

The *Folksong Symphony* has become, next to the Third Symphony, perhaps the most often performed of all Harris's larger compositions. Its success is due not only to the quality of the materials (both borrowed and original) and of their working out, but also to Harris's practicality in designing the vocal parts so that they lie within the capabilities of choruses on the high school level. This aim of providing music for amateur performance is one which the composer pursued up to his last large work, the *Bicentennial Symphony.* In addition to serving as the embodiment of this spirit, the *Folksong Symphony* provides the most potent summary of Harris's aesthetic stance toward the folk music which was so much a part of his cultural makeup.

# Fifth Symphony

In spite of its success, however, the *Folksong Symphony* falls somewhat outside the continuum represented by Harris's major purely orchestral efforts in the symphonic genre. After completing the choral work, he was eager to resume this line of development, especially in view of the success of the Third Symphony, and thus welcomed a commission from Koussevitzky in 1940 to write a new symphony for Boston. Work began in the fall of that year, but progress was slow.

In reflecting on the situation now, it appears that the labored gestation of this work, the Fifth Symphony, provides an excellent example of the way in which Harris's creative faculties were often affected by his surroundings. He needed the amplitude of ambience afforded by a large, comfortable home and many physical comforts, responding best to geographic areas of open spaces and broad vistas, for the experience of his rural upbringing could not be set aside. The composer's statement concerning the origin of the symphony is revealing in this respect:

> I had planned to write this Symphony during the late summer and fall of 1940. . . . But after working on it during the month of September, I found I was not ready to write it.
>
> And so it was not until the summer of 1942 while I was in Colorado Springs at the great mountains near by that I knew that I could write the work. We came home to Cornell University and began the Symphony in early October. It was completed on Christmas morning. . . .[4]

## A Paradigm for the 1940s

If there is any one work which can be regarded as conveying the essence of Roy Harris's style and technique during the 1940s, the Fifth Symphony is that work. Diatonic harmony (prevailingly triadic in the symphony); clear textures; melodically generated forms; directness of expression; and some of his most distinguished, accessible, and beautiful melodic writing—all these are the hallmarks of these early years of Harris's stylistic maturity.

In the Fifth Symphony, one also finds all the elements of the mature orchestral style Harris had been seeking since his earliest efforts in the medium. From the early 1940s on, he generally employs in his full orchestral scores woodwinds in threes (with the standard auxiliaries), four to eight horns (frequently playing in unison), trumpets and trombones in threes, tuba, a relatively small percussion section, and the usual strings. Also appearing in some works from the 1940s on are saxophones and the baritone horn, as well as a kind of "gamelan" consisting of piano, harp, chimes, and vibraphone that provides a bell-like chordal punctuation. Harris generally preferred to score in discrete choirs, rather than blending the various sections. The strings are usually given a complete harmonic texture, while the winds are accorded variable treatment, the composer often playing off the "sharp-tone" brasses (trumpets and trombones) against the "round-tone" instruments (horns, baritone, and tuba). And, of course, he continued in all choirs to explore and develop the reservoir of idiomatic ideas he had been accumulating for the various instruments in connection with both their uses as group members of their respective choirs and as occasional soloists.[5]

## Form

For the Fifth Symphony, Harris returned to the three-movement design represented by Symphonies Nos. 1 and 2. On several occasions he gave its three movements the titles "Prelude," "Chorale," and "Fugue," and, indeed, these titles possess a general significance in representing "characters" or "types" which recur in many of the subsequent symphonies, and in other works as well.

### First Movement

The "Prelude" is a short movement in fast tempo, exhibiting a kinship with the opening movements of *American Portrait* and Symphony No. 2. Unusually for Harris, there is virtually no extended melodic or thematic writing per se; rather, all the materials grow out of the dotted figure stated in the opening measures:[6]

EXAMPLE 40

*Symphony No. 5:* I. Opening idea

Motive x generates a number of longer ideas that function as designs repeated with variations. Additional ideas derived from x are cited in Example 13. Each of these designs is exposed and worked out within one of several sections comprising the first half of a binary form.

Through gradual intensification of rhythm, buildup of texture and dynamics, and changes in scoring, Harris manages to achieve a coherent structure that builds to a convincing high point before breaking off in the face of the vigorous march which forms the second half of the movement.

This march is based on new materials that contrast rhythmically with the incessant dotted rhythms of section A, though motive x infiltrates here as well in a fanfare figure (actually a paraphrase of an army bugle call):

EXAMPLE 41

*Symphony No. 5:* I. B section materials

The materials of section B, however, are not very distinguished. Perhaps after so much in the way of figurational designs in the A section, the listener would welcome something more truly melodic here. Harris fails to provide it. But, overall, the "Prelude" is admirably concise and provides an effective "upbeat" to the more expansive, melodically oriented slow movement that follows.

## Second Movement

The second movement constitutes the epitome of Harris's concept of the chorale. Almost entirely homophonic in texture, this type of composition, as realized here, emphasizes the long line and the cadence. The present movement comprises some of the composer's most distinguished melodic writing and, indeed, achieves one of the high points in American symphonic writing altogether. It fulfills the expectations set up in the first movement and functions as a central arch crowning the large structure of the symphony.

The movement is in three clearly defined sections. The A section features a somber, yet curiously sensuous theme:

EXAMPLE 42

*Symphony No. 5:* II. Theme I

This long line is characterized by numerous modal shifts emphasizing the dark end of Harris's melodic spectrum. It is followed in the B section by one of the most ambitious and unprecedented passages in all the contemporary symphonic literature: an enormous Gothic arch containing a rise, peak, and fall spanning one hundred and twenty measures.

EXAMPLE 43

*Symphony No. 5:* II. Theme II (segments of opening, climax, and final portion)

Not only is this line melodically distinctive, it exhibits remarkable control over dramatic timing. Perhaps more than anything else in his oeuvre, this aspiring melodic structure conveys the visionary element which is a fundamental part of Harris's makeup.

The final, C section of the movement is built not so much on a distinct thematic idea as on the continual expansion and variation of cadences:

EXAMPLE 44

*Symphony No. 5:* II. Theme III

This section is, in fact, one of the most crucial in Harris's entire output, demonstrating his treatment of harmony and cadence and the fundamental roles these aspects play for him. Here, presented with a straightforward homophonic, choralelike texture, the listener can examine clearly the skill with which the composer allows his cadential "formulas" to join in almost organic fashion in conveying a gradual and cumulative sense of growth. At the same time, one also encounters an especially good illustration of Harris's scoring in discrete orchestral choirs, each choir comprising a complete harmonic texture in itself.

## Third Movement

The "Fugue" is another in the line of polythematic contrapuntal structures exemplified by the finale of Symphony No. 2. Since completing that earlier work, Harris had gained further experience with this type of movement in such diverse compositions as the Piano Quintet (third movement), the Viola Quintet (fourth movement), and the orchestral *American Creed* (the "Free to Build" finale). The Fifth Symphony, however, exhibits in fully developed form a trend only partly evident in most of these other works, but one that was to become increasingly important in some of the later symphonies. This development is marked by a modification of the relatively strict polythematic fugue in the direction of a type which perhaps can best be called "variation-fugue." The hybrid appears to have come about partly because of the length and the diverse, and often mutually incompatible, characters of some of Harris's fugal subjects. The first subject of the present finale is an example of this:

## EXAMPLE 45

*Symphony No. 5:* III. Subject I

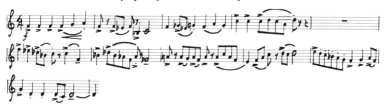

Though one of Harris's best and most memorable tunes, it lacks the pithy conciseness necessary for it to function as a true contrapuntal subject.

The composer seems to have realized the above shortcoming, at least subconsciously, for in its working out during the opening section of this large tripartite movement, the theme is passed from one group of instruments to another in a series of five contrapuntal variations. The variations convey their contrapuntal character in the manner in which the texture surrounding each statement of the theme subsequent to the first is made up virtually entirely from a network of motives extracted from the melody. Harris allows the polyphonic texture to accumulate during these variations and builds the intensity by eventually shifting the subject from the woodwinds and strings to the brass.

Subjects II and III are more concise and typically "fugal":

## EXAMPLE 46

a: *Symphony No. 5:* III. Subject II

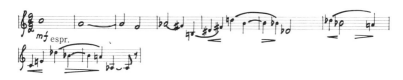

b: *Symphony No. 5:* Subject III

They are exposed in quick succession in the B section, in the process weaving one of Harris's most imaginative and ineffable passages, a music arising from a texture which creates in its vertical dimension a constantly shifting web of triadic sonorities. The feminine seductiveness of this passage is unexpected, especially following upon the vigorous, rambunctious music which has preceded it.

For the C section of the finale, Harris brings back subject I for a further series of variations, this time weaving the accompanying materials from motives extracted from all three ideas. However, in what turns out to be a typical procedure for him, he never really combines the three contrapuntally in their original forms in a true fugal development. This may result partly from a deliberate loosening up of the traditional procedure; it may also come from the incompatibility of subjects mentioned above. Whatever the reason, it is true that for some listeners this lack of contrapuntal intensification leaves a dissatisfaction, a lack of fulfillment, which seriously undermines the musicodramatic integrity of a multimovement work of this sort.

## Overview

In spite of its flaws, the generally high level of musical invention, the clarity of texture, the masterly handling of orchestral sonorities, and the exuberant spontaneity of expression found in the Fifth Symphony combine to render this work both a rewarding musical experience and a particularly valuable source for examining Harris's development.

# The Harrises in Colorado

It appears that at least partly because of the salutary effects the Colorado environment had on the composer's creative faculties, the family, now augmented by daughter Patricia, born in 1943, moved that year to Colorado Springs. They settled in a large multilevel dwelling which they christened "Holiday House." The composer, as was his wont, laid claim to what was probably the choice room and turned it into an enormous studio.

Harris assumed the position of Composer-in-Residence at The Colorado College and his wife joined the piano faculty there. Both, over the next several years, became deeply involved in the musical affairs of the college and the community and were responsible for organizing summer festivals, bringing to the area performers of national repute who gave performances and participated in workshops.

## The Legacy of Lincoln: Sixth Symphony

During this period, the composer was busy fulfilling commissions from many sources. The most important of these, from the Blue Network (which later became the American Broadcasting Corporation), was for yet another symphony. The proposed subject of the new work, Abraham Lincoln, had strong appeal for the composer. For many years Harris had capitalized, in building his public image, on the parallels between himself and Lincoln in the circumstances of their births and early childhoods. The commission stimulated him to delve into Carl Sandburg's multivolume biography of the sixteenth President, and from his research in this and other sources he developed the rather simple concept of a four-movement work, each movement of which is based upon a phrase from the "Gettysburg Address."[7]

The Sixth Symphony, subtitled "Gettysburg," which eventually emerged during the latter part of 1943 and early 1944, thus became Harris's first concrete musical involvement with a figure with which, along with Walt Whitman, he has become most identified.

### A War Symphony

Though it has received few performances, the *Gettysburg Symphony* nonetheless can be perceived, in its historical context, as one of the strongest of the war-related symphonies of the 1940s, an achievement in some ways at least as distinctive and powerful as the Sixth Symphony of Vaughan Williams and the Seventh Symphony of Shostakovich. In addition, while the Fifth Symphony constitutes a summary of Harris's development at one period during his career, the four diverse movements of the Sixth provide a broader panorama of his style, since they foreshadow in their textures and in their treatment of harmony and scoring some of the developments of the succeeding decades.

### "Awakening"

In the opening movement, "Awakening," the composer carries the pantheism that underlies the Pastoral section of the Third Symphony to its culmination, deepening and intensifying it by means of a visionary quality which is conveyed through a broad tempo, a rich and complex texture, and a soaring melody which emerges in the final pages.

The movement is in four sections and is an excellent example of the layering technique Harris sometimes uses to build a texture: section A presents snippets of melody in the strings over sustained low woodwind chords. Section B develops the linear aspect through the use of complete, though short, phrases exchanged in a dialogue between violins and solo woodwinds, with increased rhythmic animation provided by string arpeggios. In section C the woodwinds and strings continue as part of the accompaniment to a continuation of the short melodic fragments, now given to solo brasses. The vertical dimension is expanded considerably through the division of the woodwinds into a quasicontrapuntal texture in several parts (developing the string arpeggiation of the previous section). The low strings now provide both the harmonic underpinning for this section and a rhythmic intensification through their disposition in pulsing chords in half-notes, then quarter-notes.

For the final (D) section of the movement, the full-fledged melody toward which the fragmentary elements of the previous music have been leading bursts through in several long breathed phrases in the strings:

EXAMPLE 47

*Symphony No. 6:* I. Theme

As support for this melody, the woodwinds continue their complex background tapestry, the single lines of the previous section now coalescing into massive polychordal blocks woven against each other. At the same time, the melodic fragments in the brass intensify in a close-knit quasi-stretto which further enriches the texture and helps outline the harmonic foundation.

In addition to being one of Harris's most onomatopoetic conceptions in terms of the relationship of the music to the implications of the subtitle, "Awakening" is also his most expansive and impressive symphonic opening movement altogether, certainly as fine a piece of orchestral writing as he achieved during the 1940s.

## "Conflict"

The "Conflict" movement which follows is a raw unleashing of the dark, savage element in Harris's musical personality. It is also an apotheosis of the march rhythms through which he often conveys this savagery. The movement is in two large sections, corresponding respectively to a slow march and a fast march.

The first theme, delivered stridently in woodwinds and trumpets over an obsessive, hammered-out minor polychord in the strings, is one of the composer's most tortured lines:

EXAMPLE 48

*Symphony No. 6:* II. Theme I

This idea leads to a passage in which the composer's favored organum harmonies are employed to convey, somewhat uncharacteristically, a sinister presence through their outlining of a sinuous chromatic line in the top voice. This is another example of the variety of expression of which Harris's relatively limited harmonic vocabulary is capable:

EXAMPLE 49

*Symphony No. 6:* II. Theme II

The fast march which erupts convulsively out of the wild climax of the A section possess a frantic quality in its scurrying high violin idea (Theme IIIa), an idea that reveals an unexpected approach to an often cliche-ridden musical type:

EXAMPLE 50

*Symphony No. 6:* II. Theme IIIa

b: *Symphony No. 6:* II. Theme IIIb

The more lyrical theme which follows (actually a variant of theme II) is also given to the strings initially, but is later seized by the brass and developed in several paragraphs of increasingly dissonant polychordal harmonization:

EXAMPLE 51

a: *Symphony No. 6:* II. Theme IV (first statement)

b: *Symphony No. 6:* II. Theme IV (final statement)

As is often the case with Harris's aggressive pieces, the movement ends abruptly, thus underscoring the quality of savage, indiscriminate brutality which lies at the center of this music.

The element of parody, which I observed in connection with the *Folksong Symphony,* surfaces again in "Conflict:" the tortured line of Example 50 is, in reality, a paraphrase of the World War II song "The Caissons Go Rolling Along," while some of the other materials of the fast march are derived from a football fight song.

Though "Conflict" perhaps no longer sounds as startling today as it did in 1944, it is still one of Harris's most original and effective symphonic movements and provides an important reference source for many of the "rhetorical" elements which the composer uses to convey this particular side of his personality. The piece is a harbinger of the Roy Harris of social protest who emerged during the 1960s and 70s.

## "Dedication"

The "Dedication" movement constitutes a complete contrast to its predecessor. It is one of Harris's most reflective, deeply felt, and eloquent utterances. Like the second movement of the Fifth Symphony, it is ternary in structure, with an archlike musicodramatic scheme. But "Dedication" is more inward and elegiac, with a denser, richer harmonic texture that does not allow the melodic line to soar in such clear relief.

The movement is also an even more explicit example of the "layering" process discussed in connection with "Awakening." In the A section the melodic continuity is passed in slow succession from the basses up through the other members of the string choir, each division which has previously had the melody being absorbed into the accompaniment upon the entrance of a new division.

EXAMPLE 52

*Symphony No. 6:* III. Theme I

This long line (theme I) is embedded in a supporting texture that develops from bare pedal points in the opening measures to a lush polychordal fabric at the apex of the A section. The line is also punctuated, at first hesitantly, then more continuously, by a descending motive (motive x) in the first violins which itself grows into something quite elaborate:

EXAMPLE 53

*Symphony No. 6:* III. Motive x and developments

The B section comprises a new melody (theme II) in the woodwinds, harmonized in block chords and outlining a slowly descending spiral:

EXAMPLE 54

*Symphony No. 6:* III. Theme II

This is accompanied by an elaborate quasicanonic texture in the strings that is a clear outgrowth of the development of motive x in the A section.

Section C is benedictory in tone, like the corresponding portion of the slow movement of the Fifth Symphony, but with a stronger melodic profile.[8] Here Harris returns the melodic materials to the strings and continues the gradual descent established by theme II:

EXAMPLE 55

*Symphony No. 6:* III. Theme III

The metrical structure of "Dedication" reveals a simple, but carefully worked out plan: section A is in 4/4, B is in 3/4, and C is in 5/4. The "shortening" of the meter in the B section provides a greater momentum that gives the impression of a tempo change; the "expansion" of the meter in section C, on the other hand, creates a sense of broadening out, while simultaneously uniting within a single asymmetrical meter the duple and triple meters of the first two sections.

## "Affirmation"

"Affirmation" is another of Harris's contrapuntal finales. It is a triple fugue, revealing an indebtedness to the example, at least in this medium, of Symphony No. 2. This is manifest not only in its use of three subjects but also in its scheme of employing successively shorter note values for each subject. The three ideas are:

EXAMPLE 56

a: *Symphony No. 6:* IV. Subject I

b: *Symphony No. 6:* III. Subject II

c: *Symphony No. 6:* III. Subject III

There are three main sections plus a coda, another feature in common with the earlier symphony. Sections A and B expose and develop subjects I and II respectively. Section C comprises a brief exposition in stretto of subject III followed by contrapuntal developments of subjects I and II with a motive from III. The coda is based chiefly upon a changing series of reiterated polychords punctuated by references to subject I.

Though this movement possesses an admirable sense of continuity and an accumulation of tension, as well as an unpedantic variety in the contrapuntal techniques employed, it also exhibits some characteristic weaknesses. These center around Harris's failure, alluded to in connection with the Fifth Symphony finale, to devise subjects which combine naturally with one another contrapuntally. One also senses an element of haste in the movement's conception and working out and a falling off of the creative intensity which informed the first three movements. This slackening of interest during the progress of an extended composition seemed to affect Harris increasingly as he grew older.

## Overview

Taken as a whole, however, the Sixth Symphony is perhaps the richest, most varied and deeply expressive of Harris's orchestral works of the 1940s, and a crucial stepping-stone in his development.

# The Busy 1940s

The composer had little time to reflect on the new symphony after the Koussevitzky/Boston Symphony premiere in February of 1944. Though he had removed himself by more than half a continent from the hub of musical activity on the East Coast, his creative activities continued full force. He was required to produce the most varied sorts of compositions: patriotic pieces (chorus and band), folksong settings (chorus), ballets (chamber ensembles), diverse works for band alone, compositions for large and small orchestra, and concerted works (with both orchestra and band). Though the efforts of these years are uneven in quality, the opportunities they provided the composer for continued creative growth, especially in technical mastery, were invaluable.

The Harrises remained in Colorado Springs until 1948. For one year during this period, 1945, the composer was appointed to serve as Director of Music for the U. S. Office of War Information. His task centered chiefly around the dissemination overseas of American music of all kinds via recordings and sheet music. Partly as a result of his efforts, numerous concerts of various types, including those of the Boston Symphony, were transcribed on discs and broadcast to U. S. fighting forces abroad.

## Utah

In 1948 the family, which now included sons Shaun (born 1945) and Daniel (born 1947), left Colorado Springs for Logan, Utah, where the composer had accepted the position of composer-in-residence at Utah State College.

## New currents in music

During this period in the late 1940s, the first slackening of Harris's creative pace can be perceived. The country was regaining its equilibrium in the often painful readjustment period following World War II, and the frantic activity of the late 1930s and early 40s, which called forth so much from creative artists, abated somewhat. Individuals were returning from a preoccupation with national concerns to a reordering of their personal lives.

In addition, a new generation of composers with new ideas was making itself heard. Ironically for composers of Harris's generation, the new breed arose in Europe, and by the 1950s their aesthetic principles, based chiefly on an expansion of the twelve-tone principles of Schönberg, had reached into nearly every corner of Western musical culture.

Of course, theirs was not the only musical language. Composers such as Britten and Vaughan Williams in England, the Czech Martinu, Karl Amadeus Hartmann in Germany, Malipiero in Italy, and Messiaen in France (though he was to explore certain of the new developments referred to above) continued writing in their own styles and techniques. In the United States, one finds Harris and Piston, now seen as relatively conservative guardians of the former's cherished international-intercentury mainstream, continuing as before, while some of their colleagues, such as Roger Sessions and Aaron Copland were moved by the winds from the new direction.

## Tennessee

Somewhat disillusioned by what they perceived to be a lack of success in making inroads into the provincialism of the area in artistic matters during this period, the Harrises left Utah in 1949 and went to Tennessee, where they settled in Nashville while the composer took up a professorship and another composer-in-residence position at Peabody College. This was the first step in a return east that was to culminate in a five year stay (1951–56) in Pittsburgh, where the couple joined the faculty of the Pennsylvania College for Women (now Chatham College) under a grant from the Mellon Foundation.

The most noteworthy extracompositional activity in which Harris engaged during his brief period in Tennessee was the organization of the Cumberland Forest Festival, which took place during the summers of 1950–52 on the campus of the University of the South in Sewanee. For this, Harris engaged leading soloists, first-chair orchestral players, and guest conductors for a series of programs devoted to music of the twentieth century.[9]

# Seventh Symphony

The move to Pittsburgh in 1951 initiated one of the most musically productive, yet personally frustrating, periods in Harris's career. The family's life there will be discussed in the next chapter, however, in order that attention may now be turned to one of the most important musical efforts of that period, the Seventh Symphony.

Koussevitzky had commissioned the work in 1946, but the composer did not feel ready to embark again on a symphonic project just then. However, thematic materials and formal structures employed in various works of the late 1940s and early 50s, such as the Violin Concerto of 1949, eventually proved fruitful when he finally settled into the symphony in 1952, a year after Koussevitzky's death.

With the loss of the great Russian conductor, Harris had been deprived of his staunchest champion in the field of orchestral performance. Though the void was never to be filled completely for Harris and many of his colleagues who had benefited from Koussevitzky's support, other distinguished conductors proved especially responsive over the years to the Harris idiom. One of these was the Czech Rafael Kubelik, who had recently been appointed Music Director of the Chicago Symphony Orchestra. Kubelik had conducted both Harris's Third and Fifth Symphonies, and with this background he was eminently qualified to undertake the premiere of the Seventh Symphony in late 1952.

Kubelik was much impressed with the work; Harris, however, was dissatisfied and subjected the symphony to a long series of reworkings and revisions. The final version seems not to have been settled until the recording sessions for the work undertaken by Eugene Ormandy and the Philadelphia Orchestra in the fall of 1955.

## Form

The Seventh Symphony, like the celebrated Third, is cast in a single movement. This structure comprises a ternary design, the outer parts of which constitute a series of variations (a passacaglia, as Harris somewhat inaccurately calls it) on a rather lengthy theme, with the middle section formed of additional sets of variations of dancelike character on two new themes.

The subject of the so-called passacaglia, along with the principal theme of the Quintet for Piano and Strings, is one of Harris's most impressive melodies. For both it and its earlier chamber counterpart, he employed an adaptation of his autogenetic principles to closed melodic ideas, building each melody out of a series of antecedent-consequent pairs generated from a seed-motive.

The variation/expansion of both antecedent and consequent portions (especially the latter) reveals the composer's skill in achieving a statement which grows and mounts in an arch of tension and release but which never loses sight of its origin. One can observe from Example 57 (in the bracketed melodic and rhythmic motives) that Harris employs both intervallic and rhythmic means to unify his long theme:

EXAMPLE 57

*Symphony No. 7:* Passacaglia theme

Rather than treating the melody as a recurring bass line, a traditional characteristic of the passacaglia, Harris deals with it strictly in melodic terms in the manner of a theme and variations. The broad span of several variations which comprises section A, proceeding from the sumptuous polychordal string textures of the first variation through the contrapuntal savagery of the fourth, is one of Harris's most impressive conceptions. It appears to sweep forward in one huge monolithic utterance, with effortless spontaneity and mounting intensity. Taking all five variations into consideration, Harris introduces variety into his procedures by interposing among the variations in which the theme remains close to its original shape variations featuring radical changes in the melody. These latter are constructed either as a sort of free fantasia on the components of the theme (variation 2) or as a development of the seed-motive alone (variation 5).

Each of the two principal subdivisons of the B section comprises, as indicated above, a set of variations on a new theme:

EXAMPLE 58

a: *Symphony No. 7:* Theme II

b: *Symphony No. 7:* Theme III

These two ideas not only contrast with each other, but seem to bear little real relationship (except in the neighboring-note opening figure of each) to the passacaglia subject.

The composer labels the first half of section B as "variations in asymmetrical rhythms." These are chiefly in 11/8 meter. The light, frequently polyphonic texture and thinner scoring of the variations, plus the emphasis upon organum intervals in the harmony, contrast with the nearly overpowering sumptuousness and predominantly harmonic orientation of the passacaglia.

A set of "variations in symmetrical meter" (again, Harris's label) forms the second half of the B section. These are based on theme III, and the variations techniques employed here involve chiefly the addition of contrapuntal elements (both new and motives derived from theme III), the development and expansion of motives from the theme, harmonic enrichment through doubling of the theme in organum intervals, and canonic treatment.[10]

Taken together, the two sets of variations which make up the B section of the symphony constitute one of Harris's deftest, most uninhibited performances. They possess a freedom of imagination and execution which continually delights the listener with unexpected turns of phrase, new melodic and rhythmic figures, and bits of colorful scoring.

Section C features a final statement of the passacaglia subject in augmentation (in the horns and baritone horn), with ornamental counterpoint (in the violins and high woodwind), followed by a large development of the theme's consequent phrases that outlines a descending spiral over a rhythmic ostinato.

The fanfarelike brass interjections that punctuate the phrase ends of the final statement of the passacaglia subject look rhythmically contrived on paper, but in performance they reveal Harris's occasional tendency toward the cerebral being placed at the service of an utterance of great naturalness and spontaneity:

EXAMPLE 59

*Symphony No. 7:* Brass interjections

The counterpoint to the return of theme I, though primarily free and decorative, at times contains allusions to some of the other themes of the symphony, particularly the rhythm of theme II. However, it is not until the brief coda to the work that a truly explicit back-reference occurs: this section is based upon, and derives its propulsive character from, a variant of the rhythm of the opening of theme II. The relationship, coming as it does at the end of the work, helps, along with the return of the passacaglia subject, to impart an additional sense of unity to the symphony as a whole.

Harris's program note for the Seventh Symphony summarizes its essence thus:

> The work was conceived as a dynamic form with an uninterrupted time span of twenty minutes. In one sense it is a dance symphony; in another sense it is a study in harmonic and melodic rhythmic [*sic*] variations.[11]

In fact, one of the unique features of the symphony is its rhythmic organization. Each of the passacaglia variations comprising section A involves a characteristic rhythm—the passacaglia itself is an early dance type—and, of course, each of the two variations sets of section B contains its own distinctive metrical and rhythmic ideas as well. Perhaps Harris had Beethoven's Seventh Symphony in mind when composing his own seventh essay in the genre. The former work, as I have pointed out in connection with the Fifth Symphony, was a favorite of his, and both seventh symphonies constitute an "apotheosis of the dance," as Beethoven's work has sometimes been characterized. In the Harris work, the rhythmic development often follows the thematic development as the music unfolds, the consistency of an underlying rhythmic idea during a given portion of the work contributing to a sense of unity among the wide ranging variation elements of that section.

## Overview

Though the Seventh Symphony may, for some listeners, lack the searing emotional intensity of the Third Symphony and the aspiring nobility of portions of the Fifth and Sixth Symphonies, it nonetheless possesses its own equally potent features. The most important of these is a combination of the visionary with a vigorous optimism which draws the hearer into new realms of musical experience on repeated hearings. Many of Harris's works, particularly the shorter orchestral pieces, easily reveal most of their secrets fairly early. The Seventh, on the other hand, requires, and endures, repeated hearings. It shows Harris at the peak of his powers turning in what is perhaps his most virtuosic performance in the realm of orchestral writing in the creation of one of his most durable and vital symphonies, perhaps the finest altogether.

# 5

## Symphonies, Part III
## (Nos. 8 and 9 and *Canticle of the Sun*)

### The Harrises in Pittsburgh

The five years in Pittsburgh were especially busy for the Harrises. As was the case wherever they resided, the couple became engaged actively in the artistic life of the community. Again there were radio broadcasts, the most important of which were Johana's "Master Keys" series devoted to the great keyboard literature, with the Beethoven sonatas forming the core of the content. There was also another festival, probably the most ambitious of the composer's career: in 1952 he conceived a plan for a series of concerts of contemporary music which would help move Pittsburgh, otherwise known chiefly as an industrial city, into cultural prominence. The resulting event, the Pittsburgh International Festival of Contemporary Music, took place during the last week of November 1952. Forty-six composers from eighteen countries were invited to participate in performances of their music, with twelve of these being commissioned to write choral pieces for the festival.

The Pittsburgh Festival was the largest event of its kind held in this country up to that time and doubtless reaped the fruits of Harris's experiences in organizing similar events in Colorado Springs and in Sewanee.[1] It confirmed the viability of the composer's visionary ideas in matters of this sort, for the cerebral, organizing element in his makeup that contributed so much to the firm trestling of his musical structures enabled him to set down schemes such as this in great detail in terms of organization, time frame, and finances.[2]

Though the festival brought Harris a good deal of satisfaction and confirmed his eminence in the musical affairs of the area, it was also the occasion of a disgraceful event that left its mark on him for several years. Among the works performed was his Fifth Symphony. Written in wartime, the symphony had been dedicated to ". . . the peoples of the USSR." Word of this dedication, coupled with information on otherwise harmless events in the composer's background (his sympathies in the Spanish Civil War, his tenure with the Office of War Information, and his appointment of the Russian émigré Nicolas Slonimsky to the festival program board), came to the attention of certain individuals (among them a Justice of the Pennsylvania Supreme Court) who seemed to thrive on discovering subversion in every corner. (This period, one must remember, was the heyday of the House Un-American Activities Committee, chaired by Senator Joseph McCarthy.) The symphony was eventually performed at the festival with its dedication intact, the audience applauding warmly, and the whole matter was thus rendered rather academic. With the reaffirmation by various Pittsburgh civic leaders of their faith in the composer, the affair eventually evaporated.[3]

In spite of his vindication, however, Harris was bitter and irascible for a long time afterward. The sorry incident seems to have been one of the major events in his life that impinged upon his nostalgic, and idealized, vision of a rural America. Though his perpetual optimism was not stifled for long, events such as this troubled him deeply and forced him to confront some of the realities of life in America at mid-century.

One other incident, of a potentially more serious nature, darkened the Pittsburgh years: in October of 1955 the composer suffered a serious automobile accident while driving on the Pennsylvania Turnpike to New York. His right leg was shattered and there was grim concern over whether he would be able to walk again. Harris remained in a wheelchair for some months, but gradually the injury healed and he was able slowly to resume the normal pace of his activities.

## A Renewal of Recording Activity

It was during the 1950s that the first long-playing recordings of Harris's works began to appear. Among these were releases of the Third Symphony, some of the smaller orchestral pieces (*Kentucky Spring* and *Elegy and Dance*), and, under the composer's supervision, *Abraham Lincoln Walks at Midnight*, the Fantasy for Piano and Orchestra, and the Violin Sonata (these last three works also featuring Johana).

## On the Move Again; the String Congress

After the Mellon grant ended, the composer once again felt the need for a change of surroundings and took advantage of the offer of positions, first at Southern Illinois University, then at Indiana University in Bloomington, Indiana. The latter institution had an especially distinguished school of music and, as a further incentive for the move, an old friend of the Harrises, violinist Josef Gingold, served on the faculty there. Harris assumed his position in the fall of 1957, but Johana stayed on at Chatham College (the new name for Pennsylvania College for Women) until 1958. The entire family, including daughters Maureen, born in 1955, and Lane, born in 1957, was settled in Indiana by the end of 1958.

Harris's compositional activities slackened during his relatively short stay in Indiana, but the period is by no means devoid of interest in other areas. During the summer of 1958, he was sent by the U. S. Department of State, along with fellow composers Roger Sessions, Peter Mennin, and Ulysses Kay, to the Soviet Union as a cultural ambassador. He had an opportunity to meet there a number of Russian colleagues, among them Shostakovich and Krennikov, and to conduct the Moscow Radio Orchestra in his Fifth Symphony. Harris was much impressed by what he was permitted to see and hear during the visit, being particularly envious of what appeared to be a considerably more favorable climate for composers than existed in the United States.[4]

Another important event during this period was Harris's founding of the International String Congress, the first session of which took place during the summer of 1959 at Greenleaf Lake, in the composer's home state of Oklahoma. Cosponsors of the Congress were the American Federation of Musicians of the United States and Canada, who were joined by individuals in the fields of music education, entertainment, and private industry. The participants were selected at community auditions sponsored by AFM locals in the two countries involved. They were given scholarships enabling them to receive eight weeks of instruction at the Congress under such noted soloists and first-chair players as the aforementioned Josef Gingold and violist William Lincer. The students were grouped into two string orchestras, of different levels, that gave several concerts, a number of which were taped for educational broadcast.

The second session of the String Congress, with an expanded enrollment, was held in San Germán, Puerto Rico, on the campus of the Inter-American University, to which the Harrises had been invited to help in building the International Institute of Music. The composer had left Indiana University at the end of the spring term in 1959 and, after spending the summer at Greenleaf Lake, he and the family moved to San Germán in the fall. Though Harris was eventually frustrated in developing to the full his plans for music education at the University (a situation evidently repeated at other institutions at which he taught), the mild climate and the warmth of the people offered sufficient compensation for the family to regard their short stay in Puerto Rico as one of the most pleasant episodes of their lives.

## Canticle of the Sun

By the beginning of 1960, it had been over a year and a half since Harris had completed his last work, a symphonic tone poem for band titled *Ad Majorem Gloriam Universitatis Illinorum*. He was naturally anxious to resume creative activities, and it is significant that he should do so with a composition that, in some respects, marks a new development in his style. He had been commissioned by the Elizabeth Sprague Coolidge Foundation to write a work for premiere in the fall of 1961. For this, he began exploring the life of St. Francis of Assisi as a possible basis for musical treatment. Though this was certainly not the first time he had turned for extramusical stimulation to a non-Americanist subject, the two works which eventually resulted from his interest in St. Francis comprise some of the most important efforts in their respective areas of his oeuvre.

Though Harris at first began sketching a multimovement orchestral work on St. Francis, this project was set aside in favor of an extended cantata setting for high voice and chamber ensemble of the great *Canticle of the Sun* (*Cantico del sole*) attributed to the saint. The love of nature conveyed through the evocative imagery of the poem appealed strongly to the pantheistic element in Harris and, indeed, both the cantata and its companion work, the *San Francisco Symphony,* as well as portions of the *Pere Marquette Symphony,* form the summation of this aspect of his lifework.

## Form

The work forms a huge, single-movement span in which a lengthy instrumental introduction is followed by a series of alternating sections of word setting, vocalise, and instrumental interlude. Each stanza of the *Canticle* is given its own texture and harmonic color in which the outward imagery and inward meaning of the text are captured with a sensitivity unusual even for Harris. In fact, this work, with its variegated textures, instrumental timbres, and harmonies, provides one of the most important sources for the study of Harris's late style. It is also a spectacular example of his autogenetic technique of melodic generation, for all the word-setting portions appear to unfold from the same germ cell:

EXAMPLE 60

*Canticle of the Sun:* Beginnings of vocal paragraphs

In addition, the vocal writing, while quite demanding, nonetheless reveals a heightened sensitivity to the timbre and technique of the human voice and an intensification of the lyrical element in Harris's style to an altogether new level.

Harmonically, the *Canticle* is a treasury of Harris's mature polytonal vocabulary. The textures employed range from bare octaves (Example 61a), to full blown polychordal structures (Example 61c):

EXAMPLE 61

*Canticle of the Sun:* Harmonic textures

a:

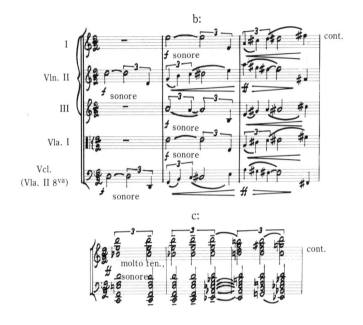

The cantata, over half an hour in length, is Harris's largest chamber work. Though its fairly regular alternation of sections is potentially predictable, the composer's ingenuity in continually devising new textures helps mitigate this. It is a warm and colorful work, and though its generous design conveys a sense of monumentality, the listener senses the composer relaxing more than usual, thereby allowing his natural spontaneity to reign.

## San Francisco Symphony

In 1961 Harris received a commission for a new symphony. By a happy coincidence, the commission came from the San Francisco Symphony Orchestra as part of a celebration of the fiftieth anniversary of the orchestra's founding. It seemed natural that the composer, having recently set the *Canticle,* would look once again to the subject of St. Francis of Assisi, the patron saint of the city of San Francisco. It was equally natural that, with his predilection for self borrowing, he would turn to the cantata for some of his musical materials.

The *San Francisco Symphony,* as the Eighth is subtitled, was written at the end of 1961 and the beginning of 1962. Like the cantata, it is a pathbreaking work, representing, for Harris, a new approach to its genre. It is infused with an unbridled pantheism and rung through with bell sounds. Its frequent fleetness of foot, the light, chamberlike textures and airy, open harmonies of many passages, and a glistening orchestration convey a special quality in relationship to its two strapping siblings (the Seventh and Ninth Symphonies) reminiscent of that between Beethoven's Fourth Symphony and its larger brethren. One critic spoke of the "gleaming, shimmering, radiant character" of the work, an observation that indeed comes very close to penetrating its heart.[5]

## Form

For the *San Francisco Symphony,* Harris decided upon a single-movement plan comprising five interconnected parts. Since he had already dealt with the *Canticle of the Sun* in the cantata, he turned largely to the life of St. Francis for the musicodramatic aspect of the symphony. Each of the five parts is a musical depiction of a specific period of or event in the saint's life. Part I is titled "Childhood and Youth"; Part II, "Renunciation," is a moving evocation of Francis's casting aside of his worldly wealth and hedonistic way of life; Part III, "The Building of the Chapel," depicts the founding of the Franciscan Order; Part IV, "The Joy of Pantheistic Beauty as a Gift of God," is an instrumental evocation of the *Canticle*; Part V, "Ecstasy After the Premonition of Death," serves as an apotheosis.

An unusual feature of the symphony is the employment of the piano in a *concertante* role. The instrument remains silent until Part IV, where, amplified, it very nearly turns the work into a piano concerto.[6] Harris also uses a C trumpet as a solo instrument in some places, apparently to represent the "voice" of St. Francis. (Though not, of course, the first such use of the instrument in his orchestral and band writing, its appearance here marks the starting point of its adoption as the norm in the symphonies from this point.) One should also mention the quasisoloistic use of the Harris "gamelan"—piano, harp, vibraphone, and chimes playing polychordal punctuation—as a further contribution to the sound world.

## Part I

Part I falls into two large sections, each comprising numerous subsections. The first half of the "movement," buoyant and skitterish, with many changes of texture and mood, features the following ideas, of which III,

entering somewhat farther along, anticipates both the materials and the
mood of Part II:

EXAMPLE 62

*Symphony No. 8:* Themes I-III

a: Theme I

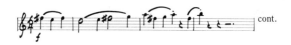

b: Theme II

c: Theme III

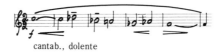

cantab., dolente

(Harris had employed both themes I and II elsewhere in his oeuvre to
represent various aspects of youth and play.) The second half of Part I,
characterizing Francis's early manhood, is purposeful and assertive. It is a
set of variations on a new theme (IV) punctuated by episodes of an aspiring
character built on contrasting materials:

EXAMPLE 63

*Symphony No. 8:* Theme IV

## Part II

Part II is one of Harris's most beautiful and impressive ascents from darkness into light. In three large sections, it is marked by the unfolding of long melodic lines over lush polychordal harmonies which gradually metamorphose from somber minor-mode poignance to major-mode radiance. There are three themes, the first given to violas, the second to solo trumpet, the third to strings in canon:

EXAMPLE 64

*Symphony No. 8:* Themes V-VII

a: Theme V

b: Theme VI

c: Theme VII

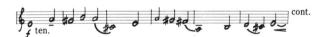

Part II culminates in a two-voice canon at various intervals, with both voices doubled initially in sixths over a polychordal accompaniment, the whole fabric penetrated by a continued spinning-out of theme VI. This section of the symphony alone, blossoming slowly from the core of Harris's visionary aspect, ought to be sufficient confirmation that the composer of the 1960s was a masterly, vital, and viable inheritor of the mantle of his counterpart of the previous decades.

## Part III

For Part III Harris resorts to his favored musical analogue for the idea of building, fugue. Here the procedure is modified, as usual, toward fugal variation. The subject (theme VIII) appears in two principal forms, though each form is varied additionally in small details:

EXAMPLE 65

*Symphony No. 8:* Theme VIII (two forms)

The frequent small variations within the subject, its vertical and horizontal expansion at various points, and the rich web of counterpart Harris weaves either from a continuation of the subject or from motives and components extracted from it, impart a truly architectural character to Part III, as though the stones of the church were being lifted and set in place and the structure taking shape before one's eyes.

There are three sections in Part III, each defined by a characteristic treatment of theme VIII. This practice of defining a large portion of a composition by a particular treatment of its ideas was common with Harris.

## Part IV

Part IV is virtually unprecedented in Harris's oeuvre. It is a large scherzo possessing a singular fleetness and sense of breathless urgency. It is also unique in that, though possessing some new materials, it is at the same time one of the composer's few extended truly developmental pieces of writing. I have observed earlier that Harris's techniques of form building are ordinarily concerned with the spinning-out of long melodic lines, the weaving together of motivic elements, and/or the erection and projection over long time spans of chord successions. There is, indeed, a continuity present in this scherzo that is fundamentally allied with one or more of the above concerns, but it is a continuity that seems carried out on different planes simultaneously, planes which often mutually intersect and interrupt one another to create a fragmentary impression. This is especially true of the outer sections.

The scherzo is essentially prefabricated, stitched together chiefly from several of the vocalise sections of the *Canticle*. In the cantata, however, these passages alternate with contrasting music which is frequently of a less florid, active character and, consequently, do not provide the persistent momentum found in the symphony, where they occur in rapid succession. The listener is presented here with a variety of rapidly changing materials, textures, and sonorities, in which themes (such as II), even entire passages, from earlier parts of the symphony reappear in company with new ideas that place these returning materials in new perspectives.

Like the preceding portions of the symphony, Part IV also falls into three sections, of which the two outer ones contain numerous subdivisions. Section one is set in motion by the piano solo paragraphs of IX:

EXAMPLE 66

*Symphony No. 8:* Theme IX

This section moves from relative stability in its opening pages to a more developmental, diversified music, with considerable tossing about of motives and rapid changes of texture. Toward its conclusion, a new idea, theme X, is tossed about in short phrases from one wind instrument to another:

EXAMPLE 67

*Symphony No. 8:* Theme X

The middle section of the scherzo (loosely corresponding to a trio) is somewhat more stable in both materials and texture than the surrounding music. It involves the spinning-out in succession of three new ideas:

EXAMPLE 68

a: *Symphony No. 8:* Theme XI

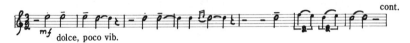

b: *Symphony No. 8:* Theme XII

c: *Symphony No. 8:* Theme XIII

The final section returns to the character of section one, but using new materials and having its events compressed into a shorter time span. The two most important ideas are XIV and XV:

EXAMPLE 69

a: *Symphony No. 8:* Theme XIV

b: *Symphony No. 8:* Theme XV

One of the most remarkable aspects of this music is the forward momentum that manages to sweep into its swift current all the diverse elements in such a way that the listener is left with a strongly unified impression. Harris partly accomplishes this by providing for each section a steady rhythmic flow and sometimes a particular harmonic color. The scherzo represents the composer at his most flexible and inventive and stands as a partial refutation of the charges of awkwardness which are sometimes leveled against him.

## Part V

Part V is the simplest portion of the symphony, comprising a set of variations with a chiming coda in which a reminiscence of theme VIII is heard:

EXAMPLE 70

*Symphony No. 8:* Theme XVI

For these variations, Harris returns to the plan of harmonic textures he had employed in the opening of the Third Symphony. In the present realization, the theme is first presented hesitantly in octaves and unisons, its phrases exchanged between various sections of the orchestra, with a contrapuntal line in the solo trumpet:

EXAMPLE 71

*Symphony No. 8:* Theme XVII

Each of the succeeding two variations presents the theme in an expanded harmonic context, first doubled in organum, then harmonized in major triads, still accompanied by the spinning-out of XVII.

The coda is dominated by bell sounds in the gamelan, which seem to draw the diverse strands of the symphony into their resonance.

## Overview

The *San Francisco Symphony* is arguably the finest of Harris's last six works in the genre. Though it lacks the singleminded concentration of energy which enables the Seventh Symphony to be perceived as a unified conception, it is nonetheless a radiant, colorful work possessing an enormous vitality and a variety of means which are masterfully controlled to present a sense of firm cohestion.

# Ninth Symphony

It is one of the ironies that occasionally marked Harris's career that he was to embark on another major symphony within a few months after the completion of the *San Francisco Symphony* after leaving such a large gap between that work and its predecessor. The Ninth Symphony was commissioned by the Philadelphia Orchestra, whose music director, Eugene Ormandy, had been a sympathetic interpreter of the composer, having performed the Third Symphony in the United States and abroad and given the premiere and recorded the final version of the Seventh. Harris was at work on the new symphony by late spring 1962, completing it that September. The first performance took place the following February in Philadelphia.

## Comparisons and Contrasts with the Eighth

Appearing in such close succession after the *San Francisco Symphony,* it was almost inevitable that the Ninth should share some of its features and even some of its materials with that work. The two compositions are especially fascinating in that they represent, in some respects, their relationships notwithstanding, opposite sides of the same coin. Whereas the light-textured Eighth is all warmth, radiance, and lyricism, the more heavily scored Ninth is by turns aggressive, bittersweet, and desperate, with a hard glare replacing the burnished glow of its predecessor.

Part of the difference may lie with the orchestras for which the two symphonies were written. With the Philadelphia Orchestra, Harris could count on a large virtuoso body capable of responding fully to the demands of one of his largest and most complex utterances. Part may also lie in the different extramusical backgrounds of the works. The Eighth, based on St. Francis, is suffused with a gentle religious mysticism and a sense of great optimism; the Ninth, on the other hand, is an Americanist work, dedicated to the City of Philadelphia as "the cradle of American Democracy." It is the "civic" Harris who sings in these pages, and one whose exuberant optimism about America has by now begun to be tempered by an awareness of how far the country had departed from his somewhat naive vision of earlier years. One senses at times, especially in the second movement, an undercurrent of personal desperation and pessimism which may disturb but which nonetheless contributes strongly to the work's power and uniqueness.

Harris provided a rather detailed program for the Ninth Symphony, giving each movement a subtitle taken from the "Preamble" to the *Constitution of the United States.* However, with the possible exception of the varied and bustling first movement, this is an instance in which his subtitles and programs do not really seem clearly reflected in the music, a situation which obtains with some other works as well.

## Prelude

The "Prelude" ("We the People") is perhaps the most successful of Harris's fast symphonic opening movements. There are four principal ideas:

EXAMPLE 72

*Symphony No. 9:* I. Themes

These are introduced during the course of the first of the three large
sections in which the movement is laid out. Thus, this section functions as a
kind of exposition. Section two is developmental, concerned chiefly with
the spinning-out of further paragraphs of theme I and development of some
of the motivic ideas. Section three is a highly varied recapitulation of
materials from the opening music.

By the above analysis, the "Prelude" may be regarded as Harris's
closest approach in the symphonic genre to the sonata-allegro form of the
Classic period symphony. However, this observation must be tempered
by the fact that the formal dynamics operate here within the context of
the additive principles employed in such pieces as the first movement of
*American Portrait*. The clearest example of the interpenetration of these
two concepts is found in the spinning-out, in section two, of theme I, this
constituting both continued exposition and, as observed above, development.

But the truly unique features of the movement are its harmonic and
rhythmic aspects. For the harmonic texture Harris restricts himself almost
entirely to organum intervals, sometimes extending them through several
multiples to create a surprisingly rich sound:

EXAMPLE 73

*Symphony No. 9:* I. Multiple-organum harmony

The use of these intervals imparts a feeling of openness and clarity to the
harmony as well as a sense of unity. But the resourceful way in which the
composer works with his limited vocabulary creates a surprising amount of
variety as well. This movement is, in fact, perhaps the most harmonically
virtuosic piece he ever created.

As for the rhythmic aspect, there are frequent shifts back and forth
between compound duple and simple triple meters, excursions into asymmetrical meters, and multiple layers of materials of differing rhythmic
characters superimposed on one another, all of which combine to convey
both a sense of great variety and an enormous forward drive.

## Chorale

The "Chorale" ("To establish a more perfect union") is very likely, along with the second movement of the Fifth Symphony, Harris's greatest symphonic slow movement. It is a summary of all the choralelike essays which comprise a special type among his works. It is also something of a departure from the norm for him in that it is his only slow movement in the genre whose climactic point occurs in its concluding pages, rather than earlier, at the peak of an arch.

The form is a large ternary design. There are two principal themes, of which I is given below (II is a variant of Example 68a):

EXAMPLE 74

*Symphony No. 9:* II. Theme I

Section one is based on theme I, which spins out, first in successively higher string divisions, then in solo trumpet and woodwinds, in several large paragraphis over a texture that unfolds from an austere organum-based string accompaniment through a rich polychordal fabric in wood-winds, to a texture formed from a combination of these two harmonic characters.

Section two forms the closest point of contact of this work with the Eighth Symphony. It is borrowed, with some modification, from measures 721–68 of that work (see Example 68). However, the halving of the tempo here in comparison with the source imparts to the passage a completely different, open plains spaciousness.

Section three resumes the momentum generated by section one, but the thematic evolution is undercut by a fragmentation of the line into shorter ideas. The movement ends with one of the most overwhelming climaxes in Harris's oeuvre, a climax in which the visionary aspiration seems undermined by an element of almost frantic striving. The sputter-ing, shell-shocked polychords in muted strings which deliver the final cadence are unexpected and disturbing, conveying a sense of profound unease rather than a calm resolution of events.

The curious tension of the "Chorale" is conveyed not only through the emotional intensity Harris generates but through the structural processes as well. As an example of this, instead of building the movement entirely on the spinning out of long lines, he disintegrates the line in the final section (as mentioned above) into motivic ideas which, in their interlinkings, form a cohesive fabric but which nonetheless fail among themselves to develop a real melodic profile.

## Contrapuntal Structures

The finale, "Contrapuntal Structures" ("To promote the general welfare"), is one of the largest of all Harris's symphonic movements, not only in duration, but in complexity and expansiveness of gesture. In a sense, it may be heard as an orchestral analogue (on a much larger scale) of the finale of the Symphony for Voices. Not only does the composer head each section of the movement with the same line from the "Inscriptions" portion of Whitman's *Leaves of Grass* ("Of Life immense in passion, pulse, power," "Cheerful for freest action formed," "The Modern Man I Sing") that he employed in the choral piece, he also uses the same structure (a triple fugue) and similar thematic materials. The first subject seems like a highly varied form of its counterpart in the earlier work, while the third subject is a variation of the ubiquitous "Modern Man I Sing" motto which had its origin in the choral symphony. Only subject II seems new, but its florid character provides at least a reminiscence of the second subject of "Inscription":

EXAMPLE 75

*Symphony No. 9:* III. Themes I-III

a: Theme I

b: Theme II

c: Theme III

"Contrapuntal Structures" consists of four sections plus a coda. Sections one through three comprise expositions of each subject in turn, while section four is a development in which elements of the three subjects are worked out together. (This is, of course, virtually identical to the procedure in the finale of the Sixth Symphony.) The movement is crowned by a rhetorical coda in which a final grandiose statement of subject III is preceded by the return of some of the subsidiary ideas of the first movement.

As is the case with Harris's previous orchestral triple fugues, the subjects are not all mutually compatible. Indeed, subject II is hardly a fugue subject at all, but rather a remarkable florid effulgence that seems amenable to development only by means of a variation in its accompanying texture and through the addition of motivic counterpoint of an ornamental nature.

The structure of the movement reveals an element of additive procedure in that each exposition after the first incorporates development of previously introduced materials. This development, unlike that in the traditional types of triple fugue, often occurs in episodes between statements of the principal subject of a given section, rather than in the form of contrapuntal combination with the subject. The exposition of subject I is the most traditionally fugal portion of the movement, comprising a profusion of entrances, stretti, rhythmic variations on the subject, sudden changes of texture, and a kaleidoscopic tour of the various sections of the orchestra. All these impart a bustling, aggressive drive and a curious edginess to the music.

By contrast, the exposition of subject II is all sensuous grace allied with a feeling of a near suspension of time. The gently and irregularly pulsing string harmonies that accompany the first two entrances of II form a soft bed on which the elaborate coloratura of the melody appears to be anchored. Subsequent subject entrances acquire an accumulation of motivic counterpoint in solo brass and woodwinds and a vertical expansion and rhythmic intensification of the accompanying string texture.

Section three, like its predecessor, also employs contrapuntal variation techniques. The several entrances of the "Modern Man" subject are given out in various brasses and woodwinds enclosed within an essentially homophonic supporting texture that undergoes rhythmic development and the acquisition of ornamental motivic accretions (derived chiefly from subject II). As in the case whenever he uses the "Modern Man" idea as a fugal subject, Harris seems unable to develop it for contrapuntal purposes and thus has to resort to various devices such as stretti, or, as here, development of subsidiary ideas.

For the final section of the movement, the composer makes an impressive sounding attempt to combine the three subjects. As can be seen from the following example (which shows the beginning of this passage), however, he has to content himself with mere suggestion when it comes to subject II:

EXAMPLE 76

*Symphony No. 9:* III. Contrapuntal combination of subjects

The coda is all bluster. Harris, not able to carry out his original intention to work up a true contrapuntal peroration, has to be satisfied with bludgeoning the listener in the hope of rendering him insensitive to what is essentially an unravelling of the underlying dynamic tension of the movement.

"Contrapuntal Structures," though uneven, nonetheless brings to a culmination the diverse combinations of fugue and variation which Harris had been exploring for over three decades. Paradoxically overwritten and underdeveloped in places, it is still a commanding affair, and careful analysis reveals a real integrity and logic underlying the construction and working out of its materials, a logic that enables one to account for the smallest motivic variant and the most elaborate strand of florid counterpoint. The movement contains a wealth of thematic, harmonic, and textural variety and provides a fascinating, and frustrating, view of Harris's uneasy combination of strengths and weaknesses.

## Overview

The Eighth and Ninth Symphonies together may be regarded as ushering in the final span of Harris's career. This was to be a period marked by creations that rank among the most original in his oeuvre. Though the pace of his production had been slowing since the early 1950s, the finest works of that decade and of the 1960s demonstrate that much of the creative potency remained and that the expressive characteristics had, in fact, deepened and became more complex.

# 6

## Symphonies, Part IV
## (Nos. 10, 11, 12, and *Bicentennial Symphony*)

### The Return Home

It is easy to assume that Roy Harris's eventual return west was predestined. With the strong Americanist bias of many of his works, his nostalgia for a rural America, and, above all, his western roots, it would seem that the big city ambience of the East Coast would be uncongenial for him.

However, Harris was no stranger to the city. One must remember that, like Whitman, his vision encompassed both the rural and the urban landscapes. He and Johana had had many exciting experiences in the East during the 1930s and early 1940s and again during the 1950s. The stimulus provided by proximity to a culture whose roots reached back to the early days of this country was a powerful one. But the commercial-industrial aspects of big cities always seemed at odds with Harris's aesthetics: for him, the developing sense of materialism during the second half of the twentieth century threatened increasingly to undermine the efforts of his generation of composers to provide a viable and durable art music for their countrymen.[1]

Harris had enjoyed some of his most productive years during the long stay in Colorado Springs in the 1940s; the move then had seemed to rejuvenate his creative faculties at a crucial moment. It was thus natural that he should have responded warmly, during the years which followed his return east, to the various invitations which emanated from out west to attend performances of his works, to conduct, and to teach. One of these resulted in his accepting in the fall of 1961 a position at the University of California, Los Angeles, as a visiting professor.

The first few years back in California were somewhat hectic. Though the appearance of both the Eighth and Ninth Symphonies within a single year (1962) attested, as I have observed, to the composer's still potent creative powers, the lack of a permanent home seems to have contributed for awhile toward inhibiting his production.

At the beginning of 1963, the Harrises were invited to join the faculty of the University of the Pacific in Stockton, California. Harris, of course, was still committed as well to his UCLA position, but nonetheless seized the opportunity to live once again in rural surroundings, and accepted the Stockton offer on a part-time basis. He purchased a house in an outlying district of Stockton, and for the next year and a half, at least during the school term, virtually lived out of a suitcase, spending his weekdays at a motel in Santa Monica (after his lease ran out on the rental property in that city) and weekends at the Stockton residence.

The University of the Pacific episode was short-lived, however. The summer of 1964 marked the family's permanent return to southern California, with Johana obtaining a position at California Institute of the Arts in Los Angeles, supplementing this activity, as usual, with private teaching. The Harrises purchased a house above the ocean in Pacific Palisades, moving to another somewhat farther inland the following summer. It was in this latter home that the composer was to spend the remaining fourteen years of his life in what turned out to be the most prolonged residence in a single place since his youth in the San Gabriel valley.

## Another Lincoln Symphony: The Tenth

In spite of the commuting during the spring and the move back to Los Angeles during the summer, 1964 was a productive year for Harris. He completed seven works, three of them substantial orchestral scores, more than during any single year since the early 1940s, and around the beginning of 1965 he began work on a new symphony which he described thus:

> The work has been contemplated for over a quarter of a century, and was finally written for the occasion of the one hundredth anniversary of Lincoln's assassination on April 14, 1865. The five-movement work was strongly influenced by Carl Sandburg's monumental study of the times and life of Abraham Lincoln.[2]

The new symphony was not the first "Lincoln" symphony to come from Harris's pen, of course, having been preceded by the 1944 Sixth Symphony. However, whereas the earlier work is based solely upon portions of the "Gettysburg Address," the Tenth Symphony (the number given to the new work) possesses a somewhat broader aim: ". . . I have chosen two moods from the youth of Lincoln, and three moods expressing his profound concern for the destiny of our democratic institutions."[3]

The Tenth Symphony also differs from its earlier counterpart in terms of scoring. Not only does it use a chorus—it also employs an instrumental apparatus consisting only of brass, percussion, and two pianos. As was the case with the *Folksong Symphony,* the choral parts were designed for the level of ability usually found in high school and community groups. In addition, the use of brass and percussion render the work more accessible to performance by organizations with limited resources.[4]

## Character and Quality

The *Abraham Lincoln Symphony* is, for the most part, an effective work. It has great vitality, color, and, in some portions of the third and fourth movements, a probing quality one does not often find in Harris's efforts in the choral/wind medium. It is uneven, though. Not only is the finale something of a letdown in inspiration and intensity (it is largely a reworking, in fact, of an occasional piece written the previous year), but the choral writing overall, with its excessive reliance on block chordal texture, lacks the wonderful flexibility of that in the *Folksong Symphony,* notwithstanding the equally modest aims of the vocal writing there.

The quality of the text has also raised some reservations. For movements three and four, Harris relied on Lincoln's writings. However, for the remaining movements he wrote his own texts. The first movement is a contrafactum of "Li'l Boy Named David" ("Li'l boy named Abraham. . ."). The finale uses chiefly the phrase "Praise and Thanksgiving for Peace," reiterated again and again—certainly not an unprecedented device, but here, because of the limitations of Harris's musical setting, somewhat wearing. It is the roughhewn, "limerick" character of the text of the second movement, however, that one either objects to violently or accepts in the spirit in which it was intended. A portion is worth quoting as a typical example of the composer's raw, homespun vein. The aim is the strightforward one of capturing the vitality of youth in the midwest of the nineteenth century and it results in one of Harris's most explicit Americanist word creations:

Abraham Lincoln was a pioneer man
Hustle with the muscle of a frontier man
Abraham Lincoln was a wrestlin' man

Hustle with the muscle of a tall, lean man
Abe was long, Abe was strong
Hustle with the muscle
Rough and tumble tussle
Strong, clean, tall, lean
Rough and tough pioneer man.

The Tenth Symphony was completed in April 1965 and given its premiere on April 14 (the date of Lincoln's death) of that year at UCLA. As the
composer indicated in his note quoted above, the symphony consists of
five movements. These are: I. Lonesome Boy, II. The Young Wrestler,
III. Abraham Lincoln's Convictions, IV. Civil War—Brother against
Brother, V. Praise and Thanksgiving for Peace.

## "Lonesome Boy"

The opening movement, employing chiefly women's voices, is a poignant
evocation of Lincoln's lonely youth in the wilderness. It contains some of
the most complex textures of the symphony. There are three sections.
The first is a setting, with Harris's own new text, of the "Li'l Boy Named
David" melody, using only the two pianos as accompaniment:

EXAMPLE 77

*Symphony No. 10:* I. Theme

The middle section develops the principal motives of the movement in a
large contrapuntal fantasia in which voices and brass are woven against
each other in a sonorous lamentation:

EXAMPLE 78

*Symphony No. 10:* I. Development figures

The final section is a tiny coda that ties the materials of the movement together through reminiscence. This movement, though simple in form, is, as I have already mentioned, enormously complex and varied in its internal articulation, possessing a richness of texture and of harmonic and instrumental color that Harris might have used to advantage more often in the symphony.

## "The Young Wrestler"

The second movement lies at the opposite pole in character, texture, and harmonic and rhythmic styles. It falls into two or three parts, depending upon one's perception, and comprises a highly varied strophic setting of the text. It uses only the men's voices of the chorus and is based upon the following theme:

EXAMPLE 79

*Symphony No. 10:* II. Theme

As is the case with nearly all of Harris's fast movements, there are a number of motives that accumulate and are developed along with the main theme. They serve here especially to articulate the major structural divisions, their developments at times forming interludes between verses and internal punctuation within sections.

Most of the materials are exposed in section A, comprising an instrumental introduction during which the most important subsidiary ideas are stated followed by a setting of the first stanza of the text to the principal theme. The remaining sections develop, in rather complex fashion, both the musical and poetic ideas of the first section. The subdivisions of each section are defined according to their concerns with either verse or refrain text.

Though "The Young Wrestler" is straightforward in expression, it is possibly even more complex in its inner workings than the first movement. But for all its variety of materials (the multiplicity of motives accounting for this), it presents to the ear a surprisingly cohesive structure. The impression of freewheeling spontaneity which emerges from Harris's tight structural control is astonishing and constitutes telling demonstration of the discipline of which he was capable.

## "Abraham Lincoln's Conviction"

In the third movement, Harris turns to Lincoln's own words for the outer
sections; for the middle section, he uses lines from the "Bill of Rights"
portion of the *Constitution*. The movement, as I have implied, is in three
parts, the first two distinguished from each other more by their choices of
text than by specific musical characteristics. For most of its duration, the
music unfolds in a fairly regular alternation of accompanied choral settings
and instrumental interludes, many of the latter foreshadowing the materials of the choral passages which immediately follow them. The choral
portions might be regarded as constituting a continual spinning-out of a
single enormous line, though the technique here is not so organic as in
*Canticle of the Sun*. The beginnings of the first two choral paragraphs are
quoted below:

EXAMPLE 80

*Symphony No. 10:* III. Beginnings of first two choral paragraphs

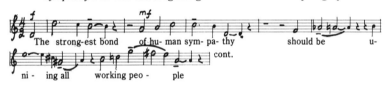

The coda, which comprises the third section, provides one of the most
touching moments in the symphony: it is based upon "When Johnny Comes
Marching Home," played in a slow triple meter by the two pianos. Over
this the chorus weaves a wordless wailing discant while the speaker
intones Lincoln's moving words beginning: "How hard . . . Oh how hard it
is to die and leave one's country no better than if one had never liv'd for
it. . . ." This coda constitutes what is perhaps the high point—the central
musicodramatic "crisis"—of the Tenth Symphony and reveals that when
Harris turned to the expression of pathos he nearly always did so with a
sure hand.

## "Civil War—Brother against Brother"

Harris's use of "Johnny" to conclude the third movement, together with
the resigned pessimism of the Lincoln text recited over the melody,

masterfully prepares for the "Civil War" movement that follows. The opening section of the ternary form into which this movement falls is built on two statements of "Johnny," the second distorted with chromatic inflections that convey almost viscerally the agony of war:

EXAMPLE 81

*Symphony No. 10:* IV. When Johnny Comes Marching Home (chromatic variant)

The chorus, after remaining silent during the opening music, enters in the second section, employing a technique Harris had used only on rare instances in the past (as in the "Tears" movement of the Symphony for Voices and the "Drums" movement of the *Walt Whitman Suite*)—choral declamation. Here he sets Lincoln's Gettysburg speech in this fashion over an ostinatolike accompaniment based chiefly on minor polychords in the pianos and a rather complex fabric of percussion rhythms:

EXAMPLE 82

*Symphony No. 10:* IV. Accompaniment texture

This texture is occasionally punctuated by interjections in the brass. In addition, Harris intensifies the drama at particularly significant phrases of the text by having the chorus break into singing, something which creates a thrilling effect in the closing words of the speech: "shall not perish from the earth."

The violence of war erupts in full measure in the final section of the movement, in which the words "Testing whether this nation can long endure" are reiterated in minor polychords in the chorus over a network of marching rhythms in the pianos and percussion and fanfares in the brass.

The "Civil War" movement, though overly repetitious in its final section (though the repetition has a musicodramatic function that can be effective), is a fine achievement, and helps elevate the Tenth Symphony above some of its shortcomings. Certainly, the unanswered question Harris raises in the reiterations of "Testing whether this nation" can be heard as an explicit manifestation of the social questioning and protest which seemed implicit in some of the darker moments of the Ninth Symphony.

## "Praise and Thanksgiving for Peace"

The final movement seems rather unfortunate after the intensity of the "Civil War" music. Though Harris intended it to convey an optimistic spirit, the material seems not strong enough to bear the weight of summarizing a thirty-five minute statement of great richness, variety, and intensity.

The movement is in five sections. These comprise an instrumental introduction based on bell sounds in the pianos and a foreshadowing of the principal melodic materials in the brass, followed by four sections featuring statements and developments of each of the large paragraphs of the principal theme in the chorus, along with the development of a bell-like idea in the pianos:

EXAMPLE 83

*Symphony No. 10:* V. Theme

Harris tightens the musicodramatic structure by eliminating, in the last two sections, the instrumental transitions that mark off some of the subdivisions of the earlier portions of the movement. His use of a persistent swinging triple meter also helps create a purposeful drive to the climax.

In spite of a diversity of textures and instrumental commentary and accompaniment, the finale is strongly unified. Various things contribute to this: the abovementioned use of a single meter, the reiteration of the text phrase "Praise and Thanksgiving," and the simultaneous unfolding throughout of what is essentially a single choral idea and the bell idea in the pianos. But there is also an impression of overrepetition, and the upbeat tone of the movement may, for some, seem defeated by such insistence.

## Overview

One might question whether the *Abraham Lincoln Symphony* really materialized as a work Harris had "contemplated for over a quarter of a century." In spite of its impressive moments, it falls short of his achievement in the Sixth. For some listeners that earlier work, along with the cantata *Abraham Lincoln Walks at Midnight,* stands as the composer's definitive tribute to the President with whom he so often identified.

# Eleventh Symphony

Following the *Abraham Lincoln Symphony,* Harris turned his back for awhile on the Americanist strain represented by works of that sort and attempted to come to grips with the more introspective, and troubled, elements of his musical personality. In the Eleventh Symphony, which materialized at the end of 1967, we find the composer at a point of psychological crisis. As he put it:

> Symphony Number Eleven has been a compulsory work. It has been the most stubborn work I have ever written: as though it were already completed in the spaces which surround me, and that my job has been to capture it—like a sculptor who has only to chip away the pieces to discover the form which granite or marble holds for him. It is as though the temper of our times has held my symphony relentlessly and unyieldingly in the restlessness, apprehension, frustration, fear, anger, hate which permeates the days and nights of our world.
>
> My problem, then, has been to find the way to communicate the gathering storm, and to hold hope for a new society—the "Great Society" which we have promised ourselves for so long. . . .
>
> Symphony Number Eleven is such an attempt. It is a symphony in the shape of an inverted arch. It is emotional rather than intellectual. The progress of emotional ethos in prescribing the form of an inverted arch is: restlessness, apprehension, fear, anger, violence to remorse, hope, expectation, and realization of a more humane world. . . .[5]

This is probably Harris's definitive statement about the profound change his concept of American society underwent during the last decades of his life, and this symphony which emerged near the end of 1967 (in response to a commission from the New York Philharmonic for the celebration of its

125th anniversary), in reflecting the change so powerfully, is one of the most curious, savage, gnarled, and disturbing affairs ever to come from his pen. One has to look back to the 1934 Trio and to the "Tears" movement of Symphony for Voices for similar utterances which fall outside the mainstream of his familiar idiom.

Though its broad gestures, large orchestral resources, and opulent string scoring grow out of the typical Harris expansiveness and fundamental optimism, the character of the materials of the Eleventh Symphony is so abstract and relatively inaccessible that it seems as though the "Modern Man" of whom Harris so often "sang" in such buoyant terms in the past is only dimly to be perceived here among the other dark objects of uncertain shape which seethe in this cauldron.

## Form

The Eleventh Symphony is in two large parts, which are sometimes regarded as distinct movements, but which actually link into an organic continuity. The listener is posed a tremendous challenge in following the tenuous, embattled thread of melodic continuity, a continuity virtually always present in Harris's music but here frequently all but submerged (at least during the first half of the work) by competing forces.

Harris's description of the symphony as an "inverted arch" identifies the musicodramatic progress in a way that needs no amplification. Each of the two parts of the work falls into three sections. The three sections of part one have a tempo scheme of fast-slow-fast. Section one presents and develops an idea in the piano solo:

EXAMPLE 84

*Symphony No. 11:* Theme I

Like the material that launched Part IV of the *San Francisco Symphony,* idea I is really too figurational and kaleidoscopic in character to be called a true theme.

Section two comprises the unfolding of theme II in three large paragraphs:

EXAMPLE 85

*Symphony No. 11:* Theme II

These paragraphs are marked by a continuation of the gradual ritardando that has been in evidence from near the beginning of the symphony and that reaches its low point in the middle of this section.

Section three is characterized by the return to a fast tempo and an attempt to continue the spinning-out of theme II, only to disintegrate into a motivic fracas that eventually results in the "collapse" of the structure onto a b-flat-minor first-inversion chord, one of Harris's darkest sonorities.

Part two is somewhat simpler in structure and more straightforward in its slow, but inexorable, accumulation of momentum. This is perhaps in character with its generally more positive, unclouded tone. The first of its three sections is a double fugue on these two subjects:[6]

EXAMPLE 86

*Symphony No. 11:* Themes III and IV

a: Theme III

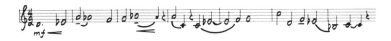

b: Theme IV

dolce, espr.

It conveys a restrained, muted sadness, with Harris masterfully creating a cause-and-effect link with the first half of the symphony through the persistence here of a soft, but nagging, timpani figure derived from an important motive of part one and suggesting that the strife of the preceding music has been banished to another dimension but nonetheless still registers faintly as a slight disturbance of the foreground events.

Section two, like its counterpart in part one, unfolds another long idea in several paragraphs:

EXAMPLE 87

*Symphony No. 11:* Theme V

dolce, poco vib., espr.

This spinning-out, however, proceeds in its harmonic aspect in reverse direction on the color spectrum, from dark to light.

The final section of the symphony is based upon a gradual unfolding of the following ideas:

EXAMPLE 88

*Symphony No. 11:* Themes VI and VII

a: Theme VI

b: Theme VII

This section continues, in intensified fashion, the very leisurely, but continual, accelerando which has operated over most of part two and which pulls back in the final pages to allow for a broadening out, thereby creating a sense of great weight and emphasis.

## The Motive

One of the most important characteristics of the Eleventh Symphony is the crucial role of the motivic elements. First, the entire work may be regarded as growing from a single cell:

EXAMPLE 89

*Symphony No. 11:* Motive x

This motive, first heard in the form of trumpet punctuation during the unfolding of idea I in the opening section of the work, is expanded intervallically near the beginning of the next section:

EXAMPLE 90

*Symphony No. 11:* Motive x expansion

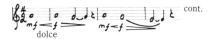

This expansion in turn serves to launch the first true melodic idea of the symphony, theme II.

Evolving simultaneously with the development of motive x is a harmonic element: in the opening pages of the work, idea I has been punctuated by polychordal string interjections which, rather than being isolated elements, are, in fact, of seminal importance, for they form the basis of the harmonization of theme II. At the same time, the line described by the top voice in the entire complex of polychordal interjections is clearly another intervallic expansion of motive x. These motivic and harmonic elements of section one thus coalesce to form the principal idea of section two.

In addition to the theme generated by motive x, there are numerous variants of the motive that operate independently of the principal materials.

There are also ideas not derived from motive x that function either as additional motives or as somewhat longer subsidiary materials and punctuate and/or weave through the principal linear continuity. The most important of these appears to be motive y, for the interval of a fourth that characterizes this figure acts as a primary disruptive force during much of part one:

EXAMPLE 91

*Symphony No. 11:* Motive y and variants

Another idea appears to be the source of a rhythmic and metrical instability that pervades portions of part one:

EXAMPLE 92

*Symphony No. 11:* Motive z

The triple-duple rhythmic character of this idea seems to be a condensation of the rhythmic asymmetry heard at the very outset of the symphony in the three-and two-note groups comprising idea I. This asymmetry is reflected on a larger scale in the phrase structure of theme II, whose first paragraph can be heard in terms of a basic 3/2 pulsation fitted across a 4/2 meter. The asymmetry erupts into the foreground in the 11/8 and 7/8 meters that occur during the final section of part one. However, the triple-duple pulsation reaches its apex of intensity, paradoxically, in the ostensibly optimistic closing pages of the symphony. Here the duple pulse of the reiterated trumpet/trombone major polychords is placed into direct confrontation with the triple pulse in the horns and strings:

EXAMPLE 93

*Symphony No. 11:* Closing ideas

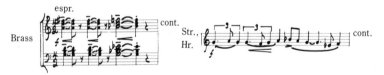

The result strikes me, at least, as hardly an easy reconciliation of two dynamic and opposing rhythmic forces which, in the long run, may provide as much of a key to the understanding of this complex work as the linear and harmonic elements.

## Overview

The Eleventh Symphony can be regarded as the opposite of another of Harris's one-movement symphonies, the Seventh. In that work, as I observed earlier, the melodic invention, ingenuity of thematic and motivic manipulation, harmonic color, and brilliance of instrumental palette manage to move the listener in spite of a curious emotional distance. In the Eleventh, on the other hand, the emotional situation prevails, with Harris creating out of sheer inner drive and necessity, it would seem, a gripping work that somehow transcends its occasional shortcomings of invention. [7]

## The *Pere Marquette Symphony*

Even before completing the full score of the Eleventh Symphony, Harris, late in 1967, began work on his next, and longest, essay in the genre. The work had been commissioned for the commemoration of the period 300 years earlier when the Jesuit Father Jacques Marquette of Laon, France, explored the central wilderness area of the United States (the discovery of the Mississippi River is attributed to him), gaining the friendship and respect of the Indian tribes in the area. A Tercentenary Commission had been established by the United States Congress in 1965 for the purpose of organizing a five-year celebration spanning the years 1968–1973, and the premiere of Harris's new symphony was planned as the opening event in the celebration.

Harris was seemingly as much interested in Marquette as an embodiment of the affirmation of the life-force as he was concerned with him as a figure of historical importance. The subject also enabled the composer to counterbalance his rather pessimistic concern with contemporary life, as exemplified in the powerful Eleventh Symphony, by turning the clock back to the pioneering spirit and the optimism of a relatively primitive America. Indeed, the *Pere Marquette Symphony* emerged as one of the last positive musical statements Harris was to make about America. It is something of a summarizing achievement, for its blend of Americanist sentiments and religious mysticism unites the nationalist and visionary characteristics of his work in a way which appears to enlarge the dimensions and enrich the substance of both these attributes.

The *Pere Marquette Symphony* (Symphony No. 12) was a rather long time in the writing. After having been premiered as a torso in February 1968, it was finally given in its definitive form in November of 1969 by the Milwaukee Symphony Orchestra under the composer's direction, with David Bender as tenor soloist/speaker.

This is the first of Harris's symphonies to employ a solo voice (aside from the brief solo in the "Tears" movement of Symphony for Voices and the short speaking part in the Tenth Symphony). It is thus, especially in the lengthy Credo setting of Part IB, a hybrid symphony/cantata and constitutes another example of the composer's flexibility of approach to the symphonic genre.

## The Chant Element Surfaces

One special feature that deserves mention is Harris's first use here of an actual Gregorian chant melody. This is significant in view of the influence the melodic profile, modal characteristics, and flowing rhythmic character of the chant had on the development of his melodic style. Yet, for all this, it was not until the present work, which comprises a summary of so many other aspects of his style, that one finally encounters an actual example of this seminal literature.

The Gregorian melody in question is an Alleluia, "Justus germinabit sicut illium," and it is used as a sort of idée fixe throughout the entire symphony. The great variety in treatment which Harris accords it reveals considerable resources in this area and results in a skillfully wrought sense of variety-within-unity. Especially noteworthy is the range of moods, from reflection, to savagery, to resignation, which his various modifications of the chant convey.

Harris never quotes the chant in its entirety or in its original form (at least as found in the *Liber Usualis*), but a substantial portion of the original is given below for comparison with some of Harris's variants:[8]

EXAMPLE 94

*Symphony No. 12:* Chant melody ("Justus germinabit" and variants)

a: Justus germinabit

b: Justus germinabit variants

## Form

The symphony is divided into two parts: I. The Old World, II. The New World. Part I consists of two movements: (Part IA) the early life of Marquette from infancy to his ordination at the age of twenty-nine; (Part IB) a setting for tenor voice and orchestra of the Nicene Creed from the Ordinary of the Mass, representing an affirmation of Marquette's own commitment as an initiate for the priesthood of the Society of Jesus. Part II contains three interconnected movements: (1) The moods of the wilderness; (2) the preachments of Marquette to the Indians, employing the first fourteen lines of the Gospel of John (in Latin); (3) Pere Marquette's death in the wilderness, employing the text of the Sanctus from the Ordinary. However, Parts IA and II group themselves around the extended Credo setting of Part IB (nearly the length of IA and II combined) to create for the listener a huge Gothic arch.

## Part IA

Part IA of the symphony is in four sections, the first built on the simultaneous spinning-out of themes I and II:

EXAMPLE 95

*Symphony No. 12:* Part IA. Themes I and II

a: Theme I

b: Theme II

Section two states and develops a new theme (III) by means of variations of its three phrases:

EXAMPLE 96

*Symphony No. 12:* Part IA. Theme III

Section three is based on three shorter ideas taken from Part I of the Eighth Symphony (see Example 62bc for variants of two of them).[9]

The last section introduces the borrowed Gregorian chant, harmonized in organum, in tandem with another idea which serves as a kind of response to each phrase of the chant. This leads to yet a further idea:

EXAMPLE 97

*Symphony No. 12:* Part IA. Themes VII and IX ("Justus germinabit" is Theme VII)

a: Theme VIII

b: Theme IX

Part IA concludes with the unexpected entrance of the tenor voice ejaculating an intense "Kyrie Eleison."

This opening portion of the *Pere Marquette Symphony* is a variation of the multisectional scheme of progressive accelerando employed in such works as the orchestral Acceleration and the Third Symphony (during its first four parts). It is also based on the plan of a gradual accumulation of textural density and detail such as is encountered in the "Awakening" movement of the Sixth Symphony, for, in addition to the principal themes, there is a network of accompanimental textures, motives, and subsidiary ideas, all of which undergo continual metamorphosis.

## Part IB

Part IB is the longest of all Harris's symphonic movements (at least within the context of the multimovement works), lasting about fifteen minutes. It is in two sections, of which the first is an orchestral passage in which the chant melody is tossed about in wild, distorted fragments through a pulsating texture built on the constant recurrence, in asymmetrically expanding and contracting paragraphs, of an underlying harmonic idea:

EXAMPLE 98

*Symphony No. 12:* Part IB. Idea I

The broadly paced Credo is one of Harris's most radiant utterances. It may mark for some the apex of his vocal writing and it certainly gives the lie to the view cited elsewhere in this study that Harris was generally ineffective when setting words to music (though his prosody is indeed awkward at times). Though the Credo lacks the variety in tempo, rhythm, and texture of the *Canticle of the Sun,* it is close in spirit to that chamber work, seeming very much like a male-voice counterpart.

The Credo setting evolves from the continual spinning-out of a single long melody, theme II, which unfolds in several paragraphs in the tenor voice, each paragraph harmonized chiefly in strings and punctuated by instrumental commentary, mostly in the brass. Though the Credo is essentially through-composed, it can be broken into subsections that correspond to the dramatic structure of the text. The first of these sets the opening lines of the Creed, which constitute the statement of beliefs up to the Crucifixion. The second subsection, beginning with the line "qui propter nos homines. . . ," describes the central act of the Crucifixion. The third subsection sets the lines from "Et resurrexit tertia die" to the end and thus conveys an increasing sense of joy in the Resurrection.

The many changes of mood, from the forthright affirmation of the opening lines, through the darkness of the Crucifixion, to the radiance of the Resurrection, are conveyed with great mastery of nuance. Cited below are some representative segments of each portion of the Credo:

EXAMPLE 99

*Symphony No. 12:* Part IB. Representative phrase-openings of the "Credo"

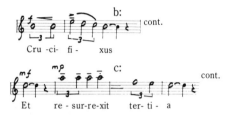

Example 99c, in particular, begins a passage that is among the most ineffable in Harris's entire oeuvre.

The element of harmonic color is crucial in realizing the changes of mood and tone in Part IB. The opening subsection is based harmonically chiefly upon organum sonorities given to the low strings. As this music unfolds, Harris begins to intermix richer major harmonies with the relatively austere organa. For the second subsection, he changes the harmonic texture to the somber coloration of minor polychords. The darkest point of the text is that which refers to the Crucifixion itself and, as expected, Harris matches this harmonically with a c-minor second-inversion chord, a sound which he generally reserves for dark, intense moments of this sort. For the final subsection, there is a brief return to organum harmonies, as though the composer were clearing the air, before a change to major polychords.

Part IB is also a summary of Harris's mastery of that aspect of harmony that arises from intervallic spacing. He achieves enormous variety in nuance of light and shade and in richness and astringency through the vertical disposition of his basically simple chord structures.

## Part II

The three interlinked "movements" of Part II are distinct from one another in materials, textures, and rhythms, though all are slow to moderate in tempo. The first movement is one of Harris's most evocative tone poems. Against a nearly static string background of organum harmonies, various motives are heard that suggest the sounds of unseen birds and animals:

EXAMPLE 100

*Symphony No. 12:* Part II. Motives

The slow, stepwise progression of the strings and the widely spaced organum intervals convey a cold, impersonal wilderness atmosphere.

The motivic development and the supporting string texture both become increasingly animated toward the end of the first movement, setting up the more strongly rhythmic character of the second movement. The voice returns in this next portion of the symphony, but now in a speaking role, delivering, in rhythmically notated speech, the lines from the Gospel of John cited earlier over an ostinato in percussion and string basses.

Motives reminiscent of the preceding wilderness movement are woven over this declamation, and its important divisions are punctuated by brass and string polychords. Near the end of the movement, Harris creates one of his most moving effects when he brings the chant back softly in the strings in long note values, first in octaves then in organum harmonies, to accompany the last few lines of text declamation. In its essentials, this movement is clearly built on the example he had provided himself in the setting of the Gettysburg speech in the Tenth Symphony and is a further manifestation of the tendency toward a greater use of speech, both choric and solo, in his vocal works from the mid-1960s on.

The final movement of Part II, rooted for the most part to a persistent b-flat-minor second-inversion chord, is a moving, ecstatic setting of the aforementioned Sanctus of the Ordinary of the Mass, spun out in two paragraphs:

EXAMPLE 101

*Symphony No. 12:* Part II. Opening of "Sanctus" setting

Though the *Pere Marquette Symphony* ends in radiance on a major polychord, the overall tone is ambiguous, suggesting, on the one hand (as Harris pointed out in his note for the premiere) the feelings of the Indians, ". . . who were overcome with grief at the failure of their devotion to keep him with them," and, on the other hand, the dying sentiments of Marquette who ". . . experienced no sorrow in leaving the trials and tribulations of life on earth. On the contrary, his last moments were lifted with the joy of his own redemption into life eternal."[10]

## Overview

Though the symphony's relatively slow pace and predominantly reflective tone may alienate some listeners who respond more readily to the wild propulsion and exuberance of some of Harris's early works, the refinement of technique demonstrated here in his control over the autogenetic unfolding of the long line, the evolution of one section from another, the interrelationships and working out of motives, and the rich and resourceful use of the diatonic harmonic vocabulary render the *Pere Marquette Symphony* a landmark in the composer's development. In some ways the symphony is Harris's *Parsifal* and almost certainly the last of his works to verge on true greatness.

# Harris in the 1970s

Harris's creative work continued through the mid-1970s, though most of the compositions of these years are occasional pieces, chiefly for chorus or solo voice and winds. In 1971 he retired from UCLA, assuming at about the same time a position as composer-in-residence at California State University, Los Angeles. During this period, Johana left Cal Arts and joined the piano faculty at UCLA.

## The Founding of the Archive: A Reawakening

Harris's position at Cal State, L. A., left him free of the chores of classroom teaching, though he did give occasional lectures. His chief teaching duties now involved a few private students, who came to the house for lessons, thus continuing the pattern of the past.

Very likely the two most significant events associated with his residence at Cal State occurred during the mid-1970s. The first was the founding at the University in February 1973, on the occasion of his 75th birthday, of the Roy Harris Archive. The development of the Archive was slow during its first five years, but in 1978 efforts on its behalf began in earnest with the formation of the Roy Harris Society, an organization established to promote the acquisition of archival materials, publication of Harris's works and of scholarly writings on the composer, and performances and recordings of the music.

All this activity coincided with a reawakening of interest in and a reevaluation of Harris's contribution to the American musical scene. While during the 1950s and 60s, especially the latter decade, there had been a strong reaction against composers of Harris's generation and aesthetic persuasion, there was now a renewed appreciation of what some regarded as a sort of "Golden Age" of American music. The happy result was that music which had been neglected for many years was now beginning to take its rightful place as a rich and vital part of the heritage of American music.

In addition, a new appreciation of tonality and of consonant harmony by composers (such as George Rochberg) who formerly seemed poles removed from this aesthetic may have contributed in a small way toward making the climate more favorable for the "reemergence" of older masters such as Harris who had so successfully adapted this vocabulary to their own needs a generation or more before. The reception of Harris's music was still mixed, but at least it was being heard more, and recorded, thus enabling listeners to gain a firmer perspective on which to base judgment.

## *Bicentennial Symphony*

The other major event of the mid-1970s was the composition of Harris's last symphony, the *Bicentennial Symphony–1976,* which was commissioned by Cal State, L. A. Since this work was planned for performance in Washington, D. C., as part of the U. S. Bicentennial Year, it was natural that the composer would turn once again to an Americanist subject. But the result was hardly the patriotic effusion many may have expected, for the strain of social concern, as realized explicitly in such works employing vocal forces as the Tenth Symphony and the still unperformed *Whether This Nation,* and implicitly in the purely orchestral Eleventh Symphony, had not altered. Harris once again turned to the Civil War for his subject, which had formed the dramatic peak of the Tenth Symphony. This time, however, he attacked the central issue of racial strife in a way that contrasts with the approach in the earlier work, where it was present more as a background element. Since completing the Tenth, Harris had confronted some of the problems of contemporary society in the aforementioned *Whether This Nation,* and that work's aggressive choral dialogues (often rendered in choric speech) and terse, direct statements, which almost seem to act as a challenge to the audience, influenced a good deal of the vocal writing and the structure of the *Bicentennial Symphony.* Another important element of *Whether This Nation* which finds its way into the symphony is the ironic juxtaposition of the noble and idealistic sentiments

of such historic documents as the "Preamble" to the *Constitution* and
Lincoln's "Gettysburg Address" with the crude expressions of reality spat
out in such lines as "Fight, fight, fight; fight for the right to keep our slaves"
(third movement of symphony).

Though the *Bicentennial Symphony* is the least substantial of all Harris's
symphonies in musical invention, a clear manifestation of the declining
powers that set in during the 1970s, it cannot be dismissed entirely, for it
constitutes one of the strongest statements on racial intolerance yet made
by an American composer. Though the work ends on a characteristically
positive note, it is doubtful if audiences wished to be reminded, during the
jingoistic excesses of the Bicentennial Year, of one of the ugliest episodes
in American history, an episode whose ramifications, in spite of decades of
progress, are still felt today. As a result, the generally negative critical
reaction to the work, though perhaps justified on musical grounds, must
also be examined in this light.

One must not assume, however, that in works of this sort Harris was
turning his back completely on the Whitmanesque ethos of his earlier
years. Rather, it appears that he had finally matured into an individual able
to take the full measure of Whitman by embracing the totality of America,
of both its light and its shadow, so powerfully conveyed in the poet's great
panoramas.

## Form

The *Bicentennial Symphony* is in five movements: I. Introduction;
"Preamble" to the *Constitution*; II. Freedom versus Slavery; III. Civil
War: Brothers Kill Brothers; IV. Emancipation Proclamation; V. Freedom.
The text is a composite of borrowed materials (from the *Constitution* and
from Lincoln) and original words.

## Overview

Musically the *Bicentennial Symphony*, as I observed earlier, is flawed—the
materials and textures are overly simple, with virtually nothing in the way
of real melodic or contrapuntal interest. There is an almost unvaried use of
block chordal texture and a tendency to rely too much on dialogue comprising an alternation of choric speech and singing. Actually, aside from some
of the orchestral introductions and interludes, there is relatively little
except the texts to distinguish one movement from another.

Thus, in spite of some occasional effective moments, such as the
orchestral introduction to the first movement and the rather moving

setting of the *Emancipation Proclamation,* the *Bicentennial Symphony* is significant chiefly for what it represents about Harris's response to the social scene of the 1960s and 70s (in terms of a broad historical perspective) rather than as a grand, valedictory symphonic statement. It is an occasional piece in the most accurate sense of the word, and even the powerful sentiments expressed in the text cannot replace the rewards of an experience of genuine musical substance. In the end, the symphony became a victim of both its creator's failing powers and of the rather frantic efforts in many areas of artistic endeavor to produce a durable creation of major importance as an outgrowth of the activities of the Bicentennial Year.

# 7

## Chamber Works, Part I
## (Works for String Ensembles)

### The Chamber Medium: a Crucible for the Development of Harris's Style and Technique

Roy Harris's involvement with the chamber medium went back almost to the beginning of his career. Works in the genre were especially important to him during that period, for these compositions, because of their smaller forces, afforded more opportunities for performance than works for larger media. But perhaps more important than performance viability was the fact that the chamber medium gave the composer a format within which to work out some of the problems of his developing technique. As indicated earlier, it was a chamber work, the String Quartet No. 1, which enabled Harris to free himself from "the room-with-a-piano-in-it bondage which might have cramped my whole life."[1] This gave him the opportunity to concentrate on the essentials of line, texture, and harmony in a medium where every voice part has the dual responsibility of functioning as an independent organism and as a vital part of the whole. The experience in writing for chamber ensembles is strongly evident in the lean, frequently contrapuntal, textures and the thematic and motivic working-out in some of the composer's orchestral scores of the 1930s (such as the Second Symphony and the *Time Suite*).

### Characteristics

Harris's chamber works tend to be more contrapuntal and rhythmically complex than his orchestral compositions. The cerebral element which has always been present in his music to some extent comes to the surface more often and renders the works in this genre more abstract and less specifically nationalistic than most of the other categories in which he

composed. They represent perhaps better than any other area of his
lifework the apt description of the composer by Arthur Farwell in his 1932
article: "Harris is a straight-out classicist, challenging the entire subsequent epoch, neo-classicist and all, from the primal standpoint of Bach
and Beethoven, but, it must be urged, such a classicist as only the present
world-scene could produce."[2]

The chamber works certainly reflect his interest in Renaissance and
Baroque polyphony, in modality, in Baroque textures and forms, and in the
aesthetics and technique of Beethoven.

## Quartet No. 1

The historical importance of the First Quartet in Harris's development has
already been cited. In addition, this work, as observed in chapter 3, proved
to be a valuable source of materials for subsequent pieces, providing some
of the principal materials for the *Symphony 1933* (first movement), the
Symphony No. 2 (finale), and the Symphony No. 3 (theme II). The quartet
has some awkward moments and possesses, overall, the quality of an
immature statement. Given the circumstances in which it was written,
these characteristics are understandable, though the work is still viable in
performance.

The composer spoke, in various program notes, about what he called
development of thematic "characteristics." The First Quartet is an excellent illustration of this, for hardly has a theme been exposed before he
begins developing and expanding it, usually through the manipulation of
motives which seem capable of calling the theme readily to mind during the
course of the musical argument.

One also finds Harris continuing here the attempt to reconcile his
emerging principles of autogenetic formal growth with some of the closed
forms of the Classic period, an attempt which was also made in some of the
early symphonies.

## Three Variations on a Theme (Quartet No. 2)

Though Harris wrote the First Quartet in silence, he did eventually have an
opportunity to experience its actual sound, for the piece was performed in
1930 by the New York Quartet at one of the Copland-Sessions concerts in
New York. It is evident that he had benefited from the lessons learned from
this first essay in the genre when it came time to write his next one: titled
Three Variations on a Theme, the Second Quartet is among the most
economical of his works, being built in its entirety on a single theme stated
in the opening measures:

EXAMPLE 102

*Three Variations on a Theme:* Theme (octave displacements and doublings omitted)

The theme itself is generated by a seed-motive (motive x) which represents, in German musical nomenclature, the initials of Elizabeth Sprague Coolidge ("Es"=Eb, "C"=C), the celebrated patroness of chamber music during the early decades of this century.

Harris demonstrates an unusual approach to variations technique in this quartet by treating different aspects of the character and structure of the theme in each of the three movements. Thus, the opening movement seizes on the short notes that articulate subdivisions of the theme as the springboard for music of a highly energetic character, with much use of cross rhythms and different accentuations within the prevailing 6/8 meter. In this movement, the theme is varied primarily through the development of motives extracted from it, particularly motive x.

Though much of the first movement is marked by a continuing development of the theme, there is also, as in the first movement of Quartet No. 1, an element of sonata-allegro form. What might correspond to an exposition ends at a climactic point in measure 118 and a kind of recapitulation starts in measure 192. This latter section includes a varied and expanded (but quite clear) return of some of the materials of the "exposition."

The second movement explores the more lyrical aspects of the theme, with Harris now treating the line to a number of increasingly elaborate expansions rather than subjecting it to the fragmentation which was a prominent feature of the preceding movement. A sample is given below:

EXAMPLE 103

*Three Variations on a Theme:* II. Violoncello expansion of theme

The movement builds to a climax in two successive waves built on gradual increases in tempo, dynamics, register, and, in the case of the second wave, rhythmic activity. It is an early attempt at the Gothic-arch structure, though here, as in the case of so many early examples of this form, the descending portion of the arch is absent, being replaced by a broken-off climax and an abrupt transition to the final section of the movement. This section is marked by a sense of repose as Harris broadens the theme out into a harmonized statement in the lower three members of the quartet over which the first violin weaves poignant reminiscences of some of the previous development. The concluding measures are among the most poetic in all Harris's oeuvre, making one wish he had been able to achieve this rapt, probing quality more often during the succeeding decades.

The finale is the most complex movement. It summarizes the procedures (at times incorporating or suggesting the actual materials) of the first two movements and adds some characteristic treatments of its own. Harris is clearly refining here the example of the finale of the First Quartet, for the movement follows essentially the same ground plan: a quasicontrapuntal structure based upon a gradual diminution in prevailing note values. Along the way, the theme is treated to an imaginative augmentation/ expansion and then a diminution which serves as the basis of a short fugal exposition:

EXAMPLE 104

*Three Variations on a Theme:* III. Augmentation and diminution of theme

a: Augmentation

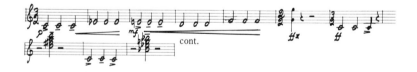

b: Diminution

Though the finale is complex and, on the first few hearings, somewhat diffuse and difficult to follow, the fact that virtually everything in it grows out of the theme or its seed-motive ultimately conveys a strong sense of unity. It is certainly a tighter, more purposefully directed structure than its counterpart in the First Quartet, though not free from some of the cerebral contrivances cited in connection with the Symphonies Nos. 1 and 2, with which it is contemporary.

Harris's attempt to explore and extract from a single melodic idea a wealth of characteristics makes the Three Variations on a Theme a landmark in his development. It points the way toward the resourcefulness and technical accomplishment of such works as the monumental Piano Quintet (also an essentially monothematic work), the Seventh Symphony, and all the other works that employ various aspects of variation technique.

## Quartet No. 3

I have observed that the first two quartets played important roles in Harris's development. With the Third Quartet, written around 1937, one finds him coming to terms with the integration of late Baroque principles of contrapuntal writing with his own developing polymodal style. The work thus serves an equally important function with respect to this aspect of his maturing. Not too long before writing it, Harris had collaborated with M. D. Herter Norton on a transcription for string quartet of J. S. Bach's *Art of the Fugue* and had doubtless immersed himself to a greater extent than ever before in the dynamics of the "passing of melodic lines through a harmonic texture" (as he often defined tonal counterpoint).

In the Third Quartet (subtitled "Four Preludes and Fugues"), Harris uses many of the traditional techniques of contrapuntal writing (stretto, inversion, etc.), but his treatment of these devices is flexible, and his exploration of modal resources beyond the major and minor scales is entirely personal. It seems appropriate that the Third Quartet, which has a partly theoretical-historical basis, should have been premiered in the fall of 1939 at a concert given for an international convention of musicologists.

The Third Quartet is a textbook of the composer's melodic, harmonic, and contrapuntal idioms. It comprises eight relatively short movements grouped in four pairs consisting of a prelude and a fugue each. The subject of each prelude is based on a specific mode and the principal subject of each fugue (except the last) is fashioned from a combination of two different modes. These latter subjects, because of their hybrid modal characteristics, display the inflections of certain scale degrees which are such a clearly recognizable aspect of Harris's style. Two of the fugue subjects are cited below to demonstrate this device of modal combination:

EXAMPLE 105

*Quartet No. 3:* Fugue subjects

a: Fugue I—Subject

b: Fugue III—Subject I

The harmonies of each movement are also conditioned by the modal characteristics of the melodic materials. The result is a great variety in mood and harmonic color, from very dark to very bright.

Each prelude is canonic, while the fugues follow the somewhat freer contrapuntal technique associated with that genre, alternating passages of exposition and episode. In many instances, the episodes of the fugues are based on materials derived from the subjects rather than on new ideas.

The four pairs of movements are laid out in a scheme which, in characteristics of tempo, resembles the four-movement design of the Classic-period quartet.

Prelude I (Dorian mode) and Fugue I (Dorian/Aeolian modes) are in moderate tempi and proceed in rhythmically straightforward fashion. Somewhat simpler and more direct in both expression and working out than the following movements, they have something of an introductory character. They also contain some of Harris's noblest and warmest writing, particularly the Prelude, whose predominant harmonic texture formed chiefly from interlocking organum sonorities reveals the composer's mastery at achieving rich and colorful results from limited means:

EXAMPLE 106

*Quartet No. 3:* Prelude I. Harmonic texture

Vln. I, Vla.

Vln. II, Vcl.

Prelude II (Lydian) and Fugue II (Lydian/Ionian) are skitterish and enigmatic. Together they comprise a sort of scherzo. In keeping with the somewhat elusive character of these pieces, the composer makes the canonic imitation in Prelude II somewhat looser than that in Prelude I. The muted fleet-footedness of this set of movements is unique in Harris's oeuvre.

Prelude III (Locrian) and Fugue III (Locrian/Phrygian) are the darkest in modal color and emotional characteristics, and correspond with a large slow movement. Fugue III is especially complex and convoluted, featuring a countersubject of uncertain modality that traces a chromatically descending line:

EXAMPLE 107

*Quartet No. 3:* Fugue III—Countersubject

The tragic intensity conveyed in these pieces is of the sort that pervades some of the composer's finest music, such as the closing pages of the Third Symphony. The visionary Harris comes to the fore here.

Prelude IV (Ionian) and Fugue IV (Subject I: Mixolydian, Subject II: Ionian), though complex, are in marked contrast to the preceding pair of movements. Striding and ebullient, their clear diatonic melodic and harmonic designs and their rhythmic propulsion bring the quartet to a dynamic close.

One problem with the Third Quartet is the difficulty of welding its eight relatively short movements into a coherent whole, even granted the larger divisions into which they naturally seem to fall. Also, the indicated tempo relationships are such that, especially with the first two pairs of movements, there is an impression of a sameness of pace. Finally, there are those for whom the Third Quartet remains, in spite of its rewards, something of a theoretical work. Part of this impression may stem from the fact that, as Harris was to demonstrate in the somewhat freer approaches of his later works, he was never truly comfortable with polyphonic writing of a traditional sort. One senses, even in the warmth and technical proficiency displayed here, a constraint on his natural musical impulses, and a sense of artificiality. Harris needed the freer fantasy possible in the hybrid fugal variations procedure of such pieces as the finale of the Fifth Sym-

phony in order to reach his own compact with the great polyphonists of the
past. However, one cannot ignore the qualities of a work which elicited a
response of this sort: "One of the few important modern quartets is
certainly Roy Harris's Third Quartet. The clean and long-breathed phrases
become dearer as one knows them better. The nostalgia which underlies
this noble music comes through."[3]

# Concerto for String Sextet

Harris wrote his Concerto for Six Groups of String Instruments, as he
once titled it, in 1932. It thus falls between the First and Second Quartets
and shares their generally polyphonic character. In fact, the Concerto is
very likely the most polyphonically complex organism Harris ever created,
the Third Quartet notwithstanding. It explores all the artifices of stretto,
inversion, augmentation, plus the composer's own approach to motivic
expansion and thematic variation. Much of the writing in the outer
movements is rhythmically convoluted and at times seems to serve more
as an example of "Augenmusik" ("eye-music") than as a rewarding listen-
ing experience.

## Form

The Concerto is in three movements. The first and last, as indicated, are
heavily contrapuntal, with a resulting emphasis upon the linear aspect; the
middle movement is a chorale, with more concern for the vertical
sonorities.

## First movement

In the opening movement, the composer approaches his thematic materials from the direction opposite that which he was to take the following
year in the Second Quartet: rather than starting with a complete theme as
a fait accompli, he gradually forms longer thematic ideas from a single germ
motive:[4]

EXAMPLE 108

*Concerto for String Sextet:* I. Theme

Of course, this was the procedure he was to follow in the opening movement of the Second Symphony two years later.

The germ motive undergoes several developments and expansions, of which the following demonstrate characteristic treatments of the A and B segments:

EXAMPLE 109

*Concerto for String Sextet:* I. Motive x developments

a: Motive xa development

b: Motive xb development

Finally it flowers into two quite different melodic ideas:[5]

EXAMPLE 110

*Concerto for String Sextet:* I. Themes derived from motive x

The "characteristics," to use Harris's term once again, of these longer ideas are developed before a varied (and broadened out) recapitulation of the opening section rounds off the movement.

This movement is clearly an outgrowth of textures and procedures employed in the "Initiative" movement of *American Portrait* (the seed-motives in both pieces are nearly identical) and shows the composer's preoccupation with exploring the possibilities of both motivic working-out and expansion of motives into longer ideas.

## Second movement: Chorale

Though the Concerto as a whole has remained virtually unknown, the Chorale which forms its second movement has come to be one of the most often played of Harris's shorter compositions. (It has nearly always been performed by a full string orchestra, minus the basses.) The chorale harmonization that frames the movement is one of his most successful early applications of the principle of common-tone harmony and of harmonies that "should represent what is in the melody, without being enslaved by the tonality in which the melody lies," to cite once again Harris's belief:[6]

EXAMPLE 111

*Concerto for String Sextet:* II. Theme (phrase marks and dynamics have been adjusted somewhat for clarity)

During the main part of the movement, the chorale melody is treated as a cantus firmus in a series of variations. Often a single statement is exchanged between various instruments, the long note values into which it is sometimes stretched rendering it little more than an organizing device, more evident to eye than ear (as in the case of some of the cantus firmi in medieval motets). Harris's willingness to unwind here from the contrapuntal and motivic abstractions of the first movement contributes to making the Chorale the most accessible and viable portion of the Concerto.

## Third Movement

The finale is a contrapuntal tour de force. It is based upon two themes, the first generated from a diatonic form of motive x, the second comprising a combination of characteristics of materials from both movements I (see Example 110b) and II:

EXAMPLE 112

*Concerto for String Sextet:* III. Themes I and II

a: Theme I

b: Theme II

Essentially a combination double fugue and variations, the movement treats its materials to a whole spectrum of contrapuntal devices. The following example is typical of both the textural complexity and of the bravura and lyricism which coexist so uneasily in this turbulent movement:

EXAMPLE 113

*Concerto for String Sextet:* III. Contrapuntal texture

The concluding pages provide another in a line of examples stretching from the early Concerto for Clarinet et al to the Viola Quintet of the way in which Harris's aspiration comes near to exploding beyond the bounds of the chamber medium:

EXAMPLE 114

*Concerto for String Sextet:* III. Climax

## Overview

In a sense, the Concerto is a last backward look at Harris's technical apprenticeship. For all its energy, it is, even in the Chorale to some extent, a contrived work. Though it can make a brilliant effect, one admires rather than loves it. But the work served its purpose in giving the composer perspectives on contrapuntal technique and thematic development that were to bear fruit in later works in which he was to develop his own more fluid approach to such matters.

# Viola Quintet

In 1940 the last of Harris's major chamber works for strings alone appeared, the Quintet for Two Violins, Two Violas, and Violoncello, commissioned by the Elizabeth Sprague Coolidge Foundation in the Library of Congress. The Viola Quintet is the most ambitious and imaginative of the composer's chamber works prior to the *Canticle of the Sun* (another Coolidge commission). It is also one of the most problematic, especially in its extended fugal finale. More than ever here, Harris seems to be occupied with abstract, intellectual concepts that sometimes rein in his natural spontaneity. However, the two middle movements, one of them a scherzo employing folk materials (which rarely appear in Harris's chamber works of this sort), are sufficiently rewarding to warrant an occasional performance of the whole work.

## First Movement

The first of the four movements that make up the work, the Prelude, is a toccatalike essay in several sections based on the gradual metamorphosis from a vigorous polyphonic texture that expands vertically and passes through various meters and accentual patterns to a bold section in block chords that is also characterized by metrical instability. Some of the principal ideas are:

EXAMPLE 115

*Viola Quintet:* I. Principal ideas

The movement from polyphony to homophony results in a tightening up of texture and rhythm as the "Prelude" progresses. In addition, one finds, in the way in which Harris moves from a relatively high tessitura in the opening sections to a lower register for the middle of the movement and back to a high tessitura for the closing pages, a relatively rare appearance of a kind of inverted Gothic arch. (But the effect here in this outgoing, virtuosic piece is quite different from the emotional ethos Harris conveyed by means of the same structure in the strife-ridden Eleventh Symphony.)

## Second Movement

The slow movement is one of the earliest of Harris's mature realizations of his more customary Gothic-arch design and is a clear forerunner, along with the third movement of the Violin Sonata, of the celebrated slow movement of the Fifth Symphony. It is in three sections, the two outer ones based upon Example 116a and relatively somber in mood and dark in harmonic color, the middle section built on a large scale autogenetic unfolding of Example 116b and employing bright harmonies:

EXAMPLE 116

*Viola Quintet:* II. Themes I and II

a: Theme I

b: Theme II

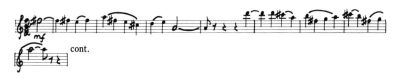

As theme II unfolds, it becomes more animated rhythmically through the gradual introduction of smaller note values and intensifies through a gradual ascent in register. However, once Harris reaches the peak of the arch he seems unclear as to how to proceed from this point, for he breaks off the climax and pads the music with several rather feeble measures of transition before beginning a descent. The descending portion of the arch, in keeping with the composer's usual procedure in working out this design, has a dark harmonic coloring.

Though the movement, particularly from the climactic portion to the end, still lacks the effortless continuity and strong sense of unity of Harris's best slow movements, it nonetheless is a considerable advance in its sure sense of direction, relative ease of unfolding, and breadth of musicodramatic scale over some of his early approaches to the arch design, such as the slow movement of *Symphony 1933.*

## Third Movement

The Scherzo features two folk tunes that Harris also employed in the orchestral interludes of the *Folksong Symphony,* written the same year as the Quintet:

EXAMPLE 117

*Viola Quintet:* III. Themes I and III

a: Theme I

b: Theme III

Theme III (a variant of "The Irish Washerwoman") is the basis of a fantastic, skirling trio that is a kind of wild apotheosis of the Irish fiddle tune. Theme I, alternating with a second, more flowing idea (Example 118), forms the principal material of the outer sections of the movement:

EXAMPLE 118

*Viola Quintet:* III. Theme II

The Scherzo maintains throughout a furtive, sotto voce character nearly unique in Harris's work and worlds removed from the down-to-earth character of the *Folksong Symphony* movements with which it shares materials.

Another unusual feature is a relatively rare appearance in Harris's music (outside of the Third Quartet) of linear polytonality, as contrasted with the chordally based sort he usually employs: when theme II returns in the highly varied recapitulation of the opening section after the trio, it is put in canon at the augmented fourth above. In addition, it remains virtually entirely in the Lydian mode in each voice. The curious juxtaposition of this rather exotic sounding melody, with its frequent emphasis in each canonic voice on the interval of the tritone, contrasts with the everyday sounds of the folk materials and contributes a further element to the rather unsettling quality of the movement.

## Fourth Movement

The finale, titled Grand Fugue, is clearly modeled after Beethoven's
*Grosse Fuge* in spirit and technique. It is a double fugue based upon the
following subjects:

EXAMPLE 119

*Viola Quintet:* IV. Subjects I and II

a: Subject I

b: Subject II

Subject I is also the motto idea of the finale of the Fifth Symphony but is
treated here as a contrapuntal subject in its own right rather than as the
head-motive of a longer idea (as in the symphony). It is really too short-
winded to make a satisfying fugue subject and, as is the case with similar
subjects of this sort, Harris seems unable to extend it to provide free
counterpoint to subsequent entrances. He thus has to content himself, for
the most part, with a series of variant forms, stretti, and augmentations
which become tiresome before long. The second subject, however, is
more promising with respect to contrapuntal working out; it just is not a
particularly distinguished melody of a sort apt to imprint itself on the
listener's mind, a vital factor in the construction of any fugue subject.

The "Grand Fugue" is a noble attempt and worth hearing. In fact, an
acquaintance with this movement is truly necessary if one wishes to
understand fully Harris's attempts to reconcile his natural inclination toward a freely unfolding form with the discipline of Baroque contrapuntal
procedure.

## Overview

The Viola Quintet reveals, possibly better than any of Harris's other
chamber works except the Piano Quintet, an apparent struggle against the
limitations in texture and sonority of the chamber medium. In his contributions in this genre one frequently senses the curious paradox of the

medium calling forth some of his noblest and most aspiring musical ideas which in turn are often at war with their surroundings and trying to break out into some larger arena. This is the source of some of the greatest strengths and some of the most troubling weaknesses in all of Roy Harris's oeuvre.

# 8

## Chamber Works, Part II
## (Works with Piano)

### The Role of the Piano in Harris's Chamber Works

Roy Harris's compositions for piano and the characteristics of his treatment of that instrument are discussed in chapter 13. It suffices here to observe that the piano figures prominently in many other areas of his oeuvre, especially the chamber works. Various factors contributed to this use, among them the bigness of some of his conceptions, the intensity of expression so often conveyed, and the effort to forge a viable harmonic style. In this latter connection, the harmonic aspect of the early compositions which do not use piano sometimes seems rather vague when generated polyphonically. However, when Harris adds the piano, the instrument is able to supply a harmonic "focus" lacking in the other, purely linear, parts.

### Treatment of the Piano in an Ensemble Role

In his chamber works, Harris wrote for the piano in much the same manner as that described for his solo works for the instrument. In compositions such as the Concerto for Piano, Clarinet, and String Quartet and the Piano Quintet, its part is fully as substantial and as demanding as those of the other instruments. In many instances, such as the scherzo of the former work and the "Cadenza" of the latter, real virtuosity is called for. In contrapuntal writing, the piano sometimes provides, as indicated above, a harmonic foundation as well as a blending factor for the diverse timbres, but it often functions as an active contrapuntal voice too.

168                                                             ROY HARRIS

Harris sometimes differentiates the treatment of his materials in the piano on the one hand and in the rest of the ensemble on the other in such a way as to create the impression of two planes of activity occurring simultaneously. The result of this is an impression of a near-orchestral sonority and complexity of texture.

## Concerto for Piano, Clarinet, and String Quartet

The Concerto is the first of Harris's major chamber works. It is also, as mentioned earlier, one of the first pieces he wrote under the tutelage of Nadia Boulanger. It was composed in 1926 in Juziers and given its premiere in Paris by Pierre Cahuzac (clarinet), the Roth Quartet, and Mme Boulanger herself as pianist.

The title Concerto alludes to both the soloist role of the clarinet (and possibly of the piano as well) and the scope of Harris's ambition in the work. There is a breadth of conception and, in the outer movements, an intensity of expression that convey a sense of aspiration, expectation, and discovery in such a way that, the flaws notwithstanding, the listener senses that he is hearing something important.

It is clear from this early chamber work that the visionary aspect was present in Harris early on, and the very immaturity of style and technique revealed here impart a special urgency to the expressive characteristics, as though the young composer were only too aware of his inability at this early stage to articulate fully his musical designs and communicate his expression to the listener.

In common with many of Harris's works of the 1920s and 30s, the Concerto manifests a conscious concern with matters of technique. One example of this is the attempt to unify the four movements of the piece by means of a recurring motive. The figure which Harris uses is the simple one of a minor second followed by a minor third. All the principal materials of the four movements are related to this. The original form generates the main themes of the first and third movements (the minor third is expanded to the brighter major third in the latter):

EXAMPLE 120

a: *Concerto for Piano, Clarinet, and String Quartet:* I. Theme (original form)

b: *Concerto for Piano, Clarinet, etc.:* III. Theme

For the second and fourth movements, the third is expanded to a fourth or a fifth and, in the case of the finale, the minor second to a major second:

EXAMPLE 121

a: *Concerto for Piano, Clarinet, etc.:* II. Theme

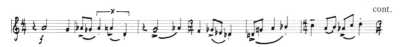

b: *Concerto for Piano, Clarinet, etc.:* IV. Theme

Here Harris seems to be equating the bright, open sounds of the wider intervals with the fast tempi and extroverted characters of the two movements in question. This is an early illustration of his technique of shaping all the elements of melody, harmony, rhythm, tempo, and scoring so as to reinforce one another in creating a distinct character.

One also finds, in addition to the cyclic characteristic of the Concerto, an early example of Harris's tendency to employ ostinati for a cumulative, climactic effect. The closing pages of the first movement show this clearly. Also present are the frequent changes of meter and the somewhat contrived rhythmic designs characteristic of a number of his early works. The second half of the finale, beginning at letter *C* in the published score, is a good example.

## First Movement

Though the four-movement design of the Concerto resembles that employed in the Classic-period sonata cycle, it nonetheless reveals a good deal of individuality in its approach to the forms and characters of the traditional components of that cycle. Thus the first movement ("Fantasia") consitutes a large written-out crescendo and gives the impression of trying out linear, rhythmic, and textural ideas that are to be explored in greater detail in the remainder of the work. The movement is built in a mosaic of several sections, each defined by a characteristic texture and a variant/expansion of the principal theme. During the course of the music, motive x is expanded until it reaches the somewhat ominous-sounding, tonally vague complex of an augmented fourth and a major second. This expansion, of course, helps create the sense of buildup in intensity which characterizes the movement. Like some of Harris's subsequent opening movements, such as the first movement of the Ninth Symphony and the "Youth" movement of the Three Symphonic Essays (and its source in the *Time Suite*), the "Fantasia" ends abruptly, as though serving as a large upbeat to the following movement.

## Second Movement

The second movement is a scherzo with changes of meter and frequent shifts of accent incorporated in a skitterish type of melody frequently favored by Harris in the fast movements of his early works (the "Speed" movement of *American Portrait* and the finale of the Piano Sonata are examples). As in a number of these compositions, the composer relies in this scherzo on highly varied repetition of a thematic idea rather than on the continuous autogenetic unfolding characteristic of his mature writing. However, so skillfully and with such plasticity does he manage this that the result comes close to suggesting his later technique. That Harris had learned something of Beethoven's device of foreshadowing events to come in a particular work is demonstrated by the chains of ascending and descending fourths which surge up and down through the ensemble in the final section of the movement, thus preparing the way, though at some remove, for the eventual eruption in the finale of the fugue subject built on this interval.

## Third Movement

The third movement is slow and lyrical. The composer is working within an essentially choralelike idiom here, but he attempts to invest the individual strands that make up his harmony with some character. This, however, is sometimes disguised by the fact that often two or more voices are moving in rhythmic unison.[1] As is the case with some other early slow movements, one can perceive here the principles of the composer's mature Gothic-arch design. He builds to his climax in the central portion of the movement by means of a succession of sections, each marked by an increasingly ostinatolike character. In common with some of the other Gothic-arch prototypes, however, the descending portion of the arch is not yet realized; rather, the middle section breaks off at its climax and is followed by a sudden change in texture, materials, and dynamics (I have already observed this in connection with compositions as late as the 1940 Viola Quintet; clearly, it took Harris a long time to work out fully the principles of his arch design.) To close the movement, Harris devises a varied recapitulation of ideas from both the opening and middle sections, a procedure that was generally uncharacteristic of his later works except for his contrapuntal finales.

This slow movement provides an excellent foil for the more dynamic outer movements by means of its nostalgic repose. It possesses an introspective quality not often associated with its composer (at least in his early years) but nonetheless very much a part of him.

## Fourth Movement

The finale is an ambitious contrapuntal study, the first in a long succession of such concluding movements (discussed in more detail in the chapters on the symphonies and in chapter 7). It is in two large parts, each fugal in procedure. The first fugue, which contains some rather extended episodes, is built on the subject cited in Example 121b; the second is based on the following radical variant of that subject:

EXAMPLE 122

*Concerto for Piano, Clarinet, etc.:* IV. Subject variant

This movement, in its presentation of the subject in variant forms, also foreshadows the variation techniques Harris was to employ in his maturity in such finales.

The movement opens with a bold introduction in the piano that appears to serve as a kind of "warming up" on the head-motive of the subject. This continues to build, with the entrance of the strings, through a series of ostinati to a broken off climax, following which the first fugue proper commences. In addition to a relatively traditional exposition, this fugue features a rather free development of various characteristics of the subject, both in episodes and as counterpoint to a final subject entrance.

The continuous sixteenth-notes in which the subject variant is disposed during the second fugue impart a greater rhythmic continuity to that section. In the final pages of the movement, Harris brings back the original form of the subject as counterpoint to materials spun out from the variant form. Though the result is somewhat contrived and awkward from a rhythmic standpoint, the earnestness of purpose and clear sighting of goal conveyed here create a noble and imposing climax. It is these final pages of the Concerto that most clearly seem to soar beyond the limitations of the chamber medium and that convey most powerfully Harris's visionary aspect.

## Overview

Though it is infiltrated with influences from other composers (e.g., the somewhat Franckian harmonic style of certain passages and the Stravinskian ostinati) and marred by flaws in technique, the Concerto still manages to sing with a distinctive voice and to carry the listener along with its youthful impulse and aggressiveness, its sense of discovery, and its conviction. It still sounds fresh and new today.

# Trio for Piano, Violin, and Violoncello

Aside from a Fantasy for woodwinds, horn, and piano composed in 1932, Harris wrote no further chamber works involving piano until 1934. The work which appeared then, the Trio for Piano, Violin, and Violoncello, is one of those compositions, like the Eleventh Symphony, that seem in some ways to stand outside the mainstream of his aesthetics. The preoccupation in the chamber work with motivic working out, development of thematic characteristics, canonic and fugal procedures, and rhythmic and metrical asymmetry was certainly not new to the composer (see especially the discussion of the somewhat earlier Concerto for String Sextet in chapter 7), but it is sometimes carried in the Trio to an extreme that renders this work one of Harris's most problematic and least accessible scores, one creating a curiously gnarled sound world that is difficult to penetrate.

## First Movement

There are three movements. The first is a driving essay characterized by rhythmic asymmetry and an austere linear texture (there are very few chords). The principal theme is based upon the interval of a third. However, the definitive form of the germ-motive seems to involve the semitone-minor third outline that is identical with the seed-motive of the Clarinet Concerto.

EXAMPLE 123
*Trio:* I. Theme

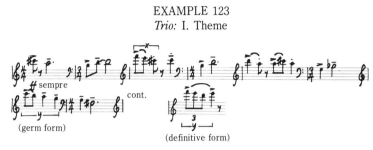

(germ form)

cont.

(definitive form)

The movement falls into a number of sections, each of which is concerned either with development of the theme itself or with treatment of one or more of its characteristics. Perhaps the most important of these characteristics after motive x is motive y, which the composer seizes on shortly after the opening of the movement to generate a kind of second theme. Harris uses both x and y as unifying devices for the entire Trio: motive x is an important component of the theme of the second movement and of the first fugue subject of the finale, while the second theme of the present movement (derived, as mentioned, from motive y) reappears as the second subject of the finale. In common with some of Harris's other early chamber works (wuch as the First Quartet), there is some varied recapitulation of whole sections in the movement.

This opening movement of the Trio is a concise, uncompromising utterance that constitutes yet another manifestation of the concern with economy of materials reflected in a number of the composer's chamber and orchestral works of this period.

## Second Movement

The second movement is meditative in character. It is based upon the same sinuous, elusive theme containing chromatic inflections on several scale degrees that Harris had used in the slow movement of the Second Symphony (completed the same year as the chamber work, see Example 2). The phrases of the initial statement of this theme are punctuated and answered by isolated phrases of a countermelody, and characteristics of both ideas are developed during the course of the three parts of the movement:

EXAMPLE 124
*Trio:* II. Countermelody

cont.

Section one comprises two complete statements of the theme, first in violin, then in piano, along with statement and development of the countermelody. Section two features a further development of the countermelody, harmonized in fourths and sixths, followed by a development of fragments of both themes. In common with some of Harris's other slow movements of the period, an incipient arch design is present here, but again the climax is broken off and followed by a contrasting section rather than by the descending portion of the arch. The final section is based on canonic treatment of the main theme. As though to balance this added complexity in the treatment of the principal idea, Harris virtually eliminates the countermelody here, providing only a whiff of a reminiscence in a benedictory chordal cadence in the closing measures.

Throughout the movement the tonality is frequently vague, though the composer does at times provide some orientation through the use of sustained or reiterated bass notes that create the effect of a succession of pedal points. The harmonic texture is still relatively sparse.

## Third Movement

The finale is a double fugue, the two subjects of which are:

EXAMPLE 125

a: *Trio:* III. Subject I

b: *Trio:* III. Subject II

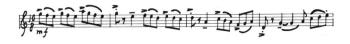

The first subject is given a stately exposition, first in the piano alone, then with each of the strings entering in turn. This noble passage, though still relatively lean in harmonic texture, nonetheless suggests a warmer, more diatonic aspect than we have heard thus far in the Trio. This is a characteristic extract:

EXAMPLE 126

*Trio:* III. Harmonic texture

The lengthy exposition builds to a broad climax that is broken off suddenly to make way for the second subject, which charges in vigorously, quite oblivious to what has preceded it. This idea is worked out at some length, then is gradually infiltrated by the first subject, which succeeds in taking command in the final pages of the movement. This is first accomplished in a broad statement in the piano, which eventually manages to pull the strings, with their somewhat frantic working-out of subject II, along with it; then in a series of stretti; finally in a broad, harmonized statement that concludes the work. Actually the two subjects of the movement do not mesh well either rhythmically or harmonically (this is most noticeable in the somewhat strained working-out of both beginning in measure 78), and the fugue as a whole reveals that the composer did not fully understand the principles of subject construction for a successful double fugue, a fault I have cited elsewhere.

## Overview

Though Harris was not particularly fond of the Trio, the work is still worth knowing, both for the genuine rewards it provides in its best moments and for a revealing glimpse of a path not followed.

# Quintet for Piano and Strings

The Quintet, one of the most monumental of all Harris's chamber compositions, was, as mentioned earlier, the immediate fruit of his marriage in 1936 to Beula Duffey (Johana) and was the first of his works written specifically with her pianistic gifts in mind.

The work is in three interlinked movements in which techniques of variation and motivic development and such procedures as canon and fugue, which Harris had explored in earlier compositions, are refined and managed with a sureness of hand and a firmness of goal that render the work one of the most accomplished efforts of the composer's early maturity. Some of the ideas underlying the composition of the Quintet were expressed by him in a 1964 note for the first long-playing recording of the work:

> The Piano Quintet was written as a conviction and prediction concerning the twelve-tone technique. At that time I was convinced, . . . that the dodecaphonic restriction of no repeated notes in a twelve-tone row was the weak link in this school of thought.
>
> Guided by these convictions, I planned my Piano Quintet as a polytonal technique, using twelve-tone melodic materals in such a way as to emphasize tonality rather than as an atonal technique to destroy tonality. . . .
>
> I cast my Piano Quintet in three traditional variation forms: Passacaglia—Cadenza—Fugue, and fashioned all the themes into twelve-tone polytonal rows. In the Fugue (a triple fugue) the first subject is presented as an eleven-tone subject in which I purposely omitted the augmented fourth or diminished fifth (*musica diabolus* [sic] of the ancients, but a supreme entity of the Viennese School) until the last section in which it is used as a structural accent.[2]

One of the most impressive aspects of the Quintet is the manner in which Harris manages to maintain a continuously ascending curve of intensity from the opening measures through to the powerful final climax. This is also characteristic of the Third Symphony, which came along two years later, and is an important factor in making these works so widely admired.

One element that contributes to this intensity curve is Harris's skillful handling of the successive climaxes of the three movements. Each of these is structured in such a way as to contribute to a macrostructure in which the first two climaxes are heard as preparations for the final one. Thus, the climax of the Passacaglia, though employing the full ensemble, nonetheless avoids an air of finality because of its disintegration of the principal theme into a reiterated motive whose development is broken off suddenly. The climax of the Cadenza is marked by the use of the piano alone; by a fantasialike treatment in which, toward the end, the theme is so broadened out as to be almost unrecognizable; and by an up-in-the-air concluding flourish. The climax of the Fugue, on the other hand, presents a bold and clear crowning statement of the principal subject in rhythmically broadened-out fashion in the full ensemble spanning more than a five-octave range, all over a set of dominant-tonic pedal points.

## Passacaglia

The Passacaglia is built on a theme (one hesitates to label such a fabric of long-breathed phrases a subject of the traditional passacaglia type) that provides an excellent example of Harris's autogenetic technique. It consists of four pairs of antecedent-consequent phrases, of which the last three are increasingly free variants of the first, the entire organism growing out of the oscillating motive heard in the opening measures:

EXAMPLE 127

*Quintet for Piano and Strings:* Theme

It is fundamentally identical in construction and overall shape with the passacaglia theme of the Seventh Symphony; in fact, the seed-motive of that later work can be perceived as a kind of intervallic expansion of the generating motive here.

The Passacaglia falls into two large sections, the first consisting of the initial statement of the theme and three variations, the second of another, more complex, set of three variations launched by a florid variant of the theme in triplet eighth-notes in the piano whose free continuation then serves as counterpoint to a four-voice canon in the strings.

The first statement of the theme is given to the strings in an imaginatively conceived texture making use of various groupings of instruments, octave doublings, and outlining of important figures with pizzicati. The piano then answers with a harmonized first variation featuring organum sonorities building to fuller chordal complexes at the apex of the line. The variations from this point on are marked by persistent canonic writing ranging from a two-voice example in which the strings are imitated by a rhythmically skeletonized, harmonized version of the theme in the piano to the four-voice close canon alluded to above. Harris also increases the rhythmic momentum through the gradual introduction of smaller note values. The intensity builds throughout the Passacaglia until the music fairly bursts the seams of the chamber medium with a fortissimo climax featuring widely spaced sonorities in the piano and frantic reiterations of the seed-motive in feverishly passionate octaves in the strings.

## Cadenza

The Cadenza that follows affords each of the instruments in turn an opportunity to explore, in virtuosic terms, various melodic, rhythmic, and emotional characteristics of the passacaglia theme, the entire ensemble ultimately coming together in a group cadenza based on a highly ornamented version of the subject (in the piano) built on octave displacement of its individual notes.

The piano cadenza that ends this middle movement of the Quintet is one of Harris's most impressive and sonorous displays of virtuoso writing for the instrument and forms perhaps the crown of the entire work. Here the composer is indebted at times to the example set by J. S. Bach in his Chaconne from the Partita No. 2 in d minor for solo violin, via the Busoni arrangement for piano (which Johana knew and played).

## Fugue

The first subject of the Fugue appears to be a short and very free paraphrase of the basic intervals and general outline of the passacaglia theme:

EXAMPLE 128

*Quintet for Piano and Strings:* III. Subject I

Harris carries this initial idea through a variety of ingeniously worked out contrapuntal textures, with passages of exposition alternating with episodes whose materials are also derived from the subject (a characteristic procedure with Harris). The composer's description of the harmonic plans of this and the succeeding fugues is worth quoting here as an illustration of his tendency to design a given section of a work in terms of specific characteristics of one or more elements of music:

> . . . The first section was conceived in organum textures. . . . The second section was conceived in fauxbourdon textures [parallel triads]. . . . The third section combines both faux-bourdon and organum textures. . . ."[3]

The giguelike subject of the second fugue is preceded, then accompanied on some of its statements, by a countersubject formed from a rhythmic variant of subject I:

EXAMPLE 129

*Quintet for Piano and Strings:* III. Subject II and countersubject

a: Subject II

b: Countersubject

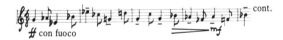

The working-out of this subject is subsequently joined by the exposition of the third subject, a somewhat cryptic idea disposed in three-and four-note phrases, chiefly in sustained, even-note values. (This idea was later used in the finale of the Fifth Symphony; see Example 46b.)

The infiltration of sixteenth-notes into one of the eighth-note components of subject II gradually grows into a pervasive characteristic that explodes in full fury in the next portion of the movement. This section contains three further statements of subject I (with the added twelfth-tone referred to in Harris's note cited earlier), the sixteenths finally sweeping the subject up in the strings. The tag-end of subject I is also developed in dancing organum intervals in the piano. This white-hot *perpetuum mobile* finally broadens out into a large-scale combination of subjects I and III that climaxes in the final statement of subject I. These last pages of the Quintet

galvanize into what is probably the most overwhelming conclusion in all of
Roy Harris's chamber oeuvre.

## Overview

One might have reservations about the contrapuntal writing in the Quintet
as a whole and the Fugue in particular. In addition to a sometimes contrived
rhythmic complexity (especially in the latter part of the Fugue), there is a
tendency to carry sequential designs on for too long. One may also find
aspects of the harmonic writing, the "sound," that seem uncharacteristic of
the mature Harris. Though he is clearly thinking in more harmonic terms
here, there are times when the vertical sonorities produced by the interweaving lines seem to coexist uneasily with his emerging harmonic idiom
based on the major and minor triad. (Some, however, may, with justification, prefer this tension to what they perceive as the somewhat blander
and more subtle effect of the mature style.)

However, the bigness of conception and boldness of gesture wedded to
the rich and powerful sonority of the piano quintet medium seem to have
ensured a freshness and viability for the piece that override its occasional
flaws. Though the Quintet is an abstract composition, it comes closer to
revealing the essentials of the Harris personality than do most of his
overtly Americanist utterances, and the striking character and power of
this personality is, indeed, another clue to the vitality and durability of this
landmark work in his development.

## *Childhood Memories of Ocean Moods*

Following the Quintet, it was to be thirty years before Harris wrote
another purely instrumental ensemble chamber work with piano (outside
of one or two pieces in the ballet and film genres). This gap was symptoma-
tic of the slackening of his writing in the chamber medium that began during
the late 1930s. *Childhood Memories of Ocean Moods,* which appeared in
1966, is the last of his compositions in the medium. It was a response to a
commission from the Laguna Arts Association of Laguna Beach, California, and this circumstance resulted in the work being the only one of his
large chamber compositions to possess an extramusical program (again,
the ballets for Hanya Holm and the one film score constitute a qualified
exception to this statement).

During his youth in southern California, Harris and his family spent a
number of vacations in the Laguna area. The impressions of the changing
moods of the sea that the composer gathered during these early years

were still potent over half a century later, if *Childhood Memories* is any indication. However, the work must also be looked upon as a tribute to Debussy, whom Harris admired perhaps more than any other twentieth-century composer. Indeed, *Childhood Memories* is a kind of latter day *La Mer*. Certainly the program is nearly identical with that of the orchestral masterwork—a depiction of the sea from dawn to dusk—and, though the sound and technique are quite different in the two works, the listener is left at the end of each with the impression of a composition that far transcends its mere descriptive characteristics.

## Form

*Childhood Memories* also differs from the earlier chamber works in its disposition in a single movement (a feature of a number of the symphonies that had been curiously absent from Harris's chamber oeuvre until now) and in the addition of a string bass to the string quartet/piano ensemble, this instrument adding weight and depth in various passages.

The work is in a large ternary form with a slow-fast-slow tempo scheme. It employs a Gothic arch design, though in this instance the arch is a somewhat lopsided one, with the bulk of the composition devoted to a continual buildup of rhythmic activity and an increase of tension. This buildup is then followed by a relatively brief final section comprising the right-hand pillar of the arch.

## Overview

*Childhood Memories of Ocean Moods* is a flawed piece. The tendency to overextend a particular idea is far too prevalent during much of the middle section, and the linear aspect, in common with much of Harris's melodic writing during his later years, is abstract and elusive. In fact, there is little real melody in the work at all; rather, the composer seems to be weaving a fabric of constantly changing patterns of shape and color, in which the individual threads are difficult to perceive except on close inspection. The piece perhaps lacks, overall, the depth of imagination and technical security of the Debussy masterpiece. Yet, in a few passages such as the final section, it is no less probing or moving.

Roy Harris's last chamber composition, though perhaps programmatically naive (as in *La Mer,* in fact)—after all, the cycle of ocean tides does not follow a tidy dawn-to-dusk pattern—is nonetheless an evocative composition, and its recollection and distillation of events far in the composer's past give the impression of a summing up. It seems an entirely sincere, and at times eloquent, tribute to the southern California in which he grew up.

Though the coastal area had changed vastly since his early years, the constancy of the sea itself must have seemed something of an antidote to the double discouragement Harris suffered during much of his last two decades from the relative neglect of his music and from the fundamental changes in a society that had seemed such a simple, unified, and congenial organism to him in the past.

# 9

# Other Works for Orchestra

## General Characteristics

In addition to an impressive roster of symphonies, the bulk of which are purely orchestral, Harris also produced a generous literature of other works in the medium. These span a period of some forty years, from the Andante of 1925 to the *Salute to Youth* of 1964, and comprise a variety of types and formats.

### The Programmatic Element

Most of these pieces have an extramusical association and could thus be regarded as belonging to the symphonic poem and concert overture genres. The programs on which Harris based them are quite varied, from the literally descriptive to the symbolic. The compositions themselves reveal a considerable range in size, complexity, and expressive characteristics. Virtually all were commissioned and most were designed to have some specific connection with the circumstances that prompted the commissions (e.g., an anniversary, a patriotic occasion, the performance capabilities of a youth orchestra).

Harris almost invariably associated certain formats, musical characters, and compositional procedures with specific types of program. For example, he usually employed fugue as a musical analogue of the concept of work or building, or of action in a general sense. Thus, the second movement, "Free to Build," of *American Creed* is a triple fugue and the composition *Work* is an elaborate fugal/variations structure. He also sometimes adopted a two-movement design for the purpose of contrasting a relatively static mood with a dynamic one. This often takes the specific programmatic form of a "dream world" (e.g., the "Free to Dream" movement of *American Creed*) versus an "action world" (e.g., the "Free to Build" movement). Occasionally, however, Harris employed this design in an abstract, non-programmatic context in the prelude and fugue format (e.g., the Prelude and Fugue for Strings).

In addition to these recurring formats and procedures, Harris developed specific responses to unique situations. For example, the *Ode to Truth*, written to celebrate the fiftieth anniversary of the founding of Stanford University in California, is built largely on canonic procedure, which is used as a musical analogue for the idea of learning.[1] In the *Ode to Consonance*, written during the mid-1950s, the composer seems to be engaging in a kind of self-portraiture, since the work explores in thoroughgoing fashion the possibilities of his mature polytonal harmonic style. The *Symphonic Epigram*, written for the twenty-fifth anniversary of the CBS network broadcasts of the New York Philharmonic Orchestra, employs alternating measures in 2/2 and 5/4 meters, whose "numerators" outline the number 25, plus representation in musical terminology of the initials CBS (C–B–Eb [Es]) and DM (Dimitri Mitropolous: D=dominant of C major/minor, E=mediant of C major). Obviously, all these devices are purely symbolic, for Harris's musical analogues have no inherent connection with the objects they are meant to represent (except possibly for the abovementioned use of canon in connection with learning, which has a historical precedent). But they are clever, sometimes resulting in a strong formal cohesion and sense of economy, and they are always placed at the disposal of genuinely musical aims.

# Forms

The majority of the orchestral works of the type considered here are in a single movement, ranging in length from about forty-five seconds (the *Fanfare for the Forces*) to over seventeen minutes (the *Cumberland Concerto for Orchestra*). As indicated above, however, there are some multimovement compositions, the favored format being two movements. There are also suitelike works in three movements (Three Symphonic Essays, *Memories of a Child's Sunday*) and one in six (*Time Suite* [the source for the Three Essays]).

## Ternary Form Types

Virtually all the forms Harris employs in the individual movements of his symphonies are represented in these other orchestral works as well.

There are straightforward ternary forms, most often ABC (*Kentucky Spring, Salute to Youth*), though on rare occasions an ABA (*When Johnny Comes Marching Home,* revised version) can be found. For most of the pieces in three-part form, Harris adopts a fast-slow-fast overall tempo scheme.

## Binary Form Types

An especially good example of the use of a binary form among these compositions is the *Ode to Friendship*. Here the opening section is created from the spinning-out in the strings of a typical Harris long line. In the second section, the strings animate rhythmically to provide ornamental counterpoint to a continuation of the linear unfolding in the brass. The two sections of this short work are clearly marked off by a change of meter and by a reversal of the roles of the orchestral choirs in the unfolding of the melodic continuity.

## Through-Composed Types

There are a number of works in what appears to be a continuously evolving form of several sections. Though sometimes an explicit unifying device is present (as in *Farewell to Pioneers* and *The Quest,* with their use of the passacaglia principle), in general the sections in these works tend to create a sense of formal cohesion by grouping into larger units, each unit containing specific features that mark it off from the others. Most often this results in another example of a two-part design, an excellent illustration of which is "Free to Dream" from *American Creed,* the first half of which, in three sections, is an evocative fantasia of an essentially meditative nature and a rather loose-limbed rhythmic aspect, the second half of which is assertive and dynamic in character and more straightforward rhythmically.

## Variation Types

Harris also, as implied above, makes use of the variations procedure in some of these works. The passacaglia examples have already been mentioned; of the type of composition in which a melodic theme is varied (as opposed to a recurring bass-line or harmonic progression), *When Johnny Comes Marching Home* is perhaps the clearest illustration.

As is the case with most of Harris's other works built in several relatively short sections, the individual variations in his compositions employing this technique can generally be grouped into larger units. For example, both *Johnny* and the *Celebration Variations* reveal clearcut ternary designs.

Other works employ the variations procedure for part of their duration.

Among them is *Kentucky Spring,* whose final section is a set of variations on a tune that Harris borrowed several times for later compositions (a version of which is found in Example 63).

## Instrumentation and Characteristics of Scoring

The miscellaneous orchestral works vary widely in the sizes of their orchestral apparati. Some, such as the *Cumberland Concerto* and the *Celebration Variations,* employ as large and elaborate an instrumentation as Harris ever used. Others, such as the Andantino and *Mirage,* use a very small orchestra of single or double woodwinds, one or two horns, strings, and, occasionally, piano. There are also compositions using a somewhat larger, though still chamber-size, ensemble. A characteristic example is *These Times,* which is scored for one of each woodwind instrument (plus most of the auxiliaries); a pair of horns; one each of trumpet, trombone, baritone, and tuba; percussion; strings; and a *concertante* piano part.

In fulfilling the commissions for these works, Harris had to be very adaptable with respect to the requirements for the instrumentation. Though there were occasions (such as the writing of the *Celebration Variations* and the *Cumberland Concerto*) on which he could indulge himself in the luxury of the resources of a large and virtuosic symphony orchestra, there were others (*Mirage* and *These Times*) when he had to draw upon considerable resourcefulness in working with a relatively limited instrumentation. Perhaps even more than the symphonies, these compositions were the genre through which Harris developed the style of orchestration "indigenous to the line and form" which I have quoted earlier as his avowed aim during the early 1930s.

## Musical Characters

Harris also had an opportunity to explore in these orchestral pieces, a wide variety of musical characters. All the aspects of his musical personality are represented in the genre: the visionary aspect (*American Creed, Ode to Truth*); the boisterous and rawboned character (*Folk Rhythms of Today, Salute to Youth*); the cerebral aspect (*Work, Symphonic Epigram*); the intimate and lyrical quality (*Memories of a Child's Sunday, Evening Piece*); the savage, intense character (*March in Time of War*); the pastoral, pantheistic quality (*Kentucky Spring*); and the poignant, elegiac aspect (*Epilogue to Profiles in Courage, Farewell to Pioneers*).

# Quality

The quality of these compositions naturally varies. Some, such as the brief *Fanfare for the Forces,* were undoubtedly composed in short order, and it is doubtful if Harris attached much importance to them (though they are effective enough in view of the composer's evidently modest aims in creating them).[2] Other works, such as *American Creed,* the *Cumberland Concerto,* the Prelude and Fugue for Strings, and *Kentucky Spring,* apparently engaged his attention more seriously, for they emerged as achievements of real substance, emotional depth, and sophistication. As was so often the case, the quality depended upon a number of factors: how many other projects were claiming the composer's attention at the time, the importance he attached to the commissions, and, of course, the pressure under which his creative juices were flowing. If the commission represented a congenial set of requirements, if it posed a new challenge, or if the occasion touched a responsive nerve, Harris would enter into the work with the same enthusiasm and intensity he would lavish on one of his symphonies.[3]

# Self-Borrowing

Harris's proclivity toward self-borrowing is especially evident in these works, and they thus provide excellent source material for the study of his compositional process. As illustrations of this borrowing, one might cite the Three Symphonic Essays, which are a selection, with some revision, of three of the movements of the *Time Suite;* the finale, "Free to Build," of *American Creed,* which is a reworking of the second half of the choral/ orchestral *Challenge 1940;* and *Horn of Plenty,* which contains a generous amount of material appropriated from the Symphonic Fantasy of ten years earlier.

In connection with this situation, one feature several of the orchestral works have in common is a kind of "satellite" relationship with some of the symphonies, by virtue of either shared materials or similarities in style and/or format. Thus, the Concert Piece of 1931 and the *Overture from the Gayety and Sadness of the American Scene* of the following year were both assembled largely of materials from the *American Portrait.* A reverse situation is that concerning *Work, Acceleration,* and *Ode to Truth,* all of which contributed materials to a symphony, the Fifth.

## Overview

However one may feel about both the variation in quality and the self-borrowing (features Harris shares with one of his celebrated colleagues, Charles Ives), one cannot deny that there is hardly a single work in this genre that is not almost instantly identifiable as springing from Roy Harris's fertile and commanding musical personality. Though a few of these pieces are modest in intent and slight in substance, it is hardly fair to characterize the better examples as mere chips from the workbench. The magnitude of Harris's achievement cannot be measured solely by the large and richly appointed rooms his symphonies and chamber compositions occupy. These shorter orchestral works constitute a literature of their own and, as such, make up an important part of the spacious Harris estate.

It is clear that the composer took to heart the suggestion Serge Koussevitzky made to him during the mid-1930s that, in addition to writing great symphonies, American composers should also provide orchestras with shorter compositions that while still giving music of substance and distinction, would, in their relative brevity, have the advantage of being able to fit into a wider variety of programming situations. For all that Harris occasionally fell short of his best in these works, the finest of them amply fulfill Koussevitzky's requirements.

# 10

# Works for Band

## A Stepchild Becomes Respectable

The recognition of the wind medium as a vehicle for music of symphonic character has come about slowly. Composers early on may have been inhibited by the relative lack of a standardized instrumentation, by the cumbersome nature of some of the ancient instruments which subsequently fell by the wayside, and by the association of the medium with music of a popular, out-of-doors character and an occasional function. The symphony orchestra, with its core of flexible string instruments, seemed to offer greater potential for a wide variety of timbres and a broad range of expression. In fact, even the modern symphonic band, with all its considerably improved resources, is still a problematic medium for the inexperienced composer in such matters as balance (with the sonic weight concentrated in the midrange) and sustaining capabilities (with the breathing considerations inherent in the winds).[1]

It was not until the early twentieth century that the large aggregation of wind instruments known as the band began to come into its own with a literature of substance and sophistication to supplement the marches and operatic transcriptions that had been its standard fare up to that time. Both the British and the French made important early contributions to this literature with such works as the two Suites of Gustav Holst, the *English Folksong Suite* and the *Toccata Marziale* of Ralph Vaughan Williams, *Dionysiaques* of Florent Schmitt, and the *Chant funéraire* of Gabriel Fauré.

In the United States, composers and audiences were slower to respond. This country had produced a popular literature of some distinction (of which the marches of John Philip Sousa are perhaps the crowning glory),

but it was not until the mid-1930s that a real body of music by American
composers for "symphonic band" began to develop.

## Harris Enters the Scene

Roy Harris was a leader in creating this literature. His first work for the
medium, *Cimarron* (1941), was one of the first compositions of its type by
any major American symphonic composer. Harris had always been receptive to the possibilities offered by a variety of media, especially when these
were revealed to him in circumstances of exceptional excellence in performance. One can therefore imagine the potent influence the ambience
surrounding the premiere of *Cimarron*—a festival involving some of the
finest college bands from three states—had on the composer. Immersed in
wind sonorities within a concentrated period of time and given the opportunity to hear his own maiden effort in the medium, he doubtless sensed
the congeniality of the band toward the more extrovert aspects of his
musical personality.

Almost immediately after this event, the composer began his initial, and
most active, period of writing for band, a period marked by infusions of
fresh stimulation from the Second Army Air Force and Fort Logan bands,
with which he came in close contact during his residence in Colorado
Springs during the 1940s.

## General Characteristics

Some of the works are entirely original (given, of course, Harris's predilection for self-borrowing), and thus conceived directly in terms of the wind
medium. A few are based on some earlier orchestral pieces (e.g., *Conflict,*
an arrangement of the second movement of the Sixth Symphony; *When
Johnny Comes Marching Home,* a recomposition of portions of the orchestral overture of the same title, along with new materials).

Virtually all the band works have titles with extramusical associations.
Even the one example with an abstract title, the Symphony for Band,
contains programmatic elements. Some of the pieces, such as *Conflict,
Comarron,* and the Symphony, have Americanist backgrounds. Others are
pantheistic in nature *(The Sun from Dawn to Dusk).* Some convey their
extramusical associations through specific musical devices (such as the
rhythms of popular character in *Rhythms of Today*). Others, like *Ad
Majorem Gloriam,* accomplish this through a more generalized means lying
closer to purely abstract expression.

# Formal Characteristics

In their principles of formal construction, Harris's band works do not differ in any substantial way from his short orchestral compositions or from the individual movements of the multimovement symphonies. All but the late (and withdrawn) *Bicentennial Aspirations* are nominally in a single movement, though the larger ones, such as the Symphony and *Ad Majorem Gloriam,* comprise sections of substantial enough length perhaps to qualify them as individual "movements" interconnected within larger single movement designs.

## Early Works

Some of the early band compositions, such as *When Johnny Comes Marching Home, Sun and Stars,* and *Rhythms of Today,* are relatively short essays in ternary form, either ABA or ABC. Most often these designs are combined with variation techniques. The three sections of *Johnny,* for example, constitute a sort of "variations continuum" on the borrowed melody, but are set off from one another by contrasts in tempo, dynamics, and harmonic coloration. The tempo scheme of all the works in ternary form is fast-slow-fast, and the variations of the final section (in the pieces which employ this technique) give the impression of resuming the activity and general style of those of the first section.

In addition to the compositions in three-part form from this period, there are others that employ different formal designs. *Cimarron* is one of these. Each of its six well-defined sections is built on one or two ideas developed in a clear-cut manner. Other works of this type are *Conflict* (a large binary form comprising a slow and a fast march for the two sections respectively) and *The Sun from Dawn to Dusk* (a brief tone poem built in the Gothic-arch design). These works, however, are somewhat more subtle and less direct in their appeal than the pieces of a more popular character discussed above. They are often in the nature of tone poems that evoke, among other things, highly charged states of the human condition (as in *Conflict,* with its graphic depiction of the physical and psychological aspects of war) and pantheism (as in *Dawn to Dusk,* with its almost literal description of the progress of the sun through the sky).

## Transitional Works

As Harris's style matured during the late 1940s and the 1950s, he appeared to move away, in his band writing, from the type of composition represented by his earlier efforts in the medium. This resulted in another, smaller, category of works, represented by compositions such as *Dark Devotion* and *Fruit of Gold*. Though possessing, like their predecessors, extramusical characteristics, these pieces nonetheless seem equally concerned with abstract principles of musical growth.

A comparison of *Fruit of Gold* of 1949 with *Cimarron* of eight years earlier provides an illustration of Harris's development in the above respect. Both works are programmatic and unfold through a succession of relatively short sections, each of which contains one or more elements developed in its successor. Of the two, *Cimarron* follows most closely the Gothic-arch design, though the descending portion of its curve is realized not so much through the means of melodic continuity as through the increasing textural simplicity and gradual relaxation in dynamics provided by the two statements of the march theme that comprise the final two sections of the work. *Fruit of Gold* opens much like *Cimarron* and, in similar fashion, builds gradually to a climax, though, unlike the earlier work, it continues this process throughout its duration to a high point that takes place only at the end of the piece. Formally, the two works differ chiefly in the shapes of their musicodramatic curves, rather than in fundamental principles.

In *Fruit of Gold,* though, Harris seems more concerned than he was in *Cimarron* with the actual detailed working-out of his materials. There is an added element of calculation lacking in the 1941 piece. In addition, the textures of some of the more active sections of *Fruit of Gold* are comparatively more complex, with more simultaneous levels of development occurring. At times, these textures may seem contrived and mechanical, and consequently less spontaneous than in *Cimarron*. The lengthy passages beginning at five measures after (9) and two measures before (18) illustrate this:

EXAMPLE 130

*Fruit of Gold:* Development textures

In *Cimarron,* where this working-out of designs possesses a strong pictorial association (as in the woodwind stretti and brass dovetailing in the section illustrating the gallop for land), it is in less danger of calling attention to itself than in a work such as *Fruit of Gold,* where the associative element is perhaps less explicit and the listener must focus chiefly upon the musical devices per se.

A work such as *Fruit of Gold,* nonetheless, did help the composer to further refine his technique of form building and to deepen his insight into the band medium. It thus paved the way for the richness and technical mastery exhibited in the two major works that followed in the 1950s.

## The Big Works of the 1950s

The two compositions just alluded to, Symphony for Band ("West Point") and *Ad Majorem Gloriam Universitatis Illinorum,* are large-scale essays (of eighteen and fifteen minutes' duration respectively) employing an exceptionally large instrumentation. They also feature the rich, predominantly polychordal harmonic idiom and the complex, at times lush, textures that characterize Harris's style during the 1950s. Both works appear to be among the relatively few band compositions he wrote out in full score (in contrast with the quasicondensed score format he employed for many of the earlier pieces), and this fact provides visual evidence of the concern for detailed working-out of complex textures and for sonority that helps set them apart from their predecessors.

### Formal Characteristics

The Symphony and *Ad Majorem* were conceived in terms of both a large macrostructure and large microstructural components. As implied earlier,

the former work can be regarded from one standpoint as exhibiting the
multimovement form of the standard symphony compressed within a
single movement. *Ad Majorem* comprises two large sections (or interlinked movements), the second of which is a large variations structure with
elements of rondo. Actually, there are no new developments either in the
invention of materials or in the handling of form in these works. What
Harris achieves here instead is an added sophistication, subtlety, and
complexity both in the initial statement of materials and in their subsequent
development.[2] He unfolds his melodic ideas through a variety of timbres in
such a way that the concept of sonority seems on an almost equal footing
with that of the materials themselves.[3]

One also finds, in the Symphony, an attempt at large-scale unification of
the various sections of a work through the device of generating many of the
themes from the same germ-idea. Thus, the triad-outline of the fanfare
that opens the work gives rise to materials as diverse as these:

EXAMPLE 131

*Symphony for Band:* Themes based on triad outline

Along with this occasional unity of thematic materials, one finds the
organic evolution of one section from another. In the Symphony, this is
carried a step further through an especially clear application of the "layering technique." The most extended example of this occurs in the slow
"movement" of the piece; each succeeding section of this portion of the

Symphony is erected, as it were, on the scaffolding provided by its predecessor, thus providing not only a continuing linear expansion and rhythmic propulsion in the horizontal aspect, but also an increase in the textural density and pitch range in the vertical aspect of the composition.

## Jazz and Popular Elements

Harris's band compositions are especially useful in assessing certain influences on his style. One of these is the folk element (as found in *When Johnny Comes Marching Home* and in the slow section of the Symphony for Band, where Harris devises for the baritone horn a theme that seems to be a clear paraphrase of "He's Gone Away"). Another is the combined influence of jazz and popular music (particularly dance music). The popular influence is, indeed, probably best approached through Harris's works for the wind medium, for it first seemed to manifest itself clearly in this area. The idiom is certainly felt in the shifting accents of Example 132a and in the slow, "bluesy" swing of Example 132b:

EXAMPLE 132

*Rhythms of Today:* Jazz elements

a: Opening section

b: Middle section

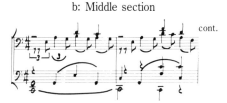

As far as jazz is concerned, Harris appeared to appropriate from it an assortment of various rhythmic, melodic, and instrumental ideas characteristic of a relatively popular, commerical type of "big-band" jazz:[4]

EXAMPLE 133

Jazz elements

a: *Rhythms of Today*

b: *Symphony for Band*

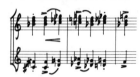

c: *Ad Majorem Gloriam*

# Conception of the Medium

One of the most recognizable contributions Harris's work in the wind medium made to his artistic growth was in allowing him to focus on the idiomatic capabilities of the brass and woodwind instruments, thus adding to the reservoir of figurations and distinctive timbral combinations he had begun to build in his orchestral works of the 1930s. In the woodwind scoring, for example, one finds figures such as the arpeggio ideas in Example 134a; for the brass there are fanfare-motives, as in Example 134b:

EXAMPLE 134

Characteristic instrumental figures

a: *Ad Majorem Gloriam*

b: *Symphony for Band*

In an alliance of harmonic color with instrumental timbre, one finds the use of polychords in close position in trumpets and trombones and harmonies in low woodwinds also becoming an important feature of Harris's style:

EXAMPLE 135

Characteristic treatments of instrumental choirs

a: *Symphony for Band*

b: *Ad Majorem Gloriam*

As a result of his experience in writing for band, Harris, during the 1940s, began to envision something of a modification of the symphony orchestra. This seemed to involve chiefly an expansion of the woodwind section. The concept was never carried out fully, but one does find elements of it in orchestral works such as the Fifth and Sixth symphonies and the *Ode to Friendship,* in the 1944 Concerto for Piano and Orchestra, and in the choral-orchestral *Blow the Man Down*. It is even more pronounced in the instrumentation of one of his last works, the *Bicentennial Symphony*. Each of these compositions has additional winds, an enlargement accomplished variously through the addition of one or more saxophones, the addition of cornets, and the division of the clarinets into sections (as in band instrumentation).[5]

# Characteristics of Instrumentation

The instrumentation of Harris's band compositions varies considerably in variety and size from work to work. Virtually all the pieces employ the standard woodwinds (flute, oboe, clarinet [often in four sections], and bassoon) and at least some of their auxiliaries (chiefly piccolo, English horn, and E-flat and bass clarinets). There are usually one or two each of the alto and tenor saxophones and one baritone saxophone. In the brass, the cornets and either the baritone horn or the euphonium are regular fixtures along with the trumpets and trombones. In his designation of the members of the tuba family, Harris is sometimes unclear. These are occasionally simply given the identification "basses" (although they are distinguished from the string bass, which is also used and written on a separate staff).

# Quality

Roy Harris's band oeuvre shows the same wide variation in quality one encounters in his short orchestral works. Obviously some of the slighter items, such as *Rhythms of Today* and *Sun and Stars,* were dashed off hurriedly and meant as occasional pieces. On the evidence of the somewhat dishevelled state in which the materials for some of the pieces have survived, it is doubtful the composer attached much importance to them. In such works, one is more likely than usual to find faults to which Harris was prone when working rapidly but at less than optimum heat. One of the most prominent of these is a tendency to become bogged down in repetitive designs. There is also, ironically, a related tendency here for the composer's idiomatic motivic ideas and figurations to become cliches through mechanical usage.

However, the larger works, such as the Symphony for Band, are important contributions to a sometimes maligned medium and stand up well today. They possess sufficient distinction in materials and sophistication in form to repay repeated hearings with rich rewards.

# An Indigenous Music for an American Institution

However precarious its balance of strengths and weaknesses may be, Harris's accomplishment in the wind medium constitutes another manifestation of his attempt to create an indigenous American music for a mode of performance which, though not American in origin, had nonetheless taken on in its characteristics of scoring and of literature a distinctive quality to which his nationalist sentiments could respond with genuine conviction. It also provided him with a means by which he could enrich his technique through the demanding discipline and insight required to produce a literature of substance for performers of widely varying abilities (a large percentage amateurs).

# 11

# Concertos and Related Works

## Origins and Types

It was inevitable as Roy Harris's growing reputation during the 1930s propelled him into the vanguard of American symphonic composers that, in addition to receiving an increasing number of commissions from symphonic organizations, he would attract the attention of performers looking for new vehicles to play with orchestras and on solo recitals.

The first of these was Jascha Heifetz, who commissioned a violin concerto on which the composer worked during 1937. Though the work was completed and partially scored, Harris withdrew it for reasons that are not clear. Nonetheless, he thought enough of some of the materials to incorporate them the following year in a composition that, ironically, was to provide perhaps the greatest success he was to enjoy during his career, the Third Symphony.

In the years that followed, Harris was to fulfill commissions from such diverse performers as William Primrose (*Soliloquy and Dance* for viola and piano and *Elegy and Paean* for viola and orchestra), E. Power Biggs (Chorale and Toccata for organ and brass), Andy Rizzo (Theme and Variations for Solo Accordion and Orchestra), Claire Coci (Fantasy for Organ, Brass, and Timpani), and Janos Starker (Sonata for Violoncello and Piano). However, at least an equal number of his concerted works was written for Johana. These comprise a rich assortment of compositions for piano and orchestra and piano and band, among them nearly half a dozen concertos and at least two large fantasia-like pieces.

# Musical Characters

The concerted works show a wide diversity in musical character. Some, such as the *Elegy and Paean* and the Chorale for organ and brass, are serious, singleminded utterances with the expansive, noble character represented by such masterpieces as the slow movement of the Fifth Symphony. Others, such as the Two-Piano Concerto, are more varied; this work, in fact, offers the listener an exceptionally wide range of expression, from playful insouciance, through lyrical sweetness, to boisterous aggressiveness.

One element that does appear to surface more often in these compositions than in the symphonies, the other orchestral pieces, and the chamber works, is humor. This is evident in the buoyant, light-hearted jazziness of many portions of the 1944 Piano Concero and in the Debussy quotations that comprise Harris's affectionate tribute to that master in the opening movement (now, unfortunately, lost) of the Amplified Piano Concerto. Perhaps the humor was a natural outgrowth of the extroverted character resulting from Harris's efforts in the fast portions of these pieces to give the soloist something distinctive and challenging to do. However, it is significant that this element appears predominantly in the concerted works for keyboard (including the organ Fantasy, in which Johana had a part in the composition). Given the often demonstrated application of her improvisational skills to weaving snatches of different tunes together in the manner of a parody, it is not unusual that the humor in the pieces her husband wrote for her would also derive much of its inspiration from and serve as a tribute to this facet of her talent.

# Formal Characteristics

## Single-Movement Designs

Harris's first approach to the single-movement form as applied to a large work of symphonic proportions (the Toccata for orchestra aside) was in the aborted violin concerto of 1938. The immediate fruit of this exploration was, as mentioned earlier, the Third Symphony, which also materialized as a one-movement design. However, Harris employed this sort of structure in a number of subsequent compositions in both the symphonic and the concerto genres, though not always in the same way each time. For example, the consistent forward momentum and steady buildup to a climax that characterize the Third Symphony are also reflected in the Concerto for Piano and Band. In the 1949 Violin Concerto, on the other hand, Harris interrupts the forward drive of the opening passacaglia for a more relaxed and dancelike music, following which the passacaglia is resumed (thus foreshadowing the format of the Seventh Symphony, which is based upon the same principal theme). In the Fantasy for Piano and Orchestra, the first half of the bipartite structure into which the single movement falls is bent back on itself through the use of the bow-form, a structural type in which materials are exposed, then recapitulated (here highly varied) in reverse order. It is only in the second half of the work that the real drive to the climax begins.

As I have described elsewhere, most of Harris's single-movement works contain distinct formal subdivisions. Thus, the piano/band Fantasia is actually a structure in two interlinked parts, or movements. The first is a slow and powerful passacaglia, with an epic character, the second a fast and dancelike music, of a playful, parodistic nature. The Fantasy for Piano and Orchestra, as indicated above, also comprises a large binary form, of which the first half is a leisurely paced exposition and varied restatement of three folk melodies, the second chiefly a set of variations on one of the melodies of the A section, the two sections being connected by an orchestral fantasia/development and a piano cadenza. The large ternary form into which the 1949 Violin Concerto falls has already been alluded to. On the other hand, the Chorale for organ and brass unfolds very gradually in autogenetic fashion in a classic Harris example of increasing dynamics, textural complexity, and rhythmic momentum, the various sections forming a continuity rather than grouping into larger units.

## Multi-Movement Types

Harris also used a two-movement design (*Elegy and Paean*) and a three-movement format (Concerto for Two Pianos, the Amplified Piano Concerto, and the 1953 Piano Concerto). All of the three-movement compositions employ the fast-slow-fast tempo scheme of the Classic- and Baroque-periods concertos, though, of course, the forms of the individual movements differ from those of these earlier types.

Among the multimovement works, the formal characteristics of the single movement vary. The slow movement of the Amplified Piano Concerto outlines a Gothic arch, while the finale exhibits characteristics of rondo form in its alternation of the boisterous, syncopated principal materials with episodes built on contrasting ideas. The opening Toccata of the Two-Piano Concerto appears to unfold in a series of sections generated by materials of both the introduction and the first section proper (the movement belongs to the autogenetic continuity type represented by the above-mentioned Chorale).

## Special Formal Characteristics: Use of Variation

Many of Harris's concerted works employ variation technique. Two, the accordion/orchestra Theme and Variations and the piano/band Concerto, use the procedure throughout. Others, such as the Fantasy for Piano and Orchestra and the 1949 Violin Concerto, use it for part of their duration, and sometimes (as in the case of the Fantasy) with more than one theme.

# Use of Folk Materials

Another special feature of the concerted works is the use of folk tunes in a number of them. This is the case with the 1944 Concerto, the piano/band Fantasia, the Two-Piano Concerto, the Fantasy for Piano and Orchestra, and the 1953 Concerto. A theme common to all of these is the tune "True Love Don't Weep." Harris always uses this melody in a variations context, its first appearance in his oeuvre occurring in the piano/band Fantasia.

# Use of the Solo Instrument

It was natural that Harris should concentrate most of his efforts in the concerted compositions on providing music for the artist whose performing style and mechanism he understood best, Johana. It appears that, in general, he lacked the ingenuity and adaptability that enabled a colleague such as Benjamin Britten to explore in virtuosic fashion the resources of instruments (such as the guitar and harp) with which he was unfamiliar in terms of playing technique. Harris was more concerned with the substance than with the gesture, without always realizing the extent to which the latter can reinforce the communication of the former.

He did manage to write idiomatically for most of the standard orchestral instruments, especially the strings and clarinet (having, of course, learned to play the latter as a youth), and for piano. However, though he could devise the types of characteristic figures I have referred to elsewhere for the various members of each instrumental choir, these seldom went beyond the most conservative ideas.[1] Even his writing for piano, though distinctive in sound, is made up chiefly of traditional devices, some of which certainly had been transmitted to him from the standard literature through Johana.

Harris usually allots the soloist the exposition of at least one of the principal themes. This is the case in both the 1949 Violin Concerto (where the soloist introduces the passacaglia theme) and the "Paean" of the *Elegy and Paean* (where the violist is given the principal theme and its continuation). Where several themes are used in a composition (as in the 1944 Piano Concerto and the Fantasy for Piano and Orchestra), the soloist usually alternates with the ensemble in exposing these ideas.

In the works employing variation, Harris naturally takes advantage of the elaborative possibilities inherent in this type to make the solo part more virtuosic. Sometimes this involves a variation on the theme itself in the solo instrument. Most often, however, the composer chooses, as his variations unfold, to give successive statements of the theme to the orchestra and to allow the soloist to decorate these with a variety of arabesque figures or with counterpoint of a more melodic nature.

There are times, as in the finale of the Amplified Piano Concerto, where the soloist engages in a dialogue with the ensemble, each protagonist having its own distinctive materials:

EXAMPLE 136

*Amplified Piano Concerto:* III. Antiphonal writing

One can deduce from this that Harris employs all the characteristics of solo/ensemble relationship of the Classic- and Romantic-period concertos. Sometimes the protagonists work together in exposing and working out materials, each in its idiomatic way; at other times an "adversary" relationship is set up that serves to throw both soloist and ensemble into stronger relief.

## Characteristics of the Ensemble

For his concerted works employing the symphony orchestra, Harris generally used the same instrumentation and the same size forces as for his

compositions for orchestra alone. Some pieces, such as the 1944 Piano
Concerto and the Concerto for Amplified Piano, possess special characteristics of instrumentation due either to the circumstances of commission
(the former work, designed for the Paul Whiteman Orchestra, employs the
saxophones and expanded clarinet section found in jazz orchestras of the
period) or to the composer's desire to explore specific timbres (the latter
work uses only brass, string basses, and percussion for the ensemble.

Two compositions, the Two-Piano Concerto and the piano/band Concerto, employ relatively large wind forces. The latter work, in fact, pits the
piano against the resources of a large symphonic band to create one of the
most sumptuous of Harris's scores of the 1940s.

## Soloist/Ensemble Balance

In neither his instrumentation nor in his scoring did Harris seem, in these
compositions, to take many special pains to forestall the problems of
balance that almost inevitably result when pitting a solo instrument against
a full orchestra or band. However, given the generally lean Harris orchestral style and its relatively sparing use of *tutti,* the solo parts in his
concerted works usually manage to register clearly. In his writing in all
genres Harris was concerned with maintaining a clear focus on the melodic
continuity by distinguishing its timbre, register, and rhythm from the
supporting elements. In the concertos and related works, when the soloist
has an important theme, it is generally accompanied lightly (as in the
opening statement of the theme of the Violin Concerto). Sometimes the
composer reduces the supporting forces to providing mere whiffs of
commentary from various sections or solo instruments from the ensemble. When, on the other hand, the ensemble has the primary materials,
ornamental figuration in the solo part is generally set off both by being
placed in a higher register and by greater rhythmic animation.

## Cadenzas

Harris was inconsistent in providing fully worked-out cadenzas for his
concerted works. There are, of course, instances of the soloist playing
relatively short passages nearly or wholly unaccompanied either in the
expositions of themes or in transitions between sections. Examples are
found in the organ/brass Chorale (measures 98–100) and the Fantasy for
Piano and Orchestra (measures 40ff.). However, the presence of large-
scale cadenzas containing further development of some of the materials in

terms of virtuosic display seems to have depended at least partly on matters of structure. For example, the inexorable forward momentum and increase in intensity (the latter achieved partly through a buildup of timbre) generated over a relatively short duration in the Concerto for Piano and Band might have been weakened by the sudden loss of timbral weight and by the introduction of the sudden changes in texture, dynamics, materials, and so forth, which accompany the appearance of a solo cadenza. In longer works the time scale provides for more contrast, and a cadenza can be used to help delineate structure, to provide a summing-up on which the listener's attention is riveted by the use of a single instrument, and to create the satisfying display of pyrotechnics soloists and audiences have come to expect as their reward.

Though the fine "Cadenza" movement of the Piano Quintet demonstrates that Harris understood well the various functions of this musical type, sadly, most of his "big" cadenzas (at least as he wrote them out) are rather short-winded, pallid affairs made up of contrived figuration that has little to do with any of the thematic materials of the works in question. Examples of this are the especially perfunctory cadenzas of the Violin Concerto and the accordion/orchestra Theme and Variations.

Though there are examples of more elaborate cadenzas (that in the finale of the Two-Piano Concerto is one), Harris seemed, for the most part, to treat this aspect of his concerted works casually, and a bit impatiently.

On at least one occasion, that of the accordion/orchestra Theme and Variations, Harris responded to a query from his publisher about the cadenza by indicating his desire to have the soloist improvise his own cadenza, in the manner of the concertos of the Classic period. Though this approach is certainly legitimate today, even following a century of tradition in writing out cadenzas, I suspect that it was simply Harris's way of evading the issue of writing idiomatically here for an instrument about which he knew little.

## Related Compositions

In addition to works such as the foregoing that were designed as solo vehicles, there are other pieces featuring a concertante part for a given instrument that, for one reason or another (intermittent use of soloist, equally important roles given to other forces), do not strictly belong in the category under discussion. Among these are the *San Francisco Symphony, These Times,* and the *Radio Piece,* in all of which the piano is featured prominently but not used as extensively and/or as virtuosically as it would be in a work of the concerto genre. In these compositions the orchestra has an equally, if not more, important role to play and sometimes the solo instrument is subsumed into the larger ensemble.

## Role in Harris's Development

Though Harris wrote relatively few concerted works, none of them, as I have observed, exploiting the solo instrument in particularly novel ways, most are compositions of genuine substance, solid craftsmanship, and no little complexity. Each solo instrument presented different problems of balance, contrast, and integration with the ensemble chosen, and, though Harris's style and technique may have lacked some degree of flexibility and variety in other connections, his lean orchestral idiom and clear, but colorful harmonic style proved remarkably adaptable in meeting the challenges presented by these works.

In addition to the minor development in scoring that Harris's division of the violin section into three parts in the accordion piece effected, the concerted compositions appear to have played a role in the development of his handling of form, as illustrated by the discussion of the variety achieved in his use of the single-movement format and of the frequent employment of variation technique. It also seems likely that the light touch evident in places in such works as the 1944 Piano Concerto, the Fantasy for Piano and Orchestra, and the Amplified Piano Concerto may have helped broaden his range of expression and the techniques associated with this.

Few of these pieces really seem to have been designed as occasional affairs. Rather, most evidently were written with the thought of providing substantial vehicles that might actually enter the standard repertoire of the instruments involved. Though, as mentioned, some of the compositions are lighthearted in character, others, such as the organ/brass Chorale, the piano/band Concerto, and the *Elegy and Paean* for viola and orchestra, are essays in the monumental, deeply expressive, visionary character many listeners feel represents Roy Harris at his best.

# 12

## Works for Solo Instruments and Piano

### Types

Harris's contributions to the literature of chamber music include a small number of works for solo instruments and piano. The compositions for solo strings, which comprise nearly all of these, are, in particular, among the more substantial works in the twentieth-century literature in the medium. There are sonatas for violin and for violoncello and a large two-movement work for viola titled *Soliloquy and Dance;* there is also a *Poem* for violin and piano, which predates these larger works and is of slighter stature.[1]

### Treatment of Strings

The three major compositions reveal especially Harris's grasp of idiomatic string writing. Indeed, with his love of the long, arching melodic line, it was natural that he would be particularly susceptible to the qualities of the string family, whose members come closest to the timbre and unique flexibility of the human voice.

In his use of the string choir in the orchestra, Harris demonstrates awareness of both the concentrated power of the various divisions playing fortissimo in unison and octaves (e.g., the closing section of the Third Symphony) and of the lush harmonic tapestry which could be woven from their use in *divisi* (e.g., the first passacaglia variation of the Seventh Symphony). He also took advantage of the tuning in perfect fifths and fourths characteristic of the string group in laying out some of his chordal writing for maximum resonance based upon the properties of the overtone system:

EXAMPLE 137

*Epilogue to Profiles in Courage—JFK:* String texture

# The Two Sonatas

## Comparisons and Contrasts

The sonatas for violin and piano (1942) and violoncello and piano (1964) are separated by more than twenty years, and a comparison of the two works reveals something of the stylistic development Harris underwent during this period. However, the sonatas also demonstrate the consistency of approach the composer often took with compositions within the same genre, regardless of their separation in time. Each work contains a fantasylike first movement in which a long line in the solo instrument passes through a variety of textures, the continuity punctuated by contrasting materials. Each also has a deeply expressive slow movement. There is an additional similarity, and a very strong one, between the materials, textures, and associated characters of the second movement of the earlier work and a major portion of the finale of the later one.

The folk element also infiltrates both compositions, an unusual situation in Harris's chamber oeuvre, as I have mentioned elsewhere. The second movement of the Violin Sonata is based on the tune "I'll Be True to My Love" and is an especially good example of the composer's skill in treating folk materials in an abstract fashion. After its initial presentation, the tune is subjected to both a variations treatment and development of its characteristic phrases:

EXAMPLE 138

a: *Violin Sonata:* II. Theme

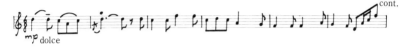

b: *Violin Sonata:* II. Theme variant

This movement clearly served as a model when the composer came to writing the finale of the Violoncello Sonata, though there is no direct use of folk tune there:

EXAMPLE 139

*Violoncello Sonata:* III. Theme I

It is clear that in creating much of the Violoncello Sonata Harris was using the violin work as a model of proven success, incorporating materials and gestures on whose effectiveness he could depend. (He did this often in works in all media.) However, characteristically, he did not slavishly appropriate the elements of the Violin Sonata that he found useful but rather rethought and reworked them. Indeed, the contrasts between the two works are as important as the similarities. For example, the short cadenza near the end of the Violin Sonata finale is a relatively traditional virtuosic showpiece that grows out of the preceding music. The cadenza of the Violoncello Sonata, however, constitutes a complete movement in itself and is more varied in character, with an added element of fantasy. Also, the piano shares in this cadenza movement, where, in the earlier example, it merely provides harmonic underpinning in the form of a sustained chord. The later cadenza also reveals an interest in sonority, arising from both instrumental timbre and from harmony, that marked Harris's music increasingly as he matured. Another contrast exists between the two finales. Whereas that of the earlier piece is a buoyantly propulsive toccata, the corresponding Violoncello Sonata movement begins with an easygoing pastoral lilt and later metamorphoses (not altogether successfully) into a savage, driving character to conclude the work on an unsettled note.

The two works also illustrate, on a small scale, Harris's flexibility in treating the Gothic-arch design. The slow movements of both employ this form, but it is articulated differently in each. In the Violin Sonata, the proportions of ascent and descent are roughly equal; the ascent is built on long-breathed phrases in the solo instrument while the descent has the melodic continuity in the piano, the violin playing animated, disconnected ideas that serve primarily as decorative counterpoint. In the violoncello work, the ascending portion of the arch is shaped more gradually and haltingly, with changes of texture along the way and a tendency for the string phrases to become more agitated and disconnected as the tension mounts. The descent is short in comparison with that in the Violin Sonata, with the melodic continuity retained in the solo instrument in a savagely impassioned outburst. Both movements have a lengthy concluding section. That of the Violin Sonata is based on a long melodic descent in the solo part while the corresponding portion of the later piece is founded on a theme in the piano, which, upon its repetition, the violoncello decorates with counterpoint.

Though the Violin Sonata seems more assured in its harmonic idiom, Harris's handling of this element in the Violoncello Sonata is somewhat more subtle and varied, achieving a wider spectrum of dark to bright sonorities.

It is partly because of this more sensitive approach to harmonic color that the music of the Violoncello Sonata seems to convey a more personal expressiveness in comparison with the somewhat externalized, but undeniably persuasive, character of its earlier companion. I have observed elsewhere the tendency for Harris's music of the 1960s to reveal a more introspective character. If this is somewhat true of even the large-scale orchestral works, whose dimensions and apparatus had always been more suited to the natural exuberance of the "civic" Harris than to reflection, it is even more true of the intimate chamber medium, and the Violoncello Sonata is a prime example of this.

In that work, Harris also reveals a heightened sensitivity to the emotional effect created by the rhythm and continuity of phrases and the interaction of different levels of activity. The most impressive example of this occurs in the closing section of the slow movement, "Elegy." As an initial stroke, Harris masterfully delays the entrance of the violoncello until near the beginning of the repetition of the harmonized piano melody. The halting, disjunct phrases of counterpoint which ensue, outlining a descending spiral to the instrument's lowest register, seem the embodiment of the deep sadness and resignation that lies at the core of this movement:

EXAMPLE 140

*Violoncello Sonata:* II. End

The contrast between the fragmentary violoncello ideas and the stolid continuity of the piano part provides an undercurrent of tension and an additional layer of complexity in the emotional makeup of this passage. The music also reveals Harris taking advantage of instrumental sonority to reinforce his "affect," the broken, disembodied sound of the violoncello harmonics at the entrance of that instrument adding to the poignance of these measures with a stifled, almost human, cry.

The transformation in the Violoncello Sonata finale from one character to another completely different one is something Harris seldom attempted within a single movement or short composition of this sort. It is, of course, difficult to give the reader a clear picture of this without citing the entire movement; however, characteristic ideas from various portions of the piece may at least convey something of this change of character. The opening violoncello idea has been cited in Example 139; some of the subsequent materials are given below:

EXAMPLE 141

*Violoncello Sonata:* III. Ideas showing musico-dramatic progress

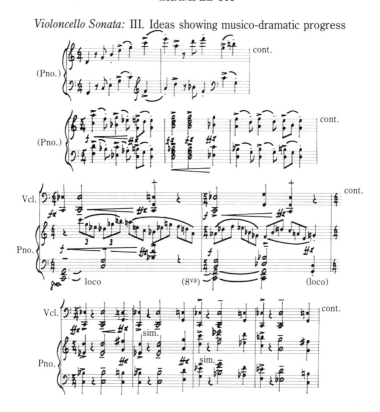

The attempt at transformation, as indicated earlier, is not completely successful, for the change is somewhat abrupt and the savage portion is not sufficiently long to balance the earlier music and achieve the dynamic impact the composer evidently intended. However, the attempt is nonetheless welcome as another of Harris's efforts during his later years to take a fresh look at matters of form.

## Overview

Of these two string works, the Violin Sonata is perhaps the more success-ful overall in terms of the distinctiveness of its materials, the mastery demonstrated in the ease and naturalness of its unfolding, and in the skillful handling of contrasts from movement to movement. Though the Violoncello Sonata is flawed in these respects, it does have the virtue of attempting more in terms of formal adventurousness, in its approach to instrumental playing techniques and sonorities, and in intensity of expres-sion. Indeed, in the "Elegy" I find what is perhaps the most deeply felt writing in all of Harris's oeuvre.

## *Soliloquy and Dance*

The *Soliloquy and Dance,* written in 1938 for violist William Primrose, is another step in Harris's exploration of contrasting characters in music. The origin of this exploration seems to have been the emotional dichotomy, touched on earlier, upon which he founded the two orchestral overtures on "When Johnny Comes Marching Home." Somewhat later, in the Prelude and Fugue for Strings, he made the contrasts in character more explicit by alloting each type a separate movement in which it could be explored to greater depth. The two-movement composition that resulted constituted a model that Harris was to use on many subsequent occasions.

In the *Soliloquy and Dance,* one finds the composer attempting to ally different form-building techniques in the two movements with distinct and contrasting characters. This treatment of the two-movement model dis-cussed above forms the basis of a number of subsequent works: *American Creed, Elegy and Paean,* and *Elegy and Dance.*[2] In all of these compo-sitions from the *Soliloquy and Dance* on, Harris contrasts a reflective world with an active one. The opening movement is sometimes sad, sometimes fantasylike in nature; the closing movement is more active and dynamic, often employing more straightforward procedures of form building and more easily grasped ("tuneful") materials.

Sometimes, as in the *Elegy and Dance,* Harris uses variation tech-niques. However, in other works (the *Soliloquy and Dance* and *American Creed*) he turns to the idea of the fugal finale. In the viola work he created an especially happy marriage between fugue and dance that resulted in a finale of exceptional drive and buoyancy and a fun-loving, unselfconscious quality that one sometimes misses in his more earnest, sober contrapuntal writing.

## "Soliloquy": The Double Arch

The "Soliloquy" employs a double Gothic-arch pattern simultaneously in the two instruments, with one arch inverted. The normal arch is in the viola, which opens in the low register and spins a long melody through a constantly rising level of pitch and dynamics and an increase in tempo to the climax. Following this the tension gradually unwinds until a return in the closing measures to the character of the opening of the piece. The piano, on the other hand, begins in the high register and gradually descends through an increasingly rich harmonic texture (and rhythmic animation— only the rhythmic aspect is not reversed in the two arches). Its climax is actually a low point, reached at the same moment as the viola's apex. After this the piano begins a gradually ascending accompaniment created by a thinning-out of texture and a waning of rhythmic activity.

The "Soliloquy" also contains some of the richest harmonic writing Harris had done up to this time. In fact, it provides a virtual guided tour through his vocabulary, moving as it does from chords built on superimposed fourths, then sixths, to a timbral climax featuring imaginatively conceived polychords, these latter revealing many unexpected harmonic relationships between their two components.

## "Dance"

The "Dance" is sparer in harmonic texture, concentrating instead upon line and rhythmic impulse. Harris described it in a letter as a "rather strict double fugue," but, in fact, it is one of his most spontaneous sounding pieces of extended contrapuntal writing and not at all rigid.

The two subjects could hardly contrast more strongly in their cultural connotations: the first is jiglike, the second chant-influenced:

EXAMPLE 142

*Soliloquy and Dance: Dance.* Subjects

But the sacred and secular coexist happily in this freewheeling essay. In fact, toward the end Harris interweaves motives from the two subjects as a substitute in the horizontal plane for their contrapuntal combination in the vertical plane. He does attempt the latter in some spots, but, as usual in his polythematic fugues, the highly contrasting subjects do not lend themselves to this contrapuntal union easily.

## Overview

In its combination of clearly drawn, strongly contrasting emotional characteristics, its plastic and expressive, at times expansive, melodic writing, and its imaginative harmonic structures and rhythmic phraseology, the *Soliloquy and Dance* remains something of a landmark in Harris's development. In it, he seemed able to focus more clearly than in some of his previous works on a precise musical definition of the Gothic arch, on various levels of textural density, on a wide spectrum of harmonic color values, and on an idiosyncratic rethinking of contrapuntal texture and fugal procedure. The lack of self-consciousness and calculation with which he accomplished this renders this work, like the Violin Sonata, one of the most viable and fresh sounding of all Harris's instrumental chamber compositions.

# 13

## Works for Piano Solo

### Origin and Extent of Literature

Considering the extent of his reliance upon the piano during the formative years of his career and the fact that for more than forty years he was married to a pianist who possessed a formidable technique and a penetrating interpretive imagination, it is surprising that Roy Harris left so few works for solo piano. Though he always had great affection for his piano compositions, an examination of their origins reveals that, aside from the early Sonata, a grandly scaled "serious" effort by a fledgling composer still attempting to make a significant mark on the musical world, most are spur-of-the-moment affairs or by-products of a larger event.

Their origins notwithstanding, the piano pieces reveal Harris's exceptional skill as a miniaturist, working concisely and unpretentiously to create clearly defined moods. For many listeners these short compositions have served as the initial introduction to his music and, indeed, they remain one of the easiest approaches to his style and technique.

### Treatment of the Piano

Though some of Harris's piano writing, such as one finds in the faster portions of the various concerted works and in solo pieces like the Sonata and Toccata, is brilliant, one could not call it truly virtuosic, except in rare instances. As in his orchestral compositions, the medium is generally employed as a means to convey ideas, rather than as an attention-getting device in itself.

Actually, though he could play, Harris was somewhat uneasy in writing for the piano. He lacked a strong keyboard technique and sometimes found it difficult to conceive ideas that lay naturally for the instrument. By the time he began to acquire some compositional technique and aesthetic principles in the mid-1920s, he found himself moving away from a conception of musical ideas in terms of the pianistic medium. As Slonimsky observed about this period: "He was now [1928] working on a piano Sonata, but found himself ill at ease writing for piano, because of his habit of thinking in terms of counterpoint. He could not very well adopt the conventional harmonic texture of pianistic technique, and he compromised by using what he called 'chordal counterpoint.' "[1] The crisis was hastened by the accident in 1929, which, as I have indicated earlier, necessitated his working away from the piano altogether during the composition of part of the First Quartet.

The "chordal counterpoint" Slonimsky refers to is one of the earliest manifestations of Harris's use of the polytonal idiom of writing upon which his mature style is based. In places in the Sonata, one does, indeed, find the composer weaving together two separate strands of chords, an effect created largely through the use of contrary motion between the two hands:

EXAMPLE 143

*Piano Sonata:* II. Chord strands

Actually, Harris did not employ the device of chordal counterpoint in his solo piano writing to the same extent as he did in his orchestral and chamber works. Rather, he gravitated as he matured, toward the following types of treatment:

## Types of Treatment

1. Homophonic presentation of a melody either as a single line in one hand against chordal accompaniment in the other or as the top right-hand voice of a texture made up of chords. The first type of this category is found in "The Wayfaring

Stranger," the second in the middle section of "Streets of Laredo" (both from the published set of *American Ballads*).

2. Embedding of the melodic material in elaborate figuration, of which the following are characteristic types:

EXAMPLE 144

Thematic materials embedded in figuration

a: *Piano Suite in Three Movements:* II.

b: *Toccata for Piano*

3. Single-line figuration either doubled in octaves or divided between the hands, of which Example 66 is a specimen. This type often serves as ornamental counterpoint in a variations context, but it sometimes acquires thematic or motivic significance.

4. A purely polyphonic style of writing is also sometimes found, though it does not predominate in Harris's solo piano music. One comes across contrapuntal textures in such pieces as the Sonata (last two movements), Toccata (the fugue that makes up the final section), and the "Recreation" movement of the Suite in Three Movements. Polyphony appears in these instances as either a relatively free unfolding of materials in two or three parts ("Recreation") or as fugal working-out (Toccata).

In spite of the Slonimsky observation cited above, from the beginning Harris seemed attracted to the piano, at least as a sonority per se, and must have found this aspect congenial to his developing concept of harmony. Much of his piano music is harmonically oriented and, in fact, his polychordal vocabulary is sometimes richer and more complex in this medium than in any other. In all the piano compositions, one finds the composer carefully laying out the harmonies for maximum resonance, taking special care to differentiate among the characteristics of the different registers of the instrument and their requirements in terms of chord voicing.

Of course, all the types of texture cited above can be found in one guise or another in the standard literature. As I have observed earlier, Harris generally did not concern himself with devising new performing techniques; rather, he adapted traditional devices to his own expressive ends. I do not know how much of the piano literature, aside from the Beethoven and Mozart sonatas learned in his youth, Harris knew by 1928 (the year of the Sonata), but there is no question that his acquaintance with it was broadened enormously after meeting Johana. In addition to exposing him to her enormous repertoire, she also gave him an insight into various pianistic devices and textures. In fact, one actually finds in Harris's piano music from this point on ideas that can be traced to specific origins in works by other composers. For instance, the principal theme of the finale of the Amplified Piano Concerto derives from the classic example of thumb/little finger substitution: the Op 25, No. 12 Étude of Chopin.[2]

In addition to the role cited above, Johana played a large part in the origin and the final working-out of many of the piano compositions her husband wrote subsequent to their marriage. For example, some of the ideas for the treatment in his various folktune settings for piano were sparked by her improvisations on these melodies at concerts and on radio. Harris nearly always consulted his wife on matters of idiomatic pianistic character and practicality. He also allowed Johana a good deal of leeway in matters of both interpretation and the notes themselves when she played his piano music. As a result, her performances have often differed from the printed scores, especially in the cuts she has made over the years (most of them in the Sonata and Toccata).

## Types of Composition

Harris's works for solo piano can be divided into two categories: (1) completely original compositions, largely, but not entirely, of an abstract nature (Sonata, Toccata, *Little Suite*); (2) compositions based upon folksong (the various *American Ballad* settings, the Suite in Three Movements [first two movements]).

## Sonata

The Sonata is the most ambitious of these works. Due to its austerity, occasional thinness of texture, and uncompromising character, it has not always been well received. A typical comment is this by Virgil Thomson: "Roy Harris' early Piano Sonata, opus 1, is a coarse work and laborious."[3] Certainly, one senses that the composer's aspiration toward a granitic, visionary expression sometimes outstrips his technical prowess here. This is especially noticeable in such things as the three-part contrapuntal development in the finale starting at the *Meno mosso* on page 14. However, the Sonata also contains some very impressive things. Arthur Farwell took pains to show the evolution of the opening measures of the work from the initial descending fourth, an evolution that can be traced through the growth of the monolithic structure of the entire first movement:[4]

EXAMPLE 145

*Piano Sonata:* I. Opening with autogenetic development of motive

Harris's exploration of chordal counterpoint in this work has already been discussed. Though the second-movement passage cited in Example 143 is perhaps the best known portion in which he employs this technique, the streams of chords in contrary motion in an extended section in the opening movement (page 4 of the published score) are an even more intensive application.[5] This type of texture creates a distinctive sound of a sort that still makes an impression today. But perhaps the most potent thing in the entire Sonata is the savage conclusion, a passage whose polytonal frictions provide the sense of granitic imperviousness toward which the young composer was striving as in so many of his early compositions:

EXAMPLE 146

*Piano Sonata:* III. Closing

## Toccata

The little Toccata, composed some twenty years after the Sonata, is a less ambitious work. It is based upon a pair of motives that are put through a series of exceptionally plastic transformations and variations:

EXAMPLE 147

a: *Toccata for Piano:* Motives

b: *Toccata for Piano:* Motive developments

# Little Suite

The *Little Suite* is an unpretentious and perfect miniature. Each of its four movements, "Bells," "Sad News," "Children at Play," and "Slumber," etches a specific mood with the precision and economy of a master engraver. The four-minute work is also an excellent introduction to Harris's harmonic style, from the various mixtures of chords built in fourths and polychords of the opening movement to the simple triads of the last.

# Folksong Settings

Harris's folksong settings for piano are generally simpler texturally but more complex harmonically than his a cappella treatments of these materials. He takes advantage of the piano sonority to create colorful, but often subtle, harmonic resonances with the diatonic melodies. In some respects his aesthetics here are akin to those of Bartok, who felt that clear, diatonic melodies can bear a relatively complex harmonic treatment. It appears that the solo medium also allowed Harris to create moods more tellingly than he sometimes managed in the more generalized ensemble mediums. Almost every one of these short pieces is a miniature tone poem that conveys the central points of the absent text in precise fashion.

As in the *Toccata,* an element of fantasy is also present in some of these pieces. This is illustrated by the free polyphonic interplay and subtle shifts of tonality in the working out of the two tunes ("Leatherwing Bat" ["The Birds' Courting Song"]and "Hop up, My Lady") in "The Bird." One even finds Harris taking advantage of the possibility working on a small time scale affords for a cryptic, attentuated mode of expression: in "Black is the Color of My True Love's Hair," the melody, in its single brief, unadorned statement, is made to seem an ornamental appendage to the dark and enigmatic chords that serve as the supporting pillars at each end of the piece. If any of Harris's piano compositions can be said to owe a debt to Debussy, it is this piece, with its impressionistic blurring of thematic outlines and its use of harmony solely for color value and mood-creating attributes.

# Overview

Aside from the Sonata, Harris's music for solo piano does not attempt to tackle the big issues of his symphonies and his more substantial chamber compositions. Most of it is unpretentious music, "Gebrauchsmusik" in the sense that it was largely conceived for a specific function. However, it contains some of the composer's finest craftsmanship and most accessible writing. As is the case with some of the a cappella choral works and other miniatures, and the patriotic pieces, it provides another example of the composer's range of expression, of his ability to render more concisely his ordinarily expansive formal procedures, and of his success in scaling down the expressive aims while still retaining a strong stylistic identity and aesthetic integrity.

# 14

## Works for Chorus

### The Literature

The magnitude of Harris's achievements in the realms of symphony and chamber music notwithstanding, it is in the area of vocal music that one finds possibly the clearest manifestation of the variety and adaptability of which he was capable. Works involving voice amount to over half of his total output and span the entirety of his long career. Harris's first known composition (now apparently lost) is a *Song Without Words* for chorus and piano, four-hands written circa 1922, while his last completed work, dating from late 1976, is a piece for solo voice, string quartet, and piano titled, appropriately, *Rejoice and Sing.* Within this fifty-four-year span one finds an enormous variety of vocal works. In the choral literature there are some twenty a cappella pieces; a dozen or so works for chorus and piano, organ, or small instrumental ensemble (often brass with piano or organ and percussion); and roughly another dozen compositions for chorus and orchestra or band.

### Categories

The majority of Harris's compositions for chorus can be divided into the following categories: (1) Walt Whitman settings, (2) folksong settings, (3) religious works (mostly psalm settings and hymns), and (4) patriotic compositions and other works relating to the social scene.

## Breadth of Accomplishment

In the Harris choral oeuvre one finds everything from the starkness of the one-page Sanctus, through the "popular" simplicity and directness of the *Freedom's Land* settings and other patriotic pieces, to the challenging complexities and subtleties of the Symphony for Voices and *Song for Occupations*. The composer seems to have found the choral medium an especially plastic one for the realization of a variety of textures and musical characters, and his work in the medium, particularly during the 1940s, helped in the development of a greater sureness of technique in responding, often under great time pressure, to commissions for a literature in all areas of works of challenging diversity.

## Style and Influences

Harris's choral composition covers a gamut of straightforward unison writing, homophonic and polyphonic textures, and choric speech. There is nothing truly novel about his approach to the medium; it is solid and conventional in the sense that the chorus is handled in much the same way as it is by most of the relatively conservative composers of his generation. There is thus a kinship not only with some of his American colleagues, such as Randall Thompson, Aaron Copland, and William Schuman, but also with such Europeans as Vaughan Williams, Walton, and Poulenc.

In relationship to his other works, one might observe that the ideas and textures of Harris's choral music seem most closely allied with the string and some of the woodwind writing in his orchestral pieces. Though he nearly always took into consideration matters of voice range, breathing, and other elements peculiar to the medium, there are times when the writing approaches an instrumental style:

EXAMPLE 148

*Symphony for Voices:* III. Subject II

In spite of the music's generally conservative cast, there is no question, however, that choral directors of the 1930s, such as John Finley Williamson, sensed something new and sometimes wildly original in works such as the Symphony and *Song for Occupations,* for Harris joined his conventional techniques with an intensity of expression in mirroring the imagery of the text (as in the onomatopoeic ostinato surges of the "Song for All Seas, All Ships" movement of the Symphony) in a way that raised them to new levels of effectiveness.

## Practical Experience

Harris's choral compositions received the benefits of an increasing store of practical experience gained through first-hand exposure to choral rehearsals and performances and close association with choral directors. The most potent of these experiences was provided by his aforementioned residence from 1934 to 1938 at the Westminster Choir School.

## Aims and Aesthetics

During his years at Westminster, Harris wrote a variety of a cappella compositions, ranging from the two large Whitman compositions mentioned above to less demanding religious pieces (the Sanctus) and folksong settings (*When Johnny Comes Marching Home, He's Gone Away* [both of these reworked later into the *Folksong Symphony*]). Virtually all of his later a cappella pieces were written for specific choirs and, in some instances, groups of choirs. In fact, the pieces designed for this last category are an even more concrete manifestation of his efforts to provide music for amateur performance than his work in the band medium.

The composer made explicit reference to his aims in this particular type of choral writing in his comments on the nature of the choral parts of the *Folksong Symphony* in the program note on that work. All the choral works, however slight, demanded a great deal of imagination and technique in designing lines and textures that possessed genuine musical interest and stylistic identity but did not exceed the capabilities of the frequently diverse levels of ability found in choral groups.

Harris seemed to demonstrate a real love for the singing voice. He made the personal and professional acquaintance of a great many solo singers and choral directors and often worked with them closely while writing the works they had commissioned from him. During my acquaintance with the composer, I heard him on more than one occasion make thoughtful and perceptive comments on singers, voice types, and vocal problems that revealed a better than average understanding of the nature of the instrument. The fundamental importance of melody in his aesthetic seems, in fact, to have grown, at least partly, from a vocal conception of line, something he exhibited many times in demonstrating his melodies by singing them aloud.

## Criticisms

The foregoing observations notwithstanding, Harris's choral technique and his general understanding of the medium have occasionally been questioned. One well-known assessment is that by Aaron Copland:

> . . . Harris has shown very little word sense thus far, either in setting prosody according to its natural speech inflection or in mirroring the meanings of words in musical images. His two long a cappella choral compositions to Whitman texts, the *Song for Occupations* and the *Symphony for Voices*, produce a somewhat stilted impression, as of something strained and unnatural in the treatment of the texts, which, perhaps, had better been left untreated in the first place. . . .[1]

This, of course, was written before Harris had produced more than a handful of relatively mature choral works. Nonetheless, there is some justification for criticism. For one thing, the homophonic, declamatory style that is such a prominent feature of the *Song for Occupations* became something of a crutch as time went on. Though it is obvious that the chorus of three or more parts is a magnificent vehicle for homophonic writing, it has traditionally been treated, since the development of a true choral literature during the Renaissance, as an essentially polyphonic medium. However, with few exceptions, such as the finale of the Symphony; *Freedom, Toleration*; and the *Whitman Triptych* for women's voices, Harris's choral polyphony often seems rather simple and casual, as though worked out somewhat impatiently. It can sometimes produce a stilted effect through the same overuse of interlocking motivic working-out that I have cited in connection with some of the early symphonies.

Along with the exceptions mentioned above, Harris seems to have accomplished his most successful polyphonic choral writing in the folksong settings. Here, given a preexistent melody as a sort of freely disposed "cantus firmus," his natural spontaneity blossoms in a freely decorative treatment of the line in the form of plastic commentary, sometimes original, sometimes derived from the folk tune in question:

EXAMPLE 149

*The Birds' Courting Song:* Folktune setting texture

Another device Harris learned to rely on excessively, especially during the 1970s, is choric speech. In late works such as *Whether this Nation* and the *Bicentennial Symphony,* the use of this technique generally enables him to convey the words in a clear and often powerful fashion. But one sometimes suspects that the composer is taking the easy way out, perhaps (in the later compositions) as a compensation for failing creative powers. In connection with his handling of prosody, the various passages in choric speech illustrate especially well one of Copland's reservations about Harris's choral writing; as one can see from the following example, he sometimes seems to treat word accent perversely indeed:

EXAMPLE 150

*Bicentennial Symphony 1976:* Prosody

However, the composer did seem to be aware of this situation early on, for, in a note to the last movement, "America," of the *Whitman Triptych,* he wrote: "The apparent reversal of stress in the text-syllables here and elsewhere in the composition arises from the fact that the presence of bars serves merely for convenience in rehearsal, as in modern editions of Renaissance works." In some instances, there is a momentary disregard for "correct" prosody in order that the key word in a line can be emphasized by placement on the correct beat. This, of course, is a technique composers such as Britten and Stravinsky (the latter in *The Rake's Progress*) employed with considerable mastery. On other occasions, however, particularly in some of the later works, Harris's disregard of word accent merely seems careless or gauche.

As far as vocal ranges are concerned, though, as inferred earlier, Harris generally keeps his parts within a reasonable span, there are times when the writing becomes ungrateful. These occasions seem to occur most frequently when there is an overemphasis on a high note, in both forte and piano passages. However, one also finds, at times, a real sensitivity to all the elements involved in the successful handling of the choral idiom. In these instances, Harris's placement of the voices, his handling of both the rhythm and accentuation of the words, and the "mirroring [of] the meanings of words in musical images," as Copland puts it, work together to produce a wonderfully effective result:

EXAMPLE 151

*Symphony for Voices:* II. Word setting

# Whitman Settings

The first tangible musical result of Harris's introduction by Arthur Farwell to the poetry of Walt Whitman was a one-movement Song Cycle for women's chorus and two pianos, based on selections from the "Children of Adam" and "Drum Taps" portions of *Leaves of Grass*. This busy piece, in which the voices are sometimes all but swamped by the frenetic activity of the pianos, is perhaps the earliest surviving composition in which features of an emerging Harris style can be discerned.

Harris's other Whitman choral compositions comprise settings of *To Thee, Old Cause; Year that Trembled; Freedom, Toleration;* and the two much larger works cited earlier, the *Song for Occupations* and the *Symphony for Voices.* [2] These last two were written within a year of each other in 1934 and 1935. Both, as mentioned, were composed for the Westminster Choir and are among the very earliest of the composer's a cappella efforts.

The *Song* is a setting of portions of Whitman's "Carol of Occupations," as it appears in the 1855 edition of *Leaves of Grass*. It is a sprawling single-movement work of a cantatalike character comprising several short interlinked sections. Written for eight-part chorus, with solo voices occasionally extracted from the group, much of the piece is built on a declamatory style of writing laid out in a rapid dialogue between various sections of the ensemble.

The *Symphony* is the most imposing of Harris's Whitman choral compositions. The first two of its three movements are based on passages from "Sea Drift," the last on the opening lines of "Inscriptions." Harris demands from his forces a near-orchestral scope of color, expression, and technique; in fact, the first two movements, "Song for All Seas, All Ships" and "Tears," are essentially choral tone poems, the sung declamation superimposed on rolling ostinato figures in the first movement creating a seascape of almost tangible immediacy, the tortured solo soprano discant over a chromatically sighing litany in the remaining women's voices and the reiterated "tears" in choric speech in the men conveying, in the second movement, a sense of muted tragedy and unfathomable loneliness. [3] The ambitious triple fugue that comprises the finale, though less graphically evocative than the music which had preceded it, nonetheless contains some of Harris's most intensively worked out and genuine (in terms of rhythmic independence of voices) polyphony.

Though the ostinati in the first movement are perhaps carried on too long and the over-insistence in the third movement on the "Modern Man" motto that forms the third subject can pall on repeated hearings, the Symphony as a whole may well transcend its occasional shortcomings. Certainly, the "Tears" movement, with its powerful evocation, is both one of the greatest of all Whitman settings and one of the masterpieces of the American choral literature.

# Folksong Settings

Roy Harris's choral settings of folk melodies span a wide range of media, more so than his completed Whitman settings. They include numerous a cappella compositions (e.g., *The Birds' Courting Song, Li'l Boy Named David, Work Song, Cindy, If I Had a Ribbon Bow, When Johnny Comes Marching Home,* and *He's Gone Away*); an extended work for chorus, speakers, soloists, and piano (*Folk Fantasy for Festivals*); and some pieces for chorus (with occasional soloists) and orchestra (*Railroad Man's Ballad* [based on "Casey Jones"] and *Blow the Man Down*).[4]

With the exception of the *Folksong Symphony* and the *Folk Fantasy,* Harris's folksong settings are less ambitious and more grateful to sing than some of the Whitman compositions. In the a cappella pieces, he generally subjects the variants he employs of the folktunes to a minimum of distortion. There is usually little embellishment within the melodies themselves, and the diatonic Harris harmonic idiom serves naturally to support the tonal implications of the tunes. However, an unexpected harmonic turn reveals from time to time a high degree of subtlety, sensitivity, and sophistication lying below the surfaces of these unpretentious works.

As in the *Folksong Symphony,* most of these settings follow the strophic layout of the source materials. However, Harris often provides a good deal of variety in the treatment of the various verses by means of contrapuntal commentary (sometimes derived from the principal melody, sometimes based on new ideas), changes in harmonization, texture, and voice parts.

The features of the large choral/orchestral settings have been illustrated in detail in the discussion of the *Folksong Symphony* in chapter 4. The two other works besides the symphony in this category, the *Railroad Man's Ballad* and *Blow the Man Down,* employ procedures similar to those of that work. In them, Harris takes advantage of the orchestra to depict extramusical sounds (the "stylized train whistle" and the rhythm of a chugging train in the former work, a sea gale in the latter).

The fantasia element is also clearly present in a composition that, after the *Folksong Symphony,* constitutes Harris's largest and most substantial folk-related composition, the *Folk Fantasy for Festivals.* This 1955–56 work, scored for soloists (among them folksinger types), speakers, double mixed chorus, and piano, is also the composer's last major composition in the genre, further use of folksong in his oeuvre being restricted to occasional quotations in compositions based chiefly on other materials.[5]

In addition to possessing the regional characteristics of the various movemements of the *Folksong Symphony,* the *Fantasy,* incorporates a somewhat wider range of techniques and a more ambitious style of choral writing. It also deals with the folk idiom within a wider frame of reference than the earlier work, for here Harris the symphonist-as-folksinger cited earlier comes to the fore. The fourth movement, "The Working Man's Pride," instead of employing actual folk tunes, is based on entirely original musical and textual materials, the folk element being derived from its portrayal of various working heroes (e.g., Paul Bunyan, Johnny Appleseed, Casey Jones).

## Religious Works

As inferred in chapter 1, Roy Harris's religious background was essentially Methodist. Johana, with her strong Irish heritage, was raised a Catholic. Harris recalled to me that around the time of his marriage to Johana, the two of them decided on a "compromise" faith that would provide some measure of compatibility with their strongly differing religious orientations. They chose the Episcopal Church, with its mixture of elements of both Protestantism and Catholicism. However, though Johana attended services from time to time, the composer seems to have refrained from active participation in religious activities except as they may have related to matters concerning his music.

Though Harris never, to my knowledge, discussed his religious views in great detail, I suspect that his studies of philosophy and sociology during the period at Berkeley around 1921 and later at UCLA resulted in both a high tolerance of the integrity of a wide variety of religious beliefs and a healthy skepticism. He recognized the value of an organized set of beliefs—after all, this was not so much different in principle from his own aesthetic and historical precepts concerning his art—and of communal activities, but he also appreciated the need for independent inquiry and faith.

This broad-mindedness is reflected in the diversity of orientation of Harris's relatively few religious works. One finds a setting of the Ordinary of the Roman Catholic Mass, a motet for the Jewish synagogue, and settings of psalms and hymns designed for Protestant services. There are also works in which the religious element functions as part of a larger scheme (e.g., the *Pere Marquette Symphony* with its extended setting of the Nicene Creed and the *Folk Fantasy* with its opening movement based on New England psalmody and religious folk melodies).

Among the religious works, the most substantial is a Mass for men's voices and organ written in 1948.[6] Though the composer achieved no

particularly original solution to the problems of the extended use of men's
voices (as Benjamin Britten managed to do a few years later in his opera
*Billy Budd*), he did try to compensate for the potential lack of timbral
variety by devising somewhat different procedures and textures for most
of the movements.

Of the composer's other religious works, the most important are the
two psalm settings. The musical imagery of Psalm 150 has appealed to
many composers, and Harris manages some felicitous touches in his own
setting. The intense plea for salvation and for sustenance against one's
enemies at the heart of Psalm 3 offers equally potent opportunities for
choral tone painting and draws forth some of Harris's most dissonant
harmonic writing:

EXAMPLE 152

*Psalm 3:* Dissonances

However, one finds in these works, as well as in the *Easter Motet* for
chorus and brass and the synagogue piece *Mi Chomocho* for tenor solo,
chorus, and organ, an overuse of block chordal writing and a rather
fragmentary, simplistic approach to polyphony, where it appears at all. All
the pieces are effective to some degree, but one feels a lack of depth and
variety. It is apparent that the folk element and the visionary power of
Whitman both had a stronger hold on Harris than did religious sentiments;
indeed, in a sense, these constituted his religion.

## Patriotic Compositions and other Works Relating to the Social Scene

One influence the writing of the a cappella choral pieces and the composition of the patriotic works discussed here had on Roy Harris's style was to
require him to work within a simpler, more direct melodic idiom, capable of
being performed by amateurs without too much difficulty. One of the

composer's most important works in the patriotic vein is a setting of Archibald MacLeish's poem "Freedom's Land." The correspondence between poet and composer reveals the earnestness and high enthusiam with which both entered into the creation of a kind of popular anthem of the sort Irving Berlin's "God Bless America" had become.[7] The melody is constructed along the clearcut, well-balanced lines of traditional phrase structure, yet the modal shifts and subtle touches in the harmony lend an unhackneyed air.

EXAMPLE 153

*Freedom's Land:* Melody

Harris got perhaps more "mileage" out of his *Freedom's Land* tune than out of anything else he ever wrote. Not only did he make several versions for different vocal combinations (a cappella chorus, accompanied women's chorus, male chorus, and versions for chorus and orchestra and band), he also used it, sometimes purely instrumentally, in other works.[8]

There are, in addition to *Freedom's Land,* compositions, mostly of larger dimensions, that, though possessing elements of patriotism, deal with the contemporary American social scene within a broader frame of reference. The earliest of these is *Challenge 1940* for baritone solo, chorus, and orchestra. But the largest, and perhaps most strongly personal, of Harris's compositions of this type is the three-movement *Whether this Nation* for chorus and band, composed in 1971. Here one finds the somewhat naive patriotic sentiments of some of the earlier essays in the genre placed in head-on confrontation with the disillusionment of his later years.

## Overview

Whatever reservations one may have about certain aspects of Roy Harris's work in the choral medium, the literature he produced here cannot be ignored. Not only does it constitute in volume a large part of his lifework, it also serves as a valuable and accessible source of observations on the origin and development of many aspects of his style and technique. In a situation similar to his work in the band medium, Harris's contributions to the choral literature may not today seem particularly venturesome. Yet he was, during the 1930s and early 1940s, regarded as something of a new and original voice in this area, and his finest efforts are infused with a genuine musicality and an understanding of the essence of the medium that should not be minimized.

# 15

## Works for Solo Voice

### Background and Position in Harris's Oeuvre

As I have pointed out earlier, whenever one had an opportunity to hear Roy Harris sing a theme from one of his symphonies or other instrumental compositions, one immediately understood, from the fervor, suppleness, and nuance which he imparted to the melody with his "composer's voice," how truly vocal was his conception of line. Harris's attitude toward the voice and his treatment of it have been discussed in chapter 14. Many of the observations made there about his choral technique and aesthetics apply also to the small, but distinctive, literature of compositions he wrote for solo voice. These works comprise some dozen items ranging from a handful of songs to a few large and striking compositions in the solo cantata genre that rank with his finest achievements. (One of these, *Canticle of the Sun,* is discussed in chapter 5 along with the Eighth Symphony because of its close relationship to that work.)

In spite of their small number, the level of quality among the compositions for solo voice is astonishingly high. Why is this? Like Schubert, Wagner, and other composers who occupied themselves with setting words to music, Harris always seemed stimulated by a potent text. This is certainly evident in some of the more impressive of his choral compositions, such as the *Symphony for Voices*. He generally missed few opportunities for grasping the central "affect" of each text and illustrating it with a corresponding melo/rhythmic idea. In addition to penetrating and conveying musically the inner meaning, he also demonstrated an occasional skill in painting individual words with representative devices.

As far as form is concerned, a poem provided Harris with a ready-made structure, a continuity that enabled him, in some works, to develop a more

flexible approach to this aspect of composition. The result was music
containing more contrasts—changes of texture, thematic ideas, tempo—
than are usually found in the logically, but sometimes doggedly, unfolding
autogenetic structures of his purely instrumental works. One of the best
examples of this flexibility, and indeed one of the high points of Harris's
oeuvre, is the cantata setting for baritone and orchestra of Whitman's
poem *Give Me the Splendid Silent Sun.* (This setting was originally intended as the opening movement of an aborted Whitman symphony on
which the composer worked during the mid-1950s.) In this work of his
maturity, one finds Harris accomplishing a welcome integration of contrasting episodes within a tightly controlled structure and a strongly paced
forward momentum. The aspect of control and unity is provided chiefly by
the vocal line, which, like that of the *Canticle,* is essentially a continued
spinning-out of the idea set in motion in the opening phrase.

## Comparisons and Contrasts with Choral Compositions

Though the voice parts in Harris's choral compositions sometimes take on
characteristics of his instrumental writing, they generally demonstrate at
least some consideration for matters of range, breathing, and balance
between conjunct and disjunct motion, as I have already observed. The
same is true of his writing for solo voice, except that here the melodic lines
tend to be more sensitively shaped and more grateful. An illustration from
one of the songs provides a demonstration of the sensitivity both to overall
mood and to individual words of which Harris was capable:

EXAMPLE 154

*Evening Song:* Vocal line examples

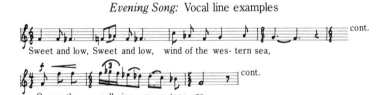

## Prosody

In general, Harris took greater care with prosody in his songs and cantatas
than in his choral works. The word accents, though sometimes handled

freely, do not conflict so obstinately with the metric accents as they do in some of the latter pieces.

## Use of the Accompanying Media

Harris employs his accompanying forces in these works in much the same fashion as in the choral works, that is, to provide harmonic support, to give additional means of representing the emotional characteristics and imagery of the text, and to provide interludes.

The most complex and colorful instrumental writing in these compositions is found in *Give Me the Splendid Silent Sun,* which is the only one to use full orchestra. The complete panoply of instrumental colors and textures that Harris's works of the 1950s display are found here: pantheistic evocations in *divisi* string arpeggios and woodwind filigrees; widely spaced string polychords suggesting the "nights perfectly quiet as on high plateaus"; savage brass interjections and nagging percussion cutting through agitated string tremolos as the poet ponders the conflict stirring in him between the enticements of nature and the ever increasing lure of the city.

## Songs

The tiny number of songs Harris bequeathed to the literature reveals a gift of considerable magnitude in this realm and causes one to regret that he did not pursue the genre more intensively. These compositions show as much as do the a cappella choral pieces and some of the solo piano works that the composer was as much at home in the world of the miniature as he was in that of large musical canvasses. The songs reveal a wide diversity in choice of texts and in musical approach and illuminate virtually every aspect of the composer's personality.

## Extended Song-settings with Chamber Ensemble

There are three works in this category. Two, a *Wedding Song* for bass solo, violin, viola, violoncello, and organ, and a *Lamentation* for soprano, viola, and piano, date from the mid-1940s; the last, *Rejoice and Sing,* for bass, string quartet, and piano comes, as mentioned before, from the 1970s and represents Harris's farewell to music.

The best of the handful of compositions in this category is the *Lamentation* of 1944. In addition to its intrinsic value, the work foreshadows in general character the more extended *Abraham Lincoln Walks at Midnight* of nearly ten years later and also prefigures, at least in principle if not in actual style, the vocalises of *Canticle of the Sun.*

The *Lamentation* too was written as an occasional piece, but it is evident that Harris poured some of his most generous melodic and harmonic inspiration into it. The work is one of his most deeply expressive utterances, unfolding with solemn pathos and great lyricism by means of the ample spinning-out of long-breathed paragraphs. Its progress from a subdued, dirgelike opening to an impassioned climax followed by a gentle winding down of tension provides another impressive illustration of the composer's Gothic-arch form. It also constitutes another summary in miniature of his harmonic idiom (similar to the "Soliloquy" of *Soliloquy and Dance*), opening with bare organum harmonies and subsequently expanding to rich polytonal aggregates. The rhythmic aspect is also illuminating in that it shows the very simple, but effective, way in which Harris gradually animates a work through the introduction of smaller and smaller subdivisons of the beat, reversing the process for the concluding portion of the work. This sort of thing is akin to the gradual reduction of note values in the finale of the Second Symphony and the augmentation of values in the last movement of the *Time Suite.*

There is an unsettling combination of seductiveness and profound sadness in the *Lamentation* that is worlds removed from the "civic" Harris who strode across the 1940s and 50s with so many big-gestured, large-scale works, and the piece is thus a valuable reminder of the complexity of personality that commentators often seem intent upon confining within a narrow, rawboned, regionalist half-frame.

## Cantatas

The four cantatas that span the twenty-year period from 1953 to 1973 constitute a happy diversity of voice types and accompanying media: *Abraham Lincoln Walks at Midnight* is scored for mezzo-soprano and piano trio; *Give Me the Splendid Silent Sun* is written for baritone and orchestra; *Canticle of the Sun* uses high voice and chamber ensemble consisting of a mixture of woodwinds, strings, and piano; *Life* employs high voice with the unconventional accompaniment of a wind ensemble.

*Abraham Lincoln Walks at Midnight* is true chamber music, an ensemble work in which the instruments are placed into a nearly equal partnership with the voice. In *Give Me the Splendid Silent Sun,* on the other hand, the orchestra is generally heard as a unit engaging in a dialogue with and supporting the soloist.

In their microstructures, both cantatas fall into a number of interlinked sections, each defined by specific textures, materials, and scoring that help to convey the changing sentiments and imagery of the texts. The Lincoln piece, aside from the lengthy passage in measures 82–109, which forms a centerpiece, may be regarded as essentially through-composed. However, the structure of the Whitman poem, with its two contrasting stanzas, demands something else. What is called for, in fact, is the kind of two-part "dream world-action world" design that came so naturally to Harris.

Perhaps only in his symphonies does one encounter the degree of variety found in Harris's solo cantatas. It seems to me that it is these compositions, rather than the choral works—fine though some of the latter are—that comprise the summit of his vocal art. Their distinctive qualities point up in an especially telling way the one-sided view that results when one concentrates exclusively on the instrumental compositions in assessing Harris's lifework.

# 16

## Farewell to a Pioneer

Roy Harris maintained an active and vigorous creative life until well into the 1970s. He also continued to conduct, teach, and fulfill speaking engagements. However, deteriorating health and a failing memory caused him to curtail much of this during his final years. The composer's ventures from the Pacific Palisades home where he had lived since 1965 became more and more infrequent. He eventually gave up driving an automobile and, though friends and family occasionally provided transportation on various occasions of business and pleasure, Harris preferred the familiarity and comfort of his studio.

He seemed increasingly ill at ease even with the routine of daily life. Indeed, he had never really had a "routine" since the very early years on the farm in San Gabriel and now, faced with desertion of his once abundant energy and a flagging of his creative powers, he was ill-equipped for a leisurely, sedentary existence. Though most admirers would have welcomed any new work from his pen, they were ready to accept the fact that he had given more than enough of himself during an immensely productive career. This acceptance by others, however, was of little comfort to a composer in whom ideas of vague shape still stirred restlessly but who lacked the capacity to bring them into the light.

In September of 1979 he suffered a fall in his studio that hospitalized him. Though the injuries sustained began to heal, it was apparent that the mishap was only a symptom of an irreversible physical decline.

## From Vanguard to Old Guard

Roy Harris's death in a Santa Monica sanitarium on October 1, 1979, ended a career that had taken him from vanguard to old guard. Though his achievements may not have had the broad international ramifications or received the publicity of the paper empire created by Schönberg and his disciples, they were no less genuine and creative. These achievements helped to transform the character of a music, to impart a new voice to the symphonic literature written by American composers. Though a precise definition of the factors that comprise this new voice, that give it its distinctive timbre, inflections, and accent, is sometimes difficult to formulate, there is no denying the immediately recognizable sound of a Harris, a Copland, a Thomson, a Schuman.

Also, beyond any nationalistic considerations, there is equally no denying in Roy Harris's oeuvre the profile of one of the most colorful and highly personal styles in the music of this century. There is nothing remarkable about the ingredients themselves: triadic harmonies, melodies shaped by the inflections of plainsong and folk tune, asymmetry of phrase at least as old as the choral polyphony of the Renaissance. Rather, the important thing is the way Harris looked at these with fresh eyes in the clear, open air and harnessed them together in a fashion that breathed with the renewed vitality of a tradition cleansed of encrustation in order that its core of truth and validity might glisten again. As he summed it up:

Throughout my lifework, my purpose has been to affirm tradition as our greatest resource, rather than to avoid it as our greatest threat.[1]

This could have served as the motto of Harris's pioneer forebears. As I observed in the preface to this book, Harris shared much with them. Though they were immersed in old values, with all the virtues and faults this entailed, they nonetheless had the courage to venture to new lands, to risk, to undergo terrible hardships, to endure. Like them, Harris, though rooted in the past, had his eye on the future. There was always a new work to write, a festival to plan, the exploration of new performing media, new designs, and, most important, new ways in which to meld the elements of the familiar vocabulary.

Though he was aware during much of the latter portion of his career that the fashion lay elsewhere, Harris also knew that one day there would be a fresh examination, a renewed appreciation. Indeed, he lived to see this happen during the last few years of his life. He was aware of the historical process that digests and provides a perspective, and he could distrust fad and understand the swings of fashion to which every vital culture is prone. Harris felt that one lifetime provided barely sufficient time to master one idiom, to say nothing of the changing succession of styles through which he felt some of his well-known colleagues had passed.

Harris believed that a serious composer should write not only lofty essays for the greatest artists of his time but should also provide music for use by committed amateurs of all persuasions. He felt that music should serve both for the purpose of spiritual and intellectual uplift and as a social, even a political stimulant. Above all, he felt that a composer should not remain aloof but should instead serve as both creative exemplar and as practical educator.

In spite of all this, however, Roy Harris's stature is still a matter of debate. The chief obstacle to a full evaluation of his achievement lies in the dual facts that only a tiny portion of his oeuvre is performed with any regularity and that scores of the majority of his works are not readily accessible. The fault for both situations lies partly with the composer, for he generally promoted only a handful of pieces that had become proven successes and, especially in later years, often neglected to follow through with preparing works for publication (especially those that had undergone revision and needed recopying).

Some critics feel that Harris failed to fulfill his early promise, revealing instead an arrested technical development and becoming mired in self-repetition. Others perceive, conversely, an increasing mastery of technique and a growing sophistication developing as his career unfolded, and believe that precisely because of this situation the music of his maturity lacks the raw, unbridled originality, vitality, and intensity of expression that characterize the early works, exhibiting in their stead a slick veneer. Some observers fault his Americanist attributes, which they feel have gone out of fashion, while others count these among his greatest strengths. Finally, there are those who are convinced that, in spite of the flaws in both man and work, the innate musicality revealed throughout his oeuvre and the breadth, vision, and generosity of impulse that inform his best music have assured Roy Harris a permanent place as one of the significant voices in the American music of this century.

# Notes and References

## Preface

1. Aaron Copland, *The New Music (1900–1960)*, rev. and enl. ed. (New York, 1968), p. 120.

2. Ibid., p. 118.

3. Roy Harris, program note on *Farewell to Pioneers, Journal of the Philadelphia Orchestra*, March 27, 1936, p. 813.

## Chapter 1

1. When Harris applied for a passport renewal upon planning a trip to Bogota, Colombia, in 1972, he was unable to locate his birth certificate and inquiries addressed to the appropriate authorities in Oklahoma failed to produce the document.

2. The Cimarron River arises in New Mexico and passes through a portion of the Oklahoma Panhandle and parts of Colorado and Kansas before dipping down into the central part of Oklahoma, passing some thirty miles northeast of Oklahoma City. Chandler lies approximately thirty miles northeast of Oklahoma City. It is the county seat of Lincoln County. The Cimarron land rush in which the composer's father took part should not be confused with the so-called Cimarron Territory, which now comprises the Panhandle.

3. Roy Harris interviews with Mark Evans, *Dialogue I,* unpublished typescript, Los Angeles, [early 1960s].

4. Virgil Thomson, review of *American Creed, New York Herald Tribune,* November 21, 1940. Reprinted in Virgil Thomson, *Music Reviewed (1940–1954)* (New York, 1967), p. 15.

5. This is reflected in both the music and the composer's program note for the "Speed" movement of the *American Portrait Symphony.* Also, in one bit of correspondence surviving from the mid-1930s, Harris proposed writing a symphony for the Chrysler Corporation for promotional purposes along the following lines: I. "Elegance" (sweeping, long melodic phrases), II. "Secure Comfort" (long flowing chorale), III. "Speed" (a scherzo), IV. "Economy" (contrapuntal fugue [*sic*], showing control, economy of means). He seemed quite serious about this (the tone of the proposal hinting that he perhaps hoped to be paid for the symphony in automobiles, presumably for life).

6. Henry Cowell, "Roy Harris," in Henry Cowell, ed., *American Composers on American Music (A Symposium)* (New York, 1962), pp. 64–65.

7. Thomson, *Music Reviewed 1940–1954,* p. 359 (from a *New York Herald Tribune* review of December 7, 1952, of the Fifth Symphony).

8. This is exemplified by his situation at both Cornell University and The Colorado College. Documents from thse institutions indicate that he did his teaching at home, while Johana Harris generally taught both classes (at the institutions) and private lessons (at home).

9. Johana Harris, "A Personal Note," quoted in David Ewen, *The New Book of Modern Composers* (New York, 1961), pp. 202–3.

10. Irene is still living. She married a violoncellist, Julian Kahn, and currently resides in Pacific Palisades, California, not far from her brother's last home.

11. The elder Broddle did not accompany them, for he had left the family not long after they had settled on the Oklahoma land.

12. Roy Harris, *Dialogue I.*

13. This house, located on West Puente Street in Covina, remained in the family for some years. Harris's mother continued to live there after Elmer passed away until her own death in 1958. The house is still standing, though it has been subjected to some alterations over the years.

14. Elkus was apparently not unsympathetic to Harris, however, for Harris claimed that some years later, at a performance of the Three Variations on a Theme (Quartet No. 2) at Mills College in Oakland, California, he reintroduced himself and admitted: "You're the greatest mistake I ever made. . . . It taught me a lesson. We don't know what people have in them by what they haven't done yet." Roy Harris interviews with Mark Evans, *Dialogue II,* unpublished typescript, Los Angeles, [early 1960s].

15. Brice Farwell, *A Guide to the Music of Arthur Farwell and to the Microfilm Collection of His Work* (Briarcliff Manor, N.Y., 1972), p. 1.

16. Roy Harris, *Dialogue II.*

17. Arthur Farwell, "Roy Harris," *Musical Quarterly* 18, no. 1 (1932):27.

18. Roy Harris, *Dialogue II.*

19. Ibid.

20. Mrs. Wertheim also ran a music publishing venture known as the Cos Cob Press, which issued a good deal of music by American composers.

21. Roy Harris, *Dialogue II.*

22. She was a fanatic admirer and promoter of the works of her immensely gifted younger sister Lili, who had died prematurely at the age of twenty-five.

23. Robert Moevs (interview with Ellen Rosond), "Nadia Boulanger (1887–1979)," *19th Century Music* 3, no. 3 (March 1980):227.

24. Virgil Thomson, *Virgil Thomson* (New York, 1967), pp. 202–3.

25. Roy Harris, "Perspective at Forty," *Magazine of Art* 32, no. 11 (November 1939):666–68.

26. Ibid., p. 668.

27. This organization had been established in 1909 by Gabriel Fauré. Its concert series was devoted primarily to works of the younger generation of European

composers, but Boulanger was responsible for adding an extra, nonsubscription, concert given over to young American composers.

28. Harris received a third Guggenheim grant in 1975.

# Chapter 2

1. Years later, when preparing live concerts and radio programs with Johana, Harris was able to draw on these early studies. He tended to take a historical style-period survey approach, employing a wide variety of materials in diverse media, sometimes arranging to have selections performed by appropriate soloists and groups to supplement Johana's interpretations of the music which lay within her repertoire.

2. Harris is sometimes compared with Shostakovich as a symphonist of bold gestures and broad musical panoramas. However, he did not really care much for the Russian's music.

3. One of the most important of these activities was the competition sponsored by the Fellowship of American Composers (of which Harris was president) which took place during the mid-1940s. The American Broadcasting Corporation offered prizes in this event to the outstanding orchestral, band, and choral entries.

4. See Schuman's tribute to his teacher in "Roy Harris (1898–1979)," in *Proceedings* of the American Academy and Institute of Arts and Letters, Second Series, no. 30, 1979, pp. 54–6.

5. One of the finest discussions of Harris's style to appear thus far, though made early in his career, is that by Arthur Farwell in "Roy Harris," *Musical Quarterly* 18, no. 1 (1932):18–32. An almost equally important, though sometimes overly generalized examination, is that by Nicolas Slonimsky in both his *Musical Quarterly* article, "Roy Harris" 33, no. 1 (1947):17–37 and in his unpublished monograph, *Roy Harris: Cimarron Composer* (Los Angeles: University of California, Los Angeles, 1951). The latter incorporates and expands upon the discussion in the former. An important discussion of Harris's treatment of harmony is Robert Evett, "The Harmonic Idiom of Roy Harris," *Modern Music,* Spring 1946, pp. 100–107. The most detailed examination given Harris's music to date is that found in Dan Stehman, "The Symphonies of Roy Harris: An Analysis of the Linear Materials and of Related Works" Ph.D. dissertation, University of Southern California, 1973.

6. H. T. Parker. Review of Roy Harris's *Symphony 1933,* c. January 27 or 28, 1934.

7. Farwell, "Roy Harris," p. 23.

8. See Harris's views on this in ibid., pp. 24–27.

9. Evett, "Harmonic Idiom," p. 104.

10. Since at least the 1940s, Harris had planned various books and series of writings on the materials and historical development of music. Though a number of

essays and articles survive touching on these topics, the major writing projects
never materialized.

11. Farwell, "Roy Harris," p. 27.
12. Evett, "Harmonic Idiom," p. 104.
13. Farwell, "Roy Harris," p. 27.
14. Evett, "Harmonic Idiom," p. 103.
15. Ibid., p. 100.
16. See the draft of Harris's letter to Stokowski on this matter in Stehman,
"Symphonies of Roy Harris," pp. 3–4, or Slonimsky, *Cimarron Composer,* p. 30.
17. See his comments on this in connection with the *Whitman Triptych* in
chapter 14. The Renaissance practice is described by Gustave Reese in *Music in
the Renaissance* (New York: W. W. Norton & Co., 1959), p. 461.

## Chapter 3

1. Roy Harris, "Composing—An Art and a Living," *Music Journal,* January
1953, p. 31.
2. Roy Harris, *Symphony–American Portrait 1929.* Note on unpublished fair
copy of score, p. 2 (Edwin A. Fleisher Collection in the Free Library of
Philadelphia).
3. For a detailed discussion of the *American Portrait,* see Stehman, "The
*Symphonies* of Roy Harris," Part I.
4. Roy Harris, quoted in Walter Piston, "Roy Harris," *Modern Music,*
January–February 1934, p. 81.
5. Farwell, *"Roy Harris,"* p. 18.
6. Among these are the nearly contemporary *When Johnny Comes Marching
Home* overture, some of the short band works of the early 1940s, and an occasional
orchestral, work such as the *Dance* of *Elegy and Dance.*
7. Roy Harris, quoted in *Speaking of Roy Harris* (Los Angeles: The Friends of
Roy Harris, University of California, Los Angeles), February 12, 1966, p. 2.
8. This type of finale is discussed in detail in chapters 4 and 5, in connection
with the Fifth, Sixth, and Ninth Symphonies.
9. Roy Harris, program note on Symphony No. 3, Boston Symphony Orchestra *Programme,* Seventeenth Program, February 24–25, 1939, pp. 777–88. A
longer and more detailed analysis by the composer is found in Slonimsky, *Cimarron
Composer,* pp. 136–40.
10. Harris mentioned to me (and a number of other individuals) his attempt to
"recapitulate" the harmonic development of Western music by means of this
vertical expansion.
11. Harris's use of the term "polytonal" is questionable because, though the
sense of tonality in his works is fluid, with frequent shifting of key centers from one
cadence point to the next, the listener is still generally aware of a single tonality
within a given phrase, regardless of the complexity of the chord structure. In this

and similar passages, the term is best understood in the purely vertical sense. See also Piston, *"Roy Harris,"* pp. 78–79.

## Chapter 4

1. Roy Harris, program note for *Folksong Symphony 1940,* quoted in Nicolas Slonimsky, *Notes* (Vanguard SRV 347 SD).

2. See chapter 14 for a discussion of these.

3. Harris's decision to reverse the positions of the two outer movements for the final version of the symphony doubtless was made at least partly on musical grounds, as the long introduction of "The Girl I Left Behind Me" seems more appropriate in an opening movement. However, the texts played a role in this as well, as the "going away" sentiments of the opening movement and the "coming home" idea of the closing movement doubtless make more sense in terms of dramatic logic, especially for a work conceived in wartime.

4. Roy Harris, program note on Symphony No. 5, Boston Symphony Orchestra *Programme,* Seventeenth Program, February 26–27, 1943, p. 724.

5. Other aspects of Harris's instrumentation and scoring are discussed in chapters 9 and 10.

6. This figure bears a strong kinship to the principal rhythmic idea of the opening movement of Beethoven's Seventh Symphony (though the latter is essentially an "upbeat" figure in contrast with the "downbeat" character of the Harris motive). Harris, a great admirer of this work, may have had it in mind when writing the present movement.

7. Harris's at times extensive preparatory reading about such figures as Lincoln and Pere Marquette (for the Twelfth Symphony) were as much for the purpose of providing a background for character and mood as for specific facts. He attempted to extract the essence of the life and career of each extramusical subject and from this created a relatively simple ground plan for the composition itself.

8. This section is actually a reworking for orchestra of the concluding portion of the third movement of the Violin Sonata. From this point on, the Sixth Symphony is based entirely on preexistent materials, something that suggests a sense of pressure and haste on the composer's part, perhaps in meeting a deadline. However, the reworked materials are in themselves distinguished and skillfully handled here, and their use does not constitute a weakness per se in the symphony.

9. Unfortunately, Harris's involvement with the Cumberland Festival, which promised to continue after his move to Pittsburgh, terminated in 1952 when he became distressed over the apparent racial policy of the University of the South. As a result, the Harrises and a number of their colleagues who were scheduled to participate in that year's festival signed a formal protest and boycotted the event.

10. Theme III actually originated in the Symphony for Band (see chapter 10), where it functioned as the subject of a fugue carried out on quite traditional lines.

11. Roy Harris, program note on Symphony No. 7 [final version], Philadelphia Orchestra *Program,* October 21–22, 1955, p. 93.

## Chapter 5

1. An account of the Pittsburgh Festival is given by Margaret Maxwell in "Contemporary Festival in Pittsburgh," *Music Journal,* January 1953, pp. 10–11, 64–66.

2. Harris's airy mismanagement of his personal finances was quite another matter and was the cause of some of the most amusing, and frustrating, incidents of his career.

3. The episode is recounted in Patricia Ashley, "Roy Harris," *Stereo Review,* December 1968, pp. 70–72.

4. To the end of his days, Harris clung naively to the idealized view of Russia he had acquired on the trip without realizing that, as an official visitor, his activities had been carefully stage managed. During his last years, I sometimes heard him talk of emigrating to Russia and/or of having all his symphonies recorded there.

5. Alfred Frankenstein, review of Symphony No. 8, *San Francisco Chronicle,* January 19, 1962, p. 36.

6. In fact, the Eighth Symphony marks the beginning of Harris's soloistic use of the piano in his symphonies, a development continued in both the Tenth Symphony (with its two pianos) and the Eleventh (with its important piano solo during the opening sections).

## Chapter 6

1. A somewhat different, though related, slant is given in an article in the *New York Herald Tribune* of February 4, 1951. Harris, who had recently come to Nashville, Tennessee, to assume his composer-in-residence position at Peabody College, was quoted as explaining that he settled in Nashville because he wanted to get away from the "New York influence." He described that city as a "cultural colony of Europe" and said he felt it was "high time to give America back to Americans" (culturally speaking).

2. Roy Harris, program note on Symphony No. 10, University of California, Los Angeles, *Abraham Lincoln Memorial Concert* program, April 14, 1965 (unpaginated).

3. Ibid.

4. Harris had second thoughts about the medium of the Tenth, however, and decided to make another version for chorus and orchestra, in order not to exclude the work from the symphonic repertoire. However, this project was only partly realized. He also made a version of movements I, II, and III for chorus and two pianos, drastically altering the choral writing in the second movement.

5. Roy Harris, program note on Symphony No. 11, New York Philharmonic Orchestra *Notes,* February 8, 9, 12, 1968, p. D. [sic.] He had planned initially to write an orchestral work based upon Tolstoy's *War and Peace.* Though this idea was abandoned, elements of it linger in the symphony's turbulent character.

6. This fugue is a reworking of the opening section of Fugue III of the Third Quartet.

7. Wilfred Mellers remarked about the Seventh Symphony: "What is new in this music is the manner in which the proliferating variations now *conflict* so violently with the noble spaciousness of the passacaglia theme that Harris's rural music acquires an undercurrent of neurotic fury, . . . The symphony is impressive, though it is difficult to imagine where Harris can go from this point." Though somewhat off the mark with regard to that earlier work, the observation does seem to have some validity when applied to the Eleventh Symphony. *Music in a New Found Land* (New York, 1965), p. 78.

8. The composer recalled for me hearing this chant for the first time during the late 1920s in France, during his studies with Boulanger. It appeared on a 78-rpm recording of plainchant by the Monks of the Abbey of Solesmes. He copied the melody, along with numerous other chants, into one of the sketchbooks that he kept during this period.

9. Harris, in fact, reworked a substantial portion of Part I of the Eighth Symphony for this section.

10. Roy Harris, program note on Symphony No. 12, Milwaukee Symphony Orchestra *Program Notes,* November 8–9, 1969, p. 3–37 (a single page, numbered as a hyphenated [series] number).

## Chapter 7

1. Roy Harris, "Perspective at Forty," *Magazine of Art,* November 1939, pp. 668–69.

2. Farwell, "Roy Harris," p. 21.

3. Edmund Scott, review of Roy Harris's String Quartet No. 3, *Christian Science Monitor,* August 12 or 13, 1939.

4. In the score, Harris cites only the "a" portion of motive x as the principal motive, but he also accords the "b" part an important role in the development, so that I have decided to extend his motive identification to incorporate both fragments.

5. The first theme cited in Ex. 110 is, of course, an early form of the theme on which the *Piano Quintet* is based (see Ex. 127).

6. Farwell, "Roy Harris," p. 27.

## Chapter 8

1. This was one of Piston's reservations about Harris's contrapuntal technique (see Walter Piston, "Roy Harris," *Modern Music,* January–February 1934, pp. 76–77).

2. Roy Harris, program note on Quintet for Piano and Strings (Contemporary Records *Contemporary Composers Series* S8012).

3. Ibid.

## Chapter 9

1. This association has a long history: witness the mensuration canons of the fifteenth-century Netherlands school of composers and the various puzzle canons in later works such as J. S. Bach's *Musical Offering* (these latter evidently originating in elements of Classical Greek rhetoric).

2. Some of the pieces such as the Fanfare, the Toccata, and the *Salute to Youth,* seem never to have been submitted to a publisher. However, Harris's waywardness in matters of this sort, especially from the 1940s on, renders contractual status an unreliable guide to his regard for a composition.

3. The *Epilogue to Profiles in Courage* of 1964 is an illustration of this. Harris had been deeply affected by the assassination of President John F. Kennedy the previous November (the "Elegy" of the Violoncello Sonata seems to have resulted in part from this) and not only spent some weeks in deep creative concentration over the relatively short work, but also took it in hand after the premiere and completely reshaped it.

## Chapter 10

1. That Harris recognized the difficulties in writing for the medium is revealed in this statement contained in his program note for the premiere of the Symphony for Band: "The writing of this work has been extraordinarily difficult for me. . . . My attention has been given, for many years, to writing for symphony orchestras wherein one can draw heavily on the sustaining quality of the strings. The problem of writing for wind instruments is much more difficult in that one must make proper allowance for breathing . . . it seems to me that a symphonic band is like a cross between a pipe organ and a chorus; yet it has a great deal more agility than a chorus and more expressive control than a pipe organ." (U. S. Military Academy Band. Program for Final Concert of the Winter Sesquicentennial Series, May 30, 1952, p. 6).

2. It must be remembered, however, that Harris's autogenetic principles imply a continual process of unfolding in which exposition and development become one.

3. This concern with sonority as a form building element is not actually new here. It may be found in such works of the 1940s as the Sixth Symphony (first movement) and the "Paean" of the *Elegy and Paean* for viola and orchestra. However, it had not figured so prominently in his band works until now.

4. His principal experiences with jazz, in a working sense, seem to have been with Paul Whiteman, on whose radio program some of his works were given in 1944, and Tommy Dorsey, for whose organization he conceived an *American Symphony* (c. 1938). This latter piece remained unfinished.

5. Harris goes into this in some detail in connection with the scoring of the original version of the Fifth Symphony in Charles O' Connell, *The Victor Book of Symphonies,* revised and enl. ed. (New York: Simon and Schuster, 1948), pp. 240–41.

## Chapter 11

1. This was not for lack of opportunity to do otherwise, for he often consulted with and received a good deal of advice from performers. For example, for the *Etude for Pedals* (for organ), Harris received a rather detailed list of suggestions from Frederick Tulan on registration and playing technique.

## Chapter 12

1. One other composition for violin and piano, dating from the 1940s and published as *Four Charming Little Pieces,* is actually a selection of scenes from the *Namesake* ballet.

2. It even underlies single-movement works (such as *Ad Majorem Gloriam*) that comprise two large connected, but contrasting, sections.

## Chapter 13

1. Slonimsky, *Cimarron Composer,* p. 23.

2. I except from this discussion the opening movement of the Amplified Piano Concerto and other pieces that deliberately employ quotation for purposes of parody.

3. Thomson, *Music Reviewed (1940–1954),* p. 105.

4. Farwell, "Roy Harris," pp. 19–21.

5. Harris, however, cut this passage from performance, apparently during the 1930s.

## Chapter 14

1. Copland, *The New Music (1900–1960),* pp. 122–23.

2. The first three were published in 1941, together with some of Harris's settings for various choral combinations of Archibald MacLeish's poem "Freedom's Land," under the series title *Songs of Democracy.* In addition, the composer reworked *Year that Trembled* and *To Thee* for the final two movements of his 1944 *Ballet on the Subject of War* (also known as the *Walt Whitman Suite*) for Hanya Holm.

3. As mentioned elsewhere, this is the piece in which Harris first employed the device of choric speech.

4. Of course, the Folksong Symphony must be included among these works. However, it is discussed in chapter 4, among the symphonies. Another work that very likely belongs in the folksetting category is Harris's a cappella treatment of the "twelve days of Christmas" idea in *A Red Bird in a Green Tree.*

5. Examples of these later works are the Ninth Symphony, whose first movement incorporates a brief reference to "I'll Be True to My Love," and the Violoncello Sonata, whose opening movement concludes with a statement of "The Raggle-Taggle Gypsy," used previously in the "Weeping Willow" movement of the

Folk Fantasy. The only post-1956 work based entirely on folksongs is the un-finished *Folksong Suite* for harp, winds, and percussion, but this torso lacks the depth and variety of the *Fantasy.*

6. The circumstances surrounding the purported commission of this work provide one of the more curious stories of Harris's sometimes colorful career. They are recounted in Slonimsky, *Cimarron Composer,* pp. 89–90.

7. In one letter, Harris, in fact, expresses a desire to write a work that would be accepted by both the public at large and the academic community, something which, he believed, had not happened with the Berlin Song.

8. An especially imaginative variation on both the melodic and harmonic aspect appears in the final pages of the Symphony for Band.

## Chapter 16

1. Roy Harris, program note on *Quintet for Piano and Strings* (Contemporary Records *Contemporary Composers Series* S8012).

# Bibliography

I have tried, in this selective bibliography, to provide a wide range of the more informative references on Roy Harris, references that provide diverse views on the composer and also, when taken together, give a broad picture of his accomplishments. For many of these, I have provided comments on special features, strengths, weaknesses, biases, etc., of which the reader should be aware when consulting them.

Countless articles have been written on Harris over the years in periodicals of national and local circulation and in books and encyclopedias. In addition, the composer himself published a number of writings. He also left, among his manuscripts and correspondence, drafts, in various stages of completion, of a variety of statements and additional articles, some of the latter quite extensive.

Since Harris's published articles often reiterate the same ideas from one to another (expected, in view of the consistency of his aesthetics), I have chosen those that I regard as containing the most cogent expression of these ideas. In addition, I have included the program notes Harris prepared for his numbered symphonies. These, I feel, will be useful both in providing the composer's own views on the genre that is given some of the most extensive coverage in this book, and also as illustrations of how Harris expressed himself on specific examples of his work, in contrast with the more general observations contained in most of his articles.

As this book goes to press, there are a number of theses and dissertations in progress, in addition to the completed studies listed, that will include discussions of various aspects of Harris's oeuvre. Also underway is *The New Grove Dictionary of Music in the United States,* to which I am contributing the Roy Harris article.

## 1. Books

Chase, Gilbert. *America's Music.* New York: McGraw-Hill, 1955, pp. 502–9. This is an attempt to place Harris within the context of his contemporaries. It is still overall one of the best books on the American musical scene. (At the time this is written, a thoroughgoing reworking of this volume is in progress for a new edition.)

Copland, Aaron. *The New Music (1900–1960),* rev. and enl. ed. New York: W. W. Norton, 1968, pp. 118–26. This is an evaluation by a fellow composer who mined some of the same musical ore. Copland provides genuine insights into some of Harris's strengths and weaknesses but seems unperceptive and/or biased in other areas, particularly those relating to Harris's form.

Cowell, Henry, ed. *American Composers on American Music (A Symposium)*. New York: Frederick Ungar, 1962, pp. 64–69. Cowell has assembled a collection of articles on several American composers, largely written by various of his colleagues. The Harris article is by Cowell himself, who is less sympathetic and more skeptical than some of Harris's other colleagues who have written about him. Included is a lengthy statement by Harris that sets forth his aesthetics in a particularly thorough manner.

Ewen, David. *The New Book of Modern Composers*. New York: Alfred A. Knopf, 1961, pp. 201–10. Of Ewen's many books of highly variable quality, this is perhaps the most useful on the topic of the American composer. It approaches each subject in four ways: (1) a biographical essay, (2) an essay on the music, (3) a personal note by a colleague or relative, (4) a statement by the composer.

Farwell, Brice. *A Guide to the Music of Arthur Farwell and to the Microfilm Collection of His Work*. Briarcliff Manor, N.Y.: Author, 1972. This is the most thorough discussion to date of the life and music of Harris's first important teacher.

Goss, Madeleine. *Modern Music Makers (Contemporary American Composers)*. New York: E. F. Dutton, 1952, pp. 283–301.

Howard, John Tasker. *Our Contemporary Composers*. New York: Thomas Crowell, 1941, pp. 132–45.

Mellers, Wilfrid. *Music in a New Found Land*. New York: Alfred A. Knopf, 1965. This constitutes an earnest, if only intermittently successful, attempt by a British writer to come to grips with the American musical scene. Mellers's views on Harris are stimulating, but ultimately he seems to fail to grasp the essence of the composer's work.

Reis, Clair. *Composers in America*, rev. and enl. ed. New York: Da Capo (Reprint of 1947 rev. and enl. ed.), 1977, pp. 167–70. The Harris chapter in this book is valuable in supplying some biographical data not found elsewhere.

Rosenfeld, Paul. *An Hour with American Music*. Philadelphia: J. B. Lippincott Co., 1929, pp. 117–25. This contains one of the earliest articles on Harris, from the pen of one of the most highly regarded of critical writers, one who seemed especially receptive to new developments.

Saminsky, Lazare. *Living Music of the Americas*. New York: Howell, Soskin, and Crown, 1949, pp. 44–49. Saminsky provides an extremely positive, though not uncritical, evaluation of Harris. His is one of the relatively few pieces of writing on the composer in which the author makes an attempt to come to grips with the music itself, rather than simply restating and/or summarizing the opinions of others.

Slonimsky, Nicolas. *Roy Harris: Cimarron Composer*. Los Angeles: University of California, Los Angeles, unpublished monograph, 1951. Slonimsky's work is the earliest attempt at a full length study of Harris, taking the composer up to c. 1950. Entertainingly and clearly written, with a good summary of the various elements of Harris's style, and many music examples, it does, however, possess some shortcomings. Among these are a tendency to overgeneralize and to categorize and enumerate without real penetration and some surprising factual lapses.

*Speaking of Roy Harris.* Los Angeles: The Friends of Roy Harris, University of California, Los Angeles, February 12, 1966. This limited edition booklet was issued in honor of the composer's sixty-eighth birthday and contains a biographical continuity, many citations of critical evaluations, comments by the composer, and photographs.

Thomson, Virgil. *Music Reviewed (1940–1954).* New York: Vintage Books, 1967. This comprises a collection of reviews of concerts Thomson covered during his tenure as music critic of the *New York Herald Tribune.* There are some incisive and provocative comments on a few of Harris's works.

Thomson, Virgil. *Virgil Thomson.* New York: Da Capo Press, 1967. Though this autobiography by one of Harris's prominent colleagues contains little on the music itself, there is some valuable information about Harris's period in France.

## 2. Articles

Ashley, Patricia. "Roy Harris." *Stereo Review,* December 1968, pp. 63–73. This is a good biographical sketch, taking the composer up through the late 1960s. It also contains a detailed account of the scandal concerning the Fifth Symphony in Pittsburgh.

Bialosky, Marshall. "Roy Harris: In Memoriam (But Keep Your Hats On)" *College Music Symposium* 22, no. 2 (1982):7–19. Bialosky gives an essentially unfavorable, though at times intelligent, assessment of Harris. His article constitutes a good summary of the negative reactions Harris's music has attracted over the years.

Curtis, William D. "Roy Harris (1898–1979)—A Discography." *Journal of the Association for Recorded Sound Collections* 13, no. 3 (1982):60–79. This constitutes the first complete Harris discography, written by a specialist in this area of research.

Evett, Robert. "The Harmonic Idiom of Roy Harris." *Modern Music,* Spring 1946, pp. 100–107. Evett, a former student of Harris, made the first real attempt to deal with the elements of the composer's harmonic idiom.

Farwell, Arthur. "Roy Harris." *Musical Quarterly* 18, no. 1 (1932):18–32. This is the pioneering essay on Harris, and is still one of the best introductions to the music, even though written before Harris's maturity. Farwell had an opportunity to participate in Harris's development during his formative years and provides many valuable insights.

Foreman, Lewis. "Roy Harris: American Symphonist." *Musical Opinion.* January 1972, pp. 180–81, 183. This is a relatively recent evaluation of Harris from a British viewpoint. It is also one of the few articles in which the later symphonies are discussed.

Gibbs, L. Chesley and Dan Stehman, "The Roy Harris Revival." *American Record Guide*: Part I, May 1979, pp. 8–13; Part II, June 1979, pp. 4–8, 57–59. The authors evaluate Harris's achievement from near the end of his career and provide critical commentary on many recordings released since the advent of the long-playing era.

Harris, Roy. "Adagio Penseroso." Raymond Swing, ed. *This I Believe (The Personal Philosophies of One Hundred Thoughtful Men and Women in all Walks of Life—Twenty of Whom Are Immortals In the History of Ideas, Eighty of Whom Are our Contemporaries of Today—Written for Edward R. Murrow)*, Vol. II. New York: Simon & Schuster, 1954, pp. 70–71.

Harris, Roy. "The Basis of Artistic Creation in Music" (no ed.). *The Bases of Artistic Creation*. New York: Octagon Books, 1969, pp. 19–29 (Rutgers University—Publications of the One Hundred Seventy-Fifth Anniversary Celebration—Number One). This is a detailed exposition of Harris's conception of what a composer must be and of his relationship to society.

Harris, Roy. "Composing—An Art and a Living." *Music Journal,* January 1953, pp. 31, 78. This is especially valuable for Harris's views on the relationship between art and commerce and on the serious composer's role in this relationship.

Harris, Roy. "Perspective at Forty." *Magazine of Art* 32, no. 11 (1939):638–39, 667–71. This is one of Harris's earliest published articles and is important for reminiscences about his early life, and, especially, his studies with Boulanger. (Slonimsky, in *Cimarron Composer,* asserts that this article is a considerably bowdlerized and truncated version of an autobiography the composer was writing at about this time and which has not been located.)

Maxwell, Margaret. "Contemporary Festival in Pittsburgh." *Music Journal,* January 1953, pp. 10–11, 64–66. Maxwell provides valuable information about the most important of the music festivals with which Harris was associated.

Moevs, Robert (interview with Ellen Rosand). "Nadia Boulanger (1887–1979)." *19th Century Music* 3, no. 3 (1980):276–78. This is a good summary of Boulanger's guiding aesthetics, from a somewhat more generalized viewpoint than that given by Harris.

Piston, Walter. "Roy Harris." *Modern Music,* January-February 1934, pp. 73–83. This is the earliest article on Harris by one of his contemporaries. Though Piston is put off by the inadequately formed technique the composer demonstrated during this period and by the naivety of some of his pronouncements, he brings considerable insight to his task and makes an honest attempt to bring out the positive aspects of Harris's works.

Reed, Peter Hugh. "Roy Harris—American Composer." *The American Music Lover* 3, no. 2 (1938):406–10. Reed's article is one of the more extensive early writings on Harris and one of the most balanced in tone.

Sabin, Robert. "Roy Harris—Still Buoyant as Composer and Teacher." *Musical*

*America,* January 15, 1957, pp. 17, 24–25. Sabin provides a view of both Harris's daily life and his professional attitudes during the 1950s. He also discusses the Seventh Symphony in some detail.

Schuman, William. "Roy Harris (1898–1979)." *Proceedings* of the American Academy and Institute of Arts and Letters, Second Series, No. 3, 1979, pp. 54–56. This is a reminiscence by one of Harris's most prominent students, given as a tribute after his death.

Slonimsky, Nicolas. "Roy Harris." *Musical Quarterly* 33, no. 1 (1947):17–37. In a sense, this is a continuation of the Farwell article of 1932, dealing with the composer at the time of his maturity. Slonimsky, however, seems to lack Farwell's ability to approach the music from the inside, sometimes, as in *Cimarron Composer,* choosing to enumerate without elucidating. But the article is valuable as a study by a long time friend and associate of Harris, and one who took time to examine a great deal of the music.

———. "The Story of Roy Harris—American Composer." *Etude,* Part I, December 1956, p. 11; Part II, January 1957, p. 12.

Strimple, Nick. "An Introduction to the Choral Music of Roy Harris." *The Choral Journal* 22, no. 9 (1982):16–19. Strimple provides considerable insight, in terms easily grasped, into Harris's choral technique and achievements, from the standpoint of an experienced choral conductor.

## 3. Encyclopedias

*Baker's Biographical Dictionary of Music and Musicians.* Fifth edition, rev. and enl. New York: G. Schirmer, 1958. With supplement 1965, edited by Nicolas Slonimsky, pp. 658–60.

Cobb, Donald. "Roy Harris." In *The New Grove Dictionary of Music and Musicians,* edited by Sadie, Stanley. Washington, D.C.: Grove's Dictionary of Music, 1980, Vol. 8, pp. 250–53. Cobb provides a reasonably well-balanced article, though he fails to convey much of the character of Harris's music, sometimes relying instead on overly generalized description. The article does contain the most extensive list of works published prior to the present volume. The bibliography, however, is inadequate.

## 4. Program Notes

Harris, Roy. Program note on *Symphony 1933.* Boston Symphony *Programme,* Fourteenth Program, January 26–27, 1934, pp. 642–57.

———. Program note on Symphony No. 2. Boston Symphony Orchestra *Programme,* Seventeenth Program, February 28–29, 1936, pp. 798–808.

———. Program note on Symphony No. 3. Boston Symphony Orchestra *Programme,* Seventeenth Program, February 24–25, 1939, pp. 777–88.

———. Program note on *Folksong Symphony.* Boston Symphony Orchestra *Programme,* Sixteenth Program, February 21–22, 1941, pp. 729–40.

———. Program note on Symphony No. 5. Boston Symphony Orchestra *Programme,* Seventeenth Program, February 26–27, 1943, pp. 720–27.

———. Program note on Symphony No. 6. Boston Symphony Orchestra *Programme,* Twenty-second Program, April 14–15, 1945, pp. 1282–1300.

———. Program note on Symphony No. 7 [final version], Philadelphia Orchestra *Program,* October 21–22, 1955, pp. 91–93.

———. Program note on Symphony No. 8. San Francisco Symphony Orchestra *Program,* January 17, 1962, n.p.

———. Program note on Symphony No. 9. Philadelphia Orchestra *Program,* Fifteenth Pair of Concerts, January 18–19, 1963, pp. 23–24.

———. Program note on Symphony No. 10. University of California, Los Angeles, *Abraham Lincoln Memorial Concert* program, April 14, 1965, p. 2.

———. Program note on Symphony No. 11. New York Philharmonic Orchestra *Notes,* February 8, 9, 12, 1968, B–D.

———. Program note on *Pere Marquette Symphony.* Milwaukee Symphony Orchestra *Program Notes,* November 8, 9, 1969, pp. 3–17 to 3–39.

———. Program note on *Bicentennial Symphony—1976. Notes on the Program,* February 10–12, 1976, pp. 30A–31B.

## 5. Theses and Dissertations

Brookhart, Charles Edward. "The Choral Music of Aaron Copland, Roy Harris, and Randall Thompson." Ph.D. dissertation, George Peabody College for Teachers, 1980. (Microfilm. Ann Arbor: University Microfilms.)

Halen, Walter John. "An Analysis and Comparison of Compositional Practices Used by Five Contemporary Composers in Works Titled Symphony." Ph.D. dissertation, Ohio State University, 1969. (Microfilm. Ann Arbor: University Microfilms.) This is the first scholarly study on the Ph.D. level of one of Harris's symphonies (the Seventh), placing it within the context of significant works in the genre by contemporaries.

King, Irvin Jean. "Neoclassical Tendencies in Seven American Piano Sonatas (1925–1945)." Ph.D. dissertation, Washington University, 1971. (Microfilm. Ann Arbor: University Microfilms.) This is an assessment of the concrete manifestations of the neo-Classic elements that are often considered to be part of Harris's style.

Kirk, Edgar L. "Toward American Music, A Study of the Life and Music of Arthur Farwell." Ph.D. dissertation, University of Rochester, 1959. (Microfilm. Ann Arbor: University Microfilms.) Though this lacks the variety and scope of Brice Farwell's later compilation (which see), it does go into the life and music in some detail.

Mize, Lou Stem. "A Study of Selected Choral Settings of Walt Whitman's Poems." Ph.D. dissertation, Florida State University, 1967. (Microfilm. Ann Arbor: University Microfilms.)

Ortolano, Williams. "The Mass and the Twentieth Century Composer." D.S.M. dissertation, University of Montreal, 1964. This study includes an examination of Harris's Mass for men's voices and organ.

Pisciotta, Louis Vincent. "Texture in the Choral Works of Selected Contemporary American Composers." Ph.D. dissertation, Indiana University, 1967. (Microfilm. Ann Arbor: University Microfilms.)

Plinkiewisch, Helen. "A Contribution to the Understanding of the Music of Charles Ives, Roy Harris, and Aaron Copland: a Report of a Type C Project." Master's thesis, Columbia University, 1955. This is one of the earliest works by a university scholar to deal with Harris and is especially valuable in that it views the composer in relation to two of his most important contemporaries.

Service, Alfred Roy, Jr. "A study of the Cadence as a Factor in Music Intelligibility in Selected Piano Sonatas by American Composers." Ph.D. dissertation, State University of Iowa, 1958. (Microfilm. Ann Arbor: University Microfilms.) Service provides the only other study, aside from the Evett article on the harmonic style, of Harris's treatment of the cadence and its relationship to the definition of form.

Stehman, Dan. "The Symphonies of Roy Harris: An Analysis of the Linear Materials and of Related Works." Ph.D. dissertation, University of Southern California, 1973. (Microfilm. Ann Arbor: University Microfilms.) This is the single most extensive scholarly work yet written on Harris. Though it concentrates on the symphonies, many other compositions are discussed in some detail. There is also an extended section on the elements of Harris's style and technique, but this material is in need of expansion. There are, in addition, several factual details that require updating.

Wolf, Henry. "The Twentieth Century Piano Sonata." Ph.D. dissertation, Boston University, 1957. (Microfilm. Ann Arbor: University Microfilms.) This includes a discussion of Harris's Piano Sonata within the context of other works in the genre by several of his colleagues.

## 6. Documents

Harris, Roy (interviews with Mark Evans). *Dialogues I and II*. Los Angeles: unpublished typescript, n.d. (very likely from the early 1960s). The origin and purpose of this interview are uncertain, the format suggesting possible use in a series of radio broadcasts. However, the manuscript contains a good deal of reminiscence about the composer's early years and about formative influences on his music.

Harris, Roy (interviews with Donald Schippers and Adelaide Tusler). *Oral History* (7/6/62–3/14/69): thirty and one-half hours of oral interview tapes. Los Angeles: University of California. This potentialy important document came to light too late to be examined in connection with the present study. A written transcription of the tapes is currently being prepared.

# List of Works

The following list is taken from the draft of a thematic catalog I am preparing. It is the most nearly complete and accurate list yet published, based on the best information that has come to light. One should keep in mind, however, that Harris ›ecame increasingly careless about preserving and documenting his oeuvre as time ›nt on, a situation aggravated by many changes of residence. Thus, a number of ›rks known from various sources to have existed have disappeared, while other ›positions previously unknown continue to turn up unexpectedly. Even for ›s for which materials exist bibliographic data are sometimes incomplete.

› list is organized by year and alphabetically by title within each year. Where a ›ed work was revised substantially prior to publication but after having been performed, the year of revision, where known, is indicated as well. ›at cannot be dated accurately are listed at the end.

›ositions that have been published are given a copyright date. If a piece ›eprinted, or published in a new edition, only the current printing and ›e listed. I also give the format (e.g., score, study score, parts, etc.) in ›‹ is issued. Out of print items are designated "op."

›d compositions available on rental only or published works now out of ›hich rental materials are available are so identified.

›ntracted to a publisher have no publication data supplied.

›me of Harris's compositions vary from one source to another. He ›ed titles deliberately, sometimes simply misremembered them ›ts of works for various published articles. Each title on the ›he best of my knowledge, the definitive title by which the ›e work in question to be known. A variant title is also listed in ›as become widely known. A subtitle is given in parentheses ›. I have included the medium as part of the main title in those ›certos, sonatas) where it traditionally appears as such. In ›ave not listed titles, where they exist, of the individual ›vement work.

Harris's transcriptions and arrangements of pieces by ›cription, I mean the transferring of material from one ›nimal changes in musical content; by arrangement, I ›ting of material (such as supplying a harmonization, ›etc.); this may also involve a transfer of medium.

However, I have treated Harris's settings of folk and related materials as original compositions, since these (being in the nature of common musical property) are so often appropriated by composers for this purpose.

I have not attempted to include works by other composers that Harris edited for publication. Though many have turned up, several are still unlocated. This is a gray area in Harris's oeuvre, involving not only the finding of still missing items but also the determination of his actual contribution to these editions.

## 1. Publishers

Arrow Music Press, Inc. (reissued Cos Cob publications; see Associated Music Publishers).

Associated Music Publishers, Inc. (AMP). 866 3rd Ave., New York, NY, 10022 (owns, in addition, all items formerly issued by Arrow Music Press).

Belwin Mills Publishing Corp. (BM). Melville, NY, 11747 (purchased Mills Music, Inc.; also owns the *Cumberland Concerto,* formerly controlled by G. Ricordi).

Columbia University Press.

Cos Cob Press (see Arrow Music Press, Associated Music Publishers).

Carl Fischer, Inc. (CF). 62 Cooper Square, New York, NY, 10003.

Harold Flammer, Inc. (see Shawnee Press).

Golden Music Publishers (GMP).

Mills Music, Inc. (see Belwin Mills).

G. Ricordi & Co. (see Belwin Mills).

G. Schirmer, Inc. 866 3rd Ave., New York, NY, 10022.

Shawnee Press, Inc. (owns the Harold Flammer issue of "Chorale" from Conce for String Sextet).

World Library Publications.

## 2. Compositions

### 1922
*Song Without Words* for chorus and two pianos. Not located.

### 1925
Andante for orchestra.

Fantasy for chorus, violin, violoncello, and piano. Also known as *Peña Hv* located.

*Songs of a Rainy Day* for string quartet. Also known as *Impressions of a R* Four movements. Not located.

### 1926
Concerto for Piano, Clarinet, and String Quartet. Four movements. AMP, n.d. Score; op. Rental.

### 1927
*Song Cycle on Words by Whitman* for women's chorus and two piar

**1928**
Sonata for Piano. Three movements. New York: AMP, 1931. Score.

**1929**
*Symphony—American Portrait 1929*. Four movements. Withdrawn.
String Quartet No. 1. Four movements.

**1930**
Concert Piece for orchestra.

**1931**
Toccata for orchestra.

**1932**
Andantino for small orchestra. Two versions, of which the second uses additional woodwinds and horn. Version 1: 1931; version 2: 1932.
Concerto for String Sextet (two violins, two violas, two violoncellos). Three movements. II. "Chorale"—Delaware Water Gap, Pa: Shawnee Press, n.d. Score and parts. (The "Chorale" may be performed by a full string orchestra, minus basses.) There is also a transcription of the "Chorale" for organ by George Lynn. Bryn Mawr, Pa: Theodore Presser Co., 1969. Score.
Fantasy for woodwinds, horn, and piano. Also known as Sextet.
*Overture–From the Gayety and Sadness of the American Scene* for orchestra. Withdrawn.

**1933**
*Symphony 1933* (Symphony No. 1) for orchestra. Three movements. New York: CF. Rental.
Three Variations on a Theme (String Quartet No. 2). Three movements. New York: GS, 1939. Score; op. Rental.

**1934**
*Four Minutes-20 Seconds* for flute and string quartet. New York: Mills, 1942. Score; op.
*A Song for Occupations* for a cappella chorus. New York: GS, 1935. Score; op.
Symphony No. 2 for orchestra. Three movements.
Trio for Piano, Violin, and Violoncello. Three movements. New York: AMP, 1936. Score, parts; op. Rental.

**1935**
*Farewell to Pioneers* (A Symphonic Elegy) for orchestra. New York: GS, 1935. Full score; op. Rental.
*Poem* for violin and piano. Final version not located.
Symphony for Voices on poems of Walt Whitman for a cappella chorus. Three movements. New York: GS, 1939. Choral and piano score (for rehearsal) of each movement published separately; op.
*When Johnny Comes Marching Home (An American Overture)* for orchestra. New York: GS, 1935. Study score (revised version).

**1936**
Prelude and Fugue for string orchestra. New York: GS, 1936. Full score and parts; op. Rental.
Quintet for Piano and Strings. Also known, in revised form for piano and full string orchestra (minus basses), as Concerto for Piano and Strings and Passacaglia, Cadenza, and Fugue. Three movements. New York: GS, 1940. Score and parts.

**1937**
Sanctus for a cappella chorus. New York: GS, 1939. Score; op.
String Quartet No. 3 (Four Preludes and Fugues). Eight movements. New York: GS. Rental. Originally published in study score by Mills Music, but turned over to GS on a prior claim basis.
Three Symphonic Essays for orchestra. New York: GS. Rental. Comprises, with some reworking, III., V., and IV., in that order, of *Time Suite.*
*Time Suite* for orchestra. Seven movements. Of the *Time Suite,* per se, only I., IV., and VI. have been located. For III. and V., as well as a reworking of IV., see Three Symphonic Essays.
*When Johnny Comes Marching Home (A Free Choral Paraphrase)* for a cappella chorus. New York: GS, 1935, 1939. Score; op.

**1938**
Concerto for Violin and Orchestra. One movement. Withdrawn.
*Sad Song* for jazz band. Intended as the second movement of an *American Symphony,* which Harris originally projected as his Symphony No. 4. Only the present movement seems to have been completed.
*Soliloquy and Dance* for viola and piano. New York: GS, 1941. Score and part; op.
Symphony No. 3 for orchestra. One movement. New York: GS, 1939, 1940. Study score (recently reprinted in larger format by GS).

**1939**
*He's Gone Away* for a cappella chorus. New York: GS, 1939. Score; op. (Tentatively assigned to 1939.)
*Little Suite* for piano. Four movements. New York: GS, 1939. Score.
Prelude and Fugue for strings and four trumpets. An arrangement, with four newly-composed trumpet parts, of Prelude and Fugue I of String Quartet No. 3.
Toccata for piano. Withdrawn. Explores some of the same materials as the later, published Toccata.

**1940**
*American Creed* for orchestra. Also known as *Creed.* Two movements. New York: BM. Rental.
*Challenge 1940* for bass solo, chorus, and orchestra. New York: GS. Rental.
*Evening Song* for voice and piano. New York: BM, 1981. Score. Published as III. of Four Songs.

*Folksong Symphony* (Symphony No. 4) for chorus and orchestra. Seven movements. New York: GS, 1940, 1942; op. Rental. Vocal scores of I., II., IV., VI., and VII. Final version made in 1942. The aforementioned movements were issued in both an early version and a final version.

*La Primavera* for voice and piano. New York: BM, 1981. Score. Published as II. of Four Songs.

*Psalm 3* for a cappella chorus. The authenticity of this work has not been verified, though Harris had some vague recollection of it.

Quintet for Two Violins, Two Violas, and Violoncello. Also known as Viola Quintet. Four movements.

*A Red-Bird in a Green Tree* for a cappella chorus. New York: BM, 1979. Score.

*To Thee, Old Cause* for a cappella chorus. New York: BM, 1979. Score.

*Whitman Triptych* for women's chorus a cappella. Three movements. New York: GS, 1940. Score; op.

*Year that Trembled* for a cappella chorus. New York: BM, 1979. Score.

### 1941

*Acceleration* for orchestra. New York: BM. Rental.

*Cimarron* (Symphonic Overture) for band. New York: BM. Rental.

*Evening Piece* for orchestra. New York: BM. Rental. Originally II. of Three Pieces for Orchestra.

Four Songs for voice and piano. I. "Waitin," II. "La Primavera," III. "Evening Song," IV. "Freedom's Land" (version for solo voice/unison chorus and piano). New York: BM, 1981. Score. A republication of I., III., and IV. (originally issued separately by Mills Music) and a new publication of II.

*Freedom's Land* for baritone solo, chorus, and orchestra. New York: BM. Rental.

*Freedom's Land* for male chorus a cappella. New York: BM, 1979. Score.

*Freedom's Land* for solo voice or unison chorus and piano. New York: BM, 1981. Score. Published as IV. of Four Songs.

*Freedom's Land* for women's chorus a cappella (with piano or organ ad lib.). New York: BM, 1979. Score.

*Freedom, Toleration (The Open Air I Sing)* for a cappella chorus. New York: BM, 1979. Score.

*From this Earth* (ballet) for chamber ensemble. New York: BM. Rental.

*Mirage* for orchestra. New York: BM. Rental. (Tentatively assigned to 1941.)

*Ode to Truth* for orchestra. New York: BM. Rental.

*One-Tenth of a Nation* (film score) for chamber ensemble.

*A Railroad-Man's Ballad* for chorus and orchestra. New York: BM. Rental. (Tentatively assigned to 1941.)

Three Pieces for Orchestra. A suite formed from the two dance interludes (III. and V.) of the *Folksong Symphony* and the newly composed *Evening Piece*. Never contracted as a suite.

*Wailin'* for voice and piano. New York: BM, 1981. Score. Published as I. of Four Songs.

*When Johnny Comes Marching Home (A Free Adaptation for Band)*. New York: GS.
Rental. Originally published in condensed score and parts by Mills Music, but
turned over to GS on a prior-claim basis.
*Work* for orchestra. New York: BM. Rental.

**1942**
*The Birds' Courting Song* for a cappella chorus. New York: BM, 1979. Score.
Concerto for Piano and Band. One movement. New York: BM. Rental.
*Fanfare for the Forces* for brass and percussion (with optional violins and violas).
(Tentatively assigned to 1942.)
*Four Charming Little Pieces* for violin and piano. New York: BM, II. and III: 1943;
I. and IV: 1944. Score and parts; op. Adapted from the *Namesake* ballet.
*Freedom's Land* for a cappella chorus. New York: BM, 1979. Score.
*Freedom's Land* for male chorus and band (two versions).
*Namesake* (ballet) for violin and piano. Four movements published, with some
reworking, as *Four Charming Little Pieces*.
Sonata for Violin and Piano. Four movements. New York: BM, 1974. Revised
Edition. Score and part. The four movements originally published separately
by Mills Music with the following titles: I. Fantasy, II. Dance of Spring, III.
Melody, IV. Toccata. In the BM republication, all four movements appear,
without titles, under a single cover.
Symphony No. 5 for orchestra. Three movements. New York: Mills, 1961. Study
score; op. BM. Rental. (Revised in 1945 or 1946; Harris made further
changes over the years even after publication.)
*What So Proudly We Hail (Dance Suite [ballet] Based on American Folk Songs)* for
chorus (wordless), strings, and piano. Five scenes. Only Scenes I., II., III.,
and V. have been located. Scene IV., "I'll Be True to My Love," may have
used the music of II. of the Violin Sonata.

**1943**
Chorale for organ and brass. New York: BM. Rental.
Fantasia for piano and band.
*Folk Rhythms of Today* for orchestra. New York: BM. Rental. A transcription of
Scene V. of the ballet *What So Proudly We Hail*.
*March in Time of War* for orchestra. New York: BM. Rental.
Piano Suite in Three Movements. New York: Mills, 1944. Score; op. Second
movement originally titled *Variations on an Irish Lullaby* and performed
separately by Johana Harris both prior and subsequent to the creation and
publication of the whole suite.
*Rhythms of Today* for band. Two versions, of which the second was scored by
Lawrence Intravaia c. 1946. The latter version also has some additional
passages whose origin has not been definitively determined.
*Work Song* for a cappella chorus. New York: BM, 1979. Score. (Tentatively
assigned to 1943.)

## 1944

*Children's Hour* for orchestra. New York: BM. Rental.

Chorale for orchestra. New York: BM. Rental. A transcription of the Chorale for organ and brass.

Concerto for Piano and Orchestra. One movement. New York: BM. Rental. Temporarily removed from the BM rental library pending revision and recopying of the score and parts.

*Conflict (War Piece)* for band. New York: BM. Rental. A reworking for band of Symphony No. 6.

Lamentation for soprano, viola, and piano. New York: BM, 1981. Score and viola part.

*Li'l Boy Named David* for a cappella chorus. New York: BM, 1979. Score. (Tentatively assigned to 1944.)

*Ode to Friendship* for orchestra. New York: Mills, 1946. Score; op. BM. Rental. Temporarily unavailable pending location of the parts.

*Our Fighting Sons* for unison chorus, brass, piano, organ, and timpani.

*Rock of Ages* for chorus and orchestra. New York: Mills, c. 1945. Score; op. BM. Rental. An adaptation of Scene III. of *What So Proudly We Hail.*

*Sammy's Fighting Sons* for chorus and orchestra, unison chorus, or solo voice and piano. New York: Mills, 1944. Vocal score; op. The present work and two others, *Sons of Uncle Sam* and *War Song of Democracy,* are variant versions of what is essentially the same composition. They differ from one another in text, performance medium, and some comparatively minor musical details. (Tentatively assigned to 1944.)

*Sun and Stars* for band. (Tentatively assigned to 1944.)

*The Sun from Dawn to Dusk* for band. New York: BM. Rental.

Symphony No. 6 (*Gettysburg*) for orchestra. Four movements. New York: BM. Rental.

*Take the Sun and Keep the Stars* for voice or unison chorus and band. New York: Mills, 1944; version for voice and piano. Score; op. The verse sections of this piece are variants of the words and music of *Sammy's Fighting Sons.*

Toccata for organ and brass. New York: BM. Rental.

## 1945

*American Ballads,* Set I, for piano. Five pieces. New York: CF, 1947. Score. Subsequent sets never completed, though Harris did compose additional piano ballads based on folk tunes. I., "Streets of Laredo," has been anthologized.

*Fog* for voice and piano. New York: CF, 1948. Score.

*Memories of a Child's Sunday* for orchestra. Three movements. New York: CF. Rental. Titles of the individual movements vary from one source to another.

*Variation on a Theme by Goossens–Variation VII* for orchestra. Score not located, though the parts are in the possession of the Cincinnati Symphony Orchestra (not examined). Part of series of variations by ten composers on a theme supplied by Eugene Goossens, the conductor during this period of the Cincinnati Symphony Orchestra.

*Walt Whitman Suite* for chorus, strings, and piano. Three movements. New York: BM. Rental. Originally given as a ballet and may be related to, or the same as, the *Ballet on the Subject of War* mentioned in some lists but for which no further information or musical materials have been located.

### 1946

*Blow the Man Down (A Free Improvisation on the Sailor's Ballad)* for soloists, chorus, and orchestra. New York: CF, 1947. Vocal score.

*Celebration Variations on a Timpani Theme from Howard Hanson's Third Symphony* for orchestra. New York: CF. Rental.

Concerto for Two Pianos and Orchestra. Three movements. New York: CF. Rental.

Melody for orchestra. New York: CF, 1947. Condensed score and parts.

*Radio Piece* for orchestra and piano. New York: CF, 1947. Condensed score and parts.

### 1947

Alleluia (*Motet for Easter*) for chorus, brass, and organ. There is also a version for chorus, strings, and organ, which has not been located. (Tentatively assigned to 1947.)

*Mi Chomocho (Israel)* for soloist, chorus, and organ. New York: GS, 1951 (copyright held by CF). Score. Published in anthology *Synagogue Music by Contemporary Composers*.

*The Quest (A Concert March-Passacaglia)* for orchestra. New York: CF. Rental.

Theme and Variations for Solo Accordion and Orchestra. Also, known, incorrectly, as Concerto for Accordion and Orchestra. New York: CF. Rental.

*They Say that Susan Has No Heart for Learning* (Madrigal) for three-part chorus of women's voices with piano accompaniment. New York: AMP, 1956. Score; op.

*Wedding Song* for bass solo, string trio, and organ.

### 1948

*Elegy and Paean* for viola and orchestra.

Mass for men's chorus and organ. New York: CF. Rental.

### 1949

*Cindy* for a cappella chorus. New York: CF, 1951. Score.

Concerto for Violin and Orchestra. One movement. New York: CF. Rental. (A completely different work from the 1938 violin concerto.)

*Fruit of Gold* for band. New York: CF. Rental.

*If I Had a Ribbon Bow* for a cappella chorus. New York: CF, 1951. Score.

*Kentucky Spring* for orchestra. New York: CF. Rental.

Toccata for piano. New York, CF, 1950. Score. (A different work from the 1939 toccata, though it shares some of the same materials.)

## 1950
*Dark Devotion* for band.
*Kentucky Jazz Piece* (provisional title) for band.
Lyric Studies for solo woodwinds and piano. Six pieces, one each for flute, oboe, and bassoon, three for clarinet. (There is also what appears to be a completed draft of a second piece for flute.) New York: AMP. Rental. Harris had projected additional pieces for this set before he abandoned it but did sanction the release of the existing movements.

## 1951
*Cumberland Concerto for Orchestra.* One movement. New York: BM. Rental.
Fantasy for piano and "pops" orchestra. Only fragments of what appear to be different versions have been located.
*Red Cross Hymn* for chorus and band. (Tentatively assigned to 1951.)

## 1952
*Remember November (Election Day Is Action Day)*; two versions: (1) unison chorus and piano four-hands; (2) bass soloist/speaker, male chorus, and piano two-hands. Score of second version has not been located, though it does exist on tape.
Symphony for Band (*West Point*). One movement. West Point: United States Military Academy. Loan.
Symphony No. 7 for orchestra. One movement. New York: AMP, 1956. Study score, recently reprinted. (Final version made in 1955.)

## 1953
*Abraham Lincoln Walks at Midnight (A Cantata of Lamentation)* for mezzo-soprano, violin, violoncello, and piano. New York: AMP, 1962. Score and string parts; op. Revised prior to publication, but the composer subsequently reverted, for some passages, to the immediate prepublication version.
Concerto No. 2 for Piano and Orchestra. Three movements. Score not located. Withdrawn.

## 1954
Fantasy for piano and orchestra. New York: AMP. Rental.
Symphonic Epigram for orchestra. New York: AMP. Rental.
Symphonic Fantasy for orchestra. New York: AMP. Rental.

## 1955
*Pep Song* (for the ceremony of name-changing of Pennsylvania College for Women to Chatham College) for unison chorus and piano. Piano part not located.

## 1956
*Each Hand Has Need* for chorus and organ. (Tentatively assigned to 1956.)
*Folk Fantasy for Festivals* for folk singers, soloists, speakers, double mixed chorus, and piano. Five movements. New York: AMP, I., II., III., IV.: 1957; V.: 1959. Score; I. and V. op.
*Give Me the Splendid Silent Sun (Cantata for Baritone and Orchestra).* New York:

AMP, 1962. Study score. Originally intended as the first movement of Harris's
initial attempt at a Symphony No. 8 (a Whitman symphony) but later issued as
a separate piece when that project was abandoned.

*Ode to Consonance* for orchestra. New York: AMP, 1957. Full score and parts.

*Our Tense and Wintry Minds* for unison chorus and organ. New York: Columbia
University Press, 1980. Score. Published in anthology *American Hymns Old
and New,* Vol. I.

*Read, Sweet, How Others Strove* for chorus and organ. New York: Columbia
University Press, 1980. Score. Published in anthology *American Hymns Old
and New,* Vol. I.

### 1957

*The Hustle with the Muscle* for male chorus and band.

*Psalm 150* for a cappella chorus. Golden, Colo.: GMP, 1963. Score.

### 1958

*Ad Majorem Gloriam Universitatis Illinorum* (Symphonic Tone Poem) for band.

*Elegy and Dance* for orchestra. New York: AMP, 1960—Elegy. Full score and
parts. Dance. Rental.

### 1959

*Life of Christ* for violoncello, chorus, and orchestra. Ten movements planned, of
which only I., "Kyrie," was completed.

### 1960

*Canticle of the Sun (A Cantata on the Words of St. Francis of Assisi)* for high voice
and chamber ensemble. New York: AMP. Rental.

### 1961

*Turn on the Night* (theatre music for the play by Jerome Lawrence and Robert E.
Lee) for chamber ensemble. Six newly composed movements. This incidental
music comprises newly written materials, music adapted from other Harris
works, and music improvised on the piano (the last taped by Johana Harris and
another, unnamed, pianist). The individual cues—composed, adapted, and
improvised—were recorded on tape and sent to the play's producers for
incorporation into the drama. (The play has since been retitled more than once
and performed with music provided by other composers.)

### 1962

*Sweet and Low* (provisional title) for voice and piano. Another setting of the text
employed in *Evening Song.*

Symphony No. 8 (*San Francisco Symphony*) for orchestra. Five interconnected
parts. New York: AMP. Rental.

Symphony No. 9 for orchestra. Three movements. New York: AMP, 1966. Study
score.

### 1963

*These Times* for small orchestra and piano.

**1964**

*Epilogue to Profiles in Courage–J. F. K.* for orchestra. New York: AMP. Rental.

Etudes for Pedals for organ pedals. Cincinnati: World Library Publications, 1973. Score. (Recomposed in 1972, and it is that version that is published.)

Fantasy for organ, brass, and timpani. New York: AMP, 1967. Full score and parts.

*Horn of Plenty* for orchestra. New York: AMP, 1967. Study score.

*Jubilation* (cantata) for chorus, brass, piano, and percussion.

*Salute to Youth* for orchestra. New York: AMP. Rental.

Sonata for Violoncello and Piano. Three parts, of which I. consists of two movements. For a time, Harris retitled the work Duo. He also made many revisions and reworkings, a process that extended into 1976. However, at the end of his life, he approved a version made and recorded for commercial release c. 1968 (see Discography).

**1965**

Rhythms and Spaces for string orchestra. Three movements. New York: GS. Rental. An arrangement, with some new material in I. and III., of Three Variations on a Theme (String Quartet No. 2).

Symphony No. 10 (*Abraham Lincoln Symphony*) for speaker, chorus, brass, two pianos, and percussion. Five movements. A.M.P. Rental. Temporarily unavailable pending recopying of score and parts.

**1966**

*Childhood Memories of Ocean Moods* for piano, string quartet, and doublebass.

*The Brotherhood of Man* for chorus and orchestra. A reworking of III. of Symphony No. 10.

**1967**

Symphony No. 11 for orchestra. One movement. New York: AMP. Rental.

**1968**

Concerto for Amplified Piano, Brass, String Basses, and Percussion. Three movements. New York: AMP. Rental. Available from AMP under the title Concert Piece, the title Harris gave it when he temporarily withdrew I. This movement was subsequently restored but has disappeared, thus only II. and III. are currently available. (The word "amplified" in the title refers to the use, at the first performance and in a commercial recording, of amplification to bring out the overtones of the harmonies in some passages. It may be dispensed with, however.)

**1969**

Symphony No. 12 (*Pere Marquette Symphony*) for tenor solo/speaker, and orchestra. Two parts: Part I comprising two separate movements; Part II comprising three interlinked movements.

**1970**

*Peace and Goodwill to All* for chorus, brass, organ, and percussion. A reworking of *Jubilation*.

**1971**
*Whether this Nation* for chorus and band. Three movements.

**1972**
Etudes for Pedals for organ pedals. See entry under 1964.

**1973**
*Folksong Suite* for harp, winds, and percussion. Harris planned six movements, but only four were completed.

*Gethsemane* for a cappella chorus (harmonization). Golden, Colo.: GMP, 1973. Score. A version, with new text, of Harris's harmonization of *Psalm 32* that appeared in the anthology *Singing Through the Ages*.

Harris, Shaun: Four Songs (I. "Today's a Day," II. "Misty Morning," III. "I'll Cry Out," IV. "Canadian Ships") for voice and orchestra. Roy Harris wrote orchestral accompaniments for these songs for an album by his son Shaun. Only small portions of the arrangements were actually used on the published album (See Discography).

*Life* (cantata) for soprano, winds, and percussion. Two movements. New York: AMP. Rental.

*Lincoln's Legacy* for chorus and band. A projected multimovement work, of which only I., "Lonesome Boy," was completed.

**1975**
*America, We Love Your People* for chorus and band. Three movements. (Originally titled *Covina.*)

*Bicentennial Symphony 1976* (Symphony No. 13) for chorus and orchestra. Five movements. New York: AMP. Rental. Originally numbered Symphony No. 14 (because of the composer's superstition about the number thirteen), but the official designation is Symphony No. 13.

**1976**
*Bicentennial Aspirations* for band. Three movements. Withdrawn.

*Rejoice and Sing* for bass, string quartet, and piano. Another version, for mezzo-soprano, string quartet, and piano, is lost.

**Undated Works**
Choral Fanfare for a cappella chorus.

Foster, Stephen. *Old Black Joe (Free Paraphrase)* for a cappella chorus. New York: GS. Score; op. Not located; date of publication not available.

Fugato (provisional title) in three parts, possibly for string trio.

*True Love Don't Weep* (Variations on an American Folk Song) for piano.

## 3. Arrangements and Transcriptions

**1932**
Bach, J. S. *Well-Tempered Clavier,* Book I. Prelude and Fugue XVI transcribed for small orchestra.

**1934**

Bach, J. S. *The Art of the Fugue* transcribed for string quartet by Roy Harris and M. D. Herton Norton. New York: GS, 1936. Score and parts. Omits the canons and the two pieces titled "Fuga a2. Clav."

Lully. *Phaeton*; Act I, Scene I, "Heureuse ûne ame indifferente" (aria for soprano). Accompaniment transcribed for string orchestra and piano.

———. *Thésée*; Prolog, "Revenez, revenez, amours, revenez" (aria for soprano). Accompaniment transcribed for string orchestra and piano.

Niles, John Jacob. *The Story of Norah* arranged for a cappella chorus. New York: GS, 1934. Score; op.

**1941**

*The Star Spangled Banner* harmonized and arranged for string quartet.

**1945**

Bach, J. S. Organ Preludes (I. "Komm, Gott, Shöpfer, heiliger Geist"; II. "Christ lag in Todesbanden"; III. "Das alte Jahr vergangen ist"; IV. "Liebster Jesu, wir sind hier"; V. "In Dulci Jubilo") transcribed for piano by Roy and Johana Harris. New York: Mills Music, 1946. Score; op. (Tentatively assigned to 1945.)

**Undated**

Bach, J. S. Five Chorales (I. "Bestir Thyself"; II. "In Dulci Jubilo"; III. "Joyful Sing"; IV. "God, Thou Holy God"; V. "O God Enthroned") transcribed for chorus and band. New York: BM. Rental. These appear to have been done during the early 1940s.

Sweelinck, J. P.: Fantasia in d minor transcribed for orchestra. New York: GS. Rental.

# IV. Collections

Harris, Roy and Jacob Evanson. *Singing Through the Ages* (anthology). 2 vols. (I. Melodic and Harmonic Songs, II. Contrapuntal Songs). New York: American Book Co, 1940. Op. Among its contents from several historical periods and composers, this publication includes Harris's a cappella setting of "When Johnny Comes Marching Home" (reprinted from the GS. edition) and his harmonization of *Psalm 32*, which served as the source for *Gethsemane*. It also contains numerous folk and related tunes (in monophonic form) of which Harris made settings or which he employed in various compositions.

# Discography

A complete discography of all the recordings of Roy Harris's music released to date has been prepared by William Curtis (see Bibliography). Since this discography is currently available, in order to avoid unnecessary duplication of effort, I list here only the recordings issued (or reissued) on long-playing (33 1/3 rpm) discs. These are apt to be most accessible to the general reader.

The list is arranged alphabetically by title and, for multiple recordings under each title, alphabetically by principal performer, or conductor. If a recording has been reissued, only the label and number of the latest issue are given. An out-of-print recording is designated "op."

Though some recordings have been released abroad, especially in England, only domestic issues are listed. Also, only commercially released recordings are included, except in the cases of one or two noncommercial issues that are widely available in libraries.

Many works appear on records coupled with other Harris compositions or with pieces by other composers. In order to save space, I have not listed the additional works on records containing more than one piece. If they are Harris compositions, they will, of course, be found cross-referenced under their titles elsewhere on the list.

*Abraham Lincoln Walks at Midnight (A Cantata of Lamentation)*. Nell Tangeman, mezzo-soprano; Johana Harris, piano; Samuel Thaviu, violin; Theo Salzman, violoncello. MGM E3210 (mono); op.
*American Ballads,* Set I for piano. Grant Johannesen, piano. Golden Crest CRS4111 (quad/stereo).
*Chorale* for organ and brass. Thomas Harmon, organ; James Westbrook conducting the UCLA Brass Ensemble. Varese Sarabande VC81085 (stereo).
*Cimarron (Symphonic Overture)* for band. James Westbrook conducting the UCLA Wind Ensemble. Varese Sarabande VC81100 (stereo).
*Concerto for Amplified Piano, Brass, String Basses, and Percussion.* Johana Harris, piano; Roy Harris conducting members of the United States Air Force Academy Band. Varese Sarabande VC81085 (stereo).
*Concerto for Piano and Strings* (arrangement of *Quintet for Piano and Strings*). Johana Harris, piano; Roy Harris conducting the International String Congress Orchestra. Varese Sarabande VC81100 (stereo).

*Concerto for Piano, Clarinet, and String Quartet.* Peter Basquin, piano; Lawrence Sobol, clarinet; Long Island Chamber Ensemble of New York. Grenadilla GS1007 (stereo).

*Elegy and Dance* for orchestra. Jacob Avshalomov conducting the Portland Junior Symphony. Composers Recordings CRI140 (mono/electronic stereo).

*Epilogue to Profiles in Courage–J. F. K.* for orchestra. Robert Whitney conducting the Louisville Orchestra. Louisville LOU-LS666 (mono/stereo); stereo op.

*Fanfare for the Forces.* Jorge Mester conducting the London Philharmonic Orchestra. In album titled "Fanfares." Varese Sarabande VCDM 1000.240 (stereo; digital).

*Fantasy* for organ, brass, and timpani. Thomas Harmon, organ; James Westbrook conducting the UCLA Brass Ensemble (with timpani). Varese Sarabande VC81085 (stereo).

*Fantasy* for piano and orchestra. Johana Harris, piano; Izler Solomon conducting the MGM Symphony Orchestra. MGM E3210 (mono); op.

*Fog* for voice and piano. John Kennedy Hanks, tenor; Ruth Friedberg, piano. In two-disc Duke University album DWR6417–8 (mono).

*Folksong Symphony (Symphony No. 4).*
   1. Maurice Abravanel conducting the Utah Chorale and Utah Symphony Orchestra. Angel S36091 (quad/stereo); op.
   2. Vladimir Golschmann conducting the American Festival Chorus and Orchestra. Vanguard Everyman SRV347SD (stereo).
   3. III. only. Richard Korn conducting the Hamburg Philharmonia Orchestra. Allegro-Elite 3419 (mono); op.

*Kentucky Spring* for orchestra. Robert Whitney conducting the Louisville Orchestra. Louisville LOU602 (mono); op.

*Quintet for Piano and Strings.*
   1. Johana Harris, piano; Blair Quartet. Varese Sarabande VC81123 (stereo).
   2. Johana Harris, piano; Eudice Shapiro and Nathan Ross, violins; Sanford Schonbach, viola; Edgar Lustgarten, violoncello. Contemporary ("Contemporary Composers Series") M6012/S8012 (mono/stereo); op.

*Sonata* for Piano. Roger Shields, piano. In three-disc Vox album SVBX5303 (stereo).

*Sonata for Violin and Piano.*
   1. Josef Gingold, violin; Johana Harris, piano. Columbia AML4842 (mono); op.
   2. Eudice Shapiro, violin; Johana Harris, piano. Contemporary ("Contemporary Composers Series") M6012/S8012 (mono/stereo); op.

*String Quartet No. 3 (Four Preludes and Fugues).* Blair Quartct. Varese Sarabande VC81123 (stereo).

*Symphony for Band (West Point).*
   1. Roy Harris conducting the United States Military Academy Band. Pittsburgh International Festival of Contemporary Music. ASCAP PFCM CB175 (mono); noncommercial; op. The opening section of the work is omitted on this recording.

2. James Westbrook conducting the UCLA Wind Ensemble. Varese Sarabande VC81100 (stereo).

*Symphony 1933 (Symphony No. 1)*. Serge Koussevitzky conducting the Boston Symphony Orchestra. Columbia AML5095 (mono; reissued from 78 rpm).

*Symphony No. 3.*

1. Leonard Bernstein conducting the New York Philharmonic Orchestra. Columbia ML5703/MS6303 (mono/stereo); op.
2. Howard Hanson conducting the Eastman-Rochester Symphony Orchestra. Mercury MG50421/SR90421 (mono/electronic stereo); op.
3. Walter Hendl conducting the Vienna Symphony Orchestra. Desto D404/DST6404 (mono/electronic stereo); op.
4. Serge Koussevitzky conducting the Boston Symphony Orchestra. RCA Victor LVT1016 (mono; reissued from 78 rpm); op.
5. Eugene Ormandy conducting the Philadelphia Orchestra. RCA Red Seal ARL1-1682 (stereo); op. This is the only recording to give the symphony complete, without the cuts in the "Pastoral" section.

*Symphony No. 5.*

1. William Steinberg conducting the Pittsburgh Symphony Orchestra. Pittsburgh International Festival of Contemporary Music. ASCAP PFCM CB165 (mono); noncommercial; op. For this performance, Harris substituted a portion of II. of Symphony No. 6 for the concluding portion of I. and made some slight changes in scoring for earlier portions of that movement. This version (though not the scoring changes) was later rescinded.
2. Robert Whitney conducting the Louisville Orchestra. Louisville LOU/LS655 (mono/stereo; op. For this recording, Harris restored the original first-movement conclusion. However, he made some cuts and changes in scoring that he later rescinded.

*Symphony No. 7.* Eugene Ormandy conducting the Philadelphia Orchestra. Columbia AML5095 (mono).

*Three Variations on a Theme (String Quartet No. 2)*. Emerson String Quartet. New World Records NW218 (stereo).

*Toccata* for organ and brass. Thomas Harmon, organ; James Westbrook conducting the UCLA Brass Ensemble. Varese Sarabande VC81085 (stereo).

*Trio for Piano, Violin, and Violoncello.*

1. New England Trio. HNH4070 (stereo); op.
2. University of Oklahoma Trio. University Recordings No. 1 (mono); op.

*When Johnny Comes Marching Home (An American Overture)*. Jorge Mester conducting the Louisville Orchestra. Louisville LS766 (stereo). The first recording of the revised (published) version.

# Credit Lines For Copyrighted Compositions

Example No.

| | |
|---|---|
| 7a | © 1961 by Mills Music, Inc. Copyright Renewed. Used with permission. All Rights Reserved. |
| 7b | © 1957 by Associated Music Publishers, Inc. Used by permission. |
| 9a | Copyright 1939 by G. Schirmer, Inc. Used by permission. |
| 9b | Copyright 1939 by G. Schirmer, Inc. Used by permission. |
| 10a | Copyright 1935 by G. Schirmer, Inc. Used by permission. |
| 10b | © 1956 by Associated Music Publishers, Inc. Used by permission. |
| 11abc | Copyright 1948 by Mills Music, Inc. Copyright assigned to G. Schirmer, Inc. Used by permission. |
| 12a | Copyright 1944 by Mills Music, Inc. Copyright Renewed. Used with Permission. All Rights Reserved. |
| 12b | © 1967 by Associated Music Publishers, Inc. Used by permission. |
| 13 | © 1961 by Mills Music, Inc. Copyright Renewed. Used with permission. All Rights Reserved. |
| 14 | © 1978 by Carl Fischer, Inc. Reprinted by permission of Carl Fischer, Inc. |
| 15 | © 1978 by Carl Fischer, Inc. Reprinted by permission of Carl Fischer, Inc. |
| 16 | © 1978 by Carl Fischer, Inc. Reprinted by permission of Carl Fischer, Inc. |
| 17 | © 1978 by Carl Fischer, Inc. Reprinted by permission of Carl Fischer, Inc. |
| 18 | © 1978 by Carl Fischer, Inc. Reprinted by permission of Carl Fischer, Inc. |
| 19ab | © 1978 by Carl Fischer, Inc. Reprinted by permission of Carl Fischer, Inc. |
| 20 | © 1978 by Carl Fischer, Inc. Reprinted by permission of Carl Fischer, Inc. |

| 50ab | © 1978 by Mills Music, Inc. Copyright Renewed. Used with permission. All Rights Reserved. |
| 51ab | © 1978 by Mills Music, Inc. Copyright Renewed. Used with permission. All Rights Reserved. |
| 52 | © 1978 by Mills Music, Inc. Copyright Renewed. Used with permission. All Rights Reserved. |
| 53 | © 1978 by Mills Music, Inc. Copyright Renewed. Used with permission. All Rights Reserved. |
| 54 | © 1978 by Mills Music, Inc. Copyright Renewed. Used with permission. All Rights Reserved. |
| 55 | © 1978 by Mills Music, Inc. Copyright Renewed. Used with permission. All Rights Reserved. |
| 56abc | © 1978 by Mills Music, Inc. Copyright Renewed. Used with permission. All Rights Reserved. |
| 57 | © 1956 by Associated Music Publishers, Inc. Used by permission. |
| 58ab | © 1956 by Associated Music Publishers, Inc. Used by permission. |
| 59 | © 1956 by Associated Music Publishers, Inc. Used by permission. |
| 60 | © 1961 by Associated Music Publishers, Inc. Used by permission. |
| 61abc | © 1971 by Associated Music Publishers, Inc. Used by permission. |
| 62abc | © 1971 by Associated Music Publishers, Inc. Used by permission. |
| 63 | © 1971 by Associated Music Publishers, Inc. Used by permission. |
| 64abc | © 1971 by Associated Music Publishers, Inc. Used by permission. |
| 65 | © 1971 by Associated Music Publishers, Inc. Used by permission. |
| 66 | © 1971 by Associated Music Publishers, Inc. Used by permission. |
| 67 | © 1971 by Associated Music Publishers, Inc. Used by permission. |
| 68abc | © 1971 by Associated Music Publishers, Inc. Used by permission. |
| 69ab | © 1971 by Associated Music Publishers, Inc. Used by permission. |

| | |
|---|---|
| 70 | © 1971 by Associated Music Publishers, Inc. Used by permission. |
| 71 | © 1971 by Associated Music Publishers, Inc. Used by permission. |
| 72 | © 1966 by Associated Music Publishers, Inc. Used by permission. |
| 73 | © 1966 by Associated Music Publishers, Inc. Used by permission. |
| 74 | © 1966 by Associated Music Publishers, Inc. Used by permission. |
| 75abc | © 1966 by Associated Music Publishers, Inc. Used by permission. |
| 76 | © 1966 by Associated Music Publishers, Inc. Used by permission. |
| 84 | © 1968 by Associated Music Publishers, Inc. Used by permission. |
| 85 | © 1968 by Associated Music Publishers, Inc. Used by permission. |
| 86ab | © 1968 by Associated Music Publishers, Inc. Used by permission. |
| 87 | © 1968 by Associated Music Publishers, Inc. Used by permission. |
| 88ab | © 1968 by Associated Music Publishers, Inc. Used by permission. |
| 89 | © 1968 by Associated Music Publishers, Inc. Used by permission. |
| 90 | © 1968 by Associated Music Publishers, Inc. Used by permission. |
| 91 | © 1968 by Associated Music Publishers, Inc. Used by permission. |
| 92 | © 1968 by Associated Music Publishers, Inc. Used by permission. |
| 93 | © 1968 by Associated Music Publishers, Inc. Used by permission. |
| 102 | Copyright 1939 by G. Schirmer, Inc. Used by permission. |
| 103 | Copyright 1939 by G. Schirmer, Inc. Used by permission. |
| 104ab | Copyright 1939 by G. Schirmer, Inc. Used by permission. |
| 105ab | Copyright 1948 by Mills Music, Inc. Copyright assigned to G. Schirmer, Inc. Used by permission. |

# Index

No. 12; Piano Suite in Three Movements, 221–22; Poem for violin and piano, 209; Prelude and Fugue for Strings, 184, 215; Psalm 3, 236; Psalm 150, 236; Quartet No. 1, 51–52, 59, 149–53, 156, 173, 220; Quartet No. 2, *See* Three Variations on a Theme; Quartet No. 3, 30, 39, 40–41, 62, 163, 153–56; Quest, The, 185; Quintet for Piano and Strings, 29, 43, 63, 84, 96, 153, 165, 167, 175–80, 207; Quintet for Two Violins, Two Violas, and Violoncello, 84, 156–65, 171; Radio Piece, 207; Railroad Man's Ballad, 234; Rejoice and Sing, 227, 241; Rhythms of Today, 190–91, 195, 198; Sanctus, 228–29; Salute to Youth, 183, 185–86; San Francisco Symphony, *See* Symphony No. 8; Soliloquy and Dance, 199, 209, 215–17, 242; Sonata for Piano, 62, 170, 219, 222–25; Sonata for Violin and Piano, 44, 161, 210–15; Sonata for Violoncello and Piano, 199, 210–15; Song Cycle on Words by Whitman, 233; Song Without Words, 227; Song for Occupations, 228–30, 233; Songs of Democracy, 257n2 (Chapter 14); Sun and Stars, 191, 198; Sun from Dawn to Dusk, The, 190–91; Symphonic Epigram, 184, 186; Symphonic Fantasy, 187; Symphony—American Portrait 1929, 21, 26–28, 43, 49–52, 54, 56–57, 61, 81, 158, 170, 187; Symphony No. 1, *See* Symphony 1933; Symphony 1933, 25–26, 30, 43, 51–59, 62, 64, 68, 150, 153, 162; Symphony No. 2, 28, 51, 58–62, 68, 84, 92, 149–50, 153, 157, 240; Symphony No. 3, 29, 32, 34, 42–43, 49, 62, 63–69, 79–80, 87, 96, 102, 113–14, 140, 150, 155, 176, 201–202, 209; Symphony No. 5, 26, 28–29,

33, 40, 45, 68, 79–87, 91–93, 96, 99, 102, 103, 117, 155–56, 161, 164, 179, 187, 197, 202; Symphony No. 6, 29, 50, 68, 87–93, 99, 119, 124, 131, 190, 197, 253n8; Symphony No. 7, 29, 43, 49, 96–100, 107, 144, 136–37, 153, 177, 203, 209, 255n7; Symphony No. 8, 50, 61, 104, 106–115, 117, 121, 124, 130, 140, 207–208; Symphony No. 9, 107, 124, 114–21, 170; Symphony No. 10, 49, 124–31, 137, 145, 254n4 (Chapter 6); Symphony No. 11, 29, 44, 131–37, 145, 161, 254n5 (Chapter 6); Symphony No. 12, 104, 137–44, 235; Symphony No. 13, *See* Bicentennial Symphony; Symphony for Band, 49, 190–91, 193–95, 197–98; Symphony for Voices, 49, 118, 129–30, 137, 228–30, 232–33, 239; Theme and Variations for Solo Accordion and Orchestra, 199, 207–208; These Times, 38, 186, 207; Three Symphonic Essays, 170, 184, 187; Three Variations on a Theme (Quartet No. 2), 62, 156, 150–53; Time Suite, 149, 170, 184, 187, 242; Toccata for orchestra, 51–52, 202; Toccata for organ and brass, 199; Toccata for piano, 219, 221–25; To Thee, Old Cause, 233; Trio for Piano, Violin, and Violoncello, 62, 130, 172–75; Walt Whitman Suite, 129; Wedding Song, 241; When Johnny Comes Marching Home (band work), 190–91, 195, (choral work), 229, 234, (orchestral overture), 62, 185, 215; Whether This Nation, 145, 237; Whitman Triptych, 230–31; Work, 183, 186–87; Work Song, 234